HISTORICAL STUDIES IN EDUCATION

Edited by William J. Reese and John L. Rury

William J. Reese, Carl F. Kaestle WARF Professor of Educational Policy Studies and History, the University of Wisconsin-Madison

John L. Rury, Professor of Education and (by courtesy) History, the University of Kansas

This series features new scholarship on the historical development of education, defined broadly, in the United States and elsewhere. Interdisciplinary in orientation and comprehensive in scope, it spans methodological boundaries and interpretive traditions. Imaginative and thoughtful history can contribute to the global conversation about educational change. Inspired history lends itself to continued hope for reform, and to realizing the potential for progress in all educational experiences.

Published by Palgrave Macmillan:

Democracy and Schooling in California: The Legacy of Helen Heffernan and Corinne Seeds
By Kathleen Weiler

The Global University: Past, Present, and Future Perspectives
Edited by Adam R. Nelson and Ian P. Wei

Catholic Teaching Brothers: Their Life in the English-Speaking World, 1891–1965
By Tom O'Donoghue

Science Education and Citizenship: Fairs, Clubs, and Talent Searches for American Youth, 1918–1958
By Sevan G. Terzian

The Founding Fathers, Education, and "The Great Contest": The American Philosophical Society Prize of 1797
Edited by Benjamin Justice

Education and the State in Modern Peru: Primary Schooling in Lima, 1821 – c. 1921
By G. Antonio Espinoza

Desegregating Chicago's Public Schools: Policy Implementation, Politics, and Protest, 1965–1985
By Dionne Danns

Previously Published Works

Danns, D. (2003). *Something Better for Our Children: Black Organizing in Chicago Public Schools, 1963–1971.*

DESEGREGATING CHICAGO'S PUBLIC SCHOOLS

Policy Implementation, Politics, and Protest, 1965–1985

Dionne Danns

First published in 2014 by
PALGRAVE MACMILLAN®
in the United States—a division of St. Martin's Press LLC,
175 Fifth Avenue, New York, NY 10010.

Where this book is distributed in the UK, Europe and the rest of the world,
this is by Palgrave Macmillan, a division of Macmillan Publishers Limited,
registered in England, company number 785998, of Houndmills,
Basingstoke, Hampshire RG21 6XS.

Palgrave Macmillan is the global academic imprint of the above companies
and has companies and representatives throughout the world.

Palgrave® and Macmillan® are registered trademarks in the United States,
the United Kingdom, Europe and other countries.

ISBN: 978–1–137–36091–5

Library of Congress Cataloging-in-Publication Data

Danns, Dionne.
    Desegregating Chicago's public schools : policy implementation,
  politics, and protest, 1965–1985 / Dionne Danns.
      pages cm.—(Historical studies in education)
    Includes bibliographical references and index.
    ISBN 978–1–137–36091–5 (alk. paper)
      1. School integration—Illinois—Chicago—History—20th century.
    2. Public schools—Illinois—Chicago—History—20th century. I. Title.
LC214.23.C54D36 2013
379.2′630977311—dc23   2013028961

A catalogue record of the book is available from the British Library.

Design by Newgen Knowledge Works (P) Ltd., Chennai, India.

First edition: January 2014

10 9 8 7 6 5 4 3 2 1

Contents

Illustrations

Maps

Tables

SERIES FOREWORD

In the annals of school desegregation in American history, surprisingly little attention has been given to Chicago, long recognized as one of the country's most segregated cities. This is partly because its public schools were never subject to the wrenching legal battles and court-ordered integration plans that many other urban districts experienced. Studies about why desegregation cases *didn't* happen, after all, hardly seem as compelling as those that describe the many dramatic encounters that characterized cities where legal decisions had an immediate impact on the daily lives of students, parents, and educators. In this illuminating book, however, Dionne Danns demonstrates how legal inaction can be just as revealing of the social and political forces that historically constrained equity in urban schools.

In certain respects, it is rather surprising that a major desegregation court decision was never rendered in Chicago; it was the only major city in the Great Lakes region to avoid one. As Danns clearly documents, this was largely a function of the city's importance in state and national politics, and the power wielded by its legendary mayor of the postwar era, Richard J. Daley. There certainly was no shortage of local controversy over school segregation and related questions of equity in education during this period. Activists in Chicago were national leaders in identifying the manifold ways in which racial inequality could persist in a school system that claimed to be evenhanded and "colorblind." Yet the Daley regime successfully resisted efforts by protestors and by both state and federal authorities to compel the school system to seriously expand upon limited voluntary desegregation measures.

As Danns's research shows, this situation would last well beyond the period of Daley's immediate influence. By the time of his death in 1976, the politics of desegregation had shifted dramatically, both at the national and local levels. This meant that efforts to achieve meaningful desegregation were continually stymied by a constellation of factors and circumstances, despite ample documentation of inequity and discrimination in the provision of school resources and ongoing avoidance of racial integration. As Danns notes in her conclusion, a "shifting federal agenda, local political power, stakeholder opposition and demographic transitions" combined to make school desegregation a highly elusive goal in the Windy City. Based on solid research and delivered in straightforward prose, her instructive study breaks new ground in Chicago history and historical examinations of northern school integration. We are pleased to include it in the series, and expect that other readers will find it as enlightening as we have.

WILLIAM J. REESE
and
JOHN L. RURY

Acknowledgments

I am grateful to so many people who have made this book possible. I would first like to thank my colleagues at Indiana University for providing a supportive environment, which has helped me to grow as a scholar. Andrea Walton, Barry Bull, and Edward McClellan provided insight on individual chapters. I would especially like to thank my mentor, Donald Warren, for reading an entire draft of the book. Don has continually been supportive of my work and has been far more of a mentor than I could have expected. Other colleagues at IU and elsewhere also provided valuable feedback. Thanks to Valerie Grim, Khalil Muhammad, Christopher Span, Michelle Purdy, and Timothy Lovelace. Special thanks to V. P. Franklin and Derrick Aldridge who guided me through the early drafts of the book. I would also like to thank the anonymous reviewer at Palgrave.

This project was partially supported by Indiana University's New Frontiers Program, funded by Lilly Endowment and administered by the Office of the Vice Provost for Research. A number of current and former students also assisted me with this project. I am grateful to Mahauganee Shaw, Lyndsay Spear, Juan Berumen, Jacob Hardesty, Daniel Dethrow, and Megan Houlihan for research assistance. Alexis Saba had the great joy of transcribing interviews. They were each indispensable early on in this project. Daniel Dethrow also provided valuable editing for the book. Hope Rias, Yesenia Cervera, Carolyn Weber, and Alli Fetter-Harrott also took the time to provide great feedback for some of my chapters.

I visited a number of archives to complete this research. I would like to thank the archivists and staff at the Chicago Board of Education Archives, Harold Washington Library, the National Archives (College Park and the regional Chicago site), Indiana University Library, the Chicago History Museum, Special Collections at the University of Illinois at Chicago, and the Hoover Institution at Stanford University. Three people were especially helpful: at the Indiana University Library, Lou Malcolm found a way for me to receive more microfilm additions of the *Chicago Sun-Times* through interlibrary loan; Theresa Quill created the maps for the book; and Richard Seidel at the Chicago Board of Education Archives was the most helpful, friendly, and supportive archivist I have had the pleasure to meet. He will be missed.

My family has shown me unconditional love and support throughout this project. Danda and Melissa Thomas provided me with hospitality (BTT), as I completed research at the National Archives. Some family members have been so supportive that they have been put to work. My aunt, Joan Elcock, read chapters and provided editorial feedback. My mother, Ann Danns, read the entire manuscript, provided editorial assistance, and served as a sounding board as the project developed. My father, George (Ken) Danns, read the manuscript several times while teaching numerous classes. His guidance was essential in developing the larger arguments for this book. I could not have done this without my parents. My daughter, Najerie, gave up her time with me so that I could complete various drafts of this book. Her sacrifices did not go unnoticed. She also provided valuable editing for the final draft of the book. This book is dedicated to my mother and father, my daughter Najerie, and my sister Tamara Bramlett.

Portions of this book were previously published in articles including "Northern Desegregation: A Tale of Two Cities," *History of Education Quarterly* 51 (1) (2011); "Chicago School Desegregation and the Role of the State of Illinois, 1971–1979," *American Educational History Journal* 37 (1) (2010): 55–73; and "Racial Ideology and the Sanctity of the Neighborhood School Policy in Chicago," *Urban Review* 40 (1) (2008): 64–75.

Introduction

"We charge that the Board of Education of the City of Chicago operates a public school system that is, in fact and by its own statistics, segregated and discriminatory on a racial basis and that the education offered Chicago's Negro children is not only separate from, but inferior to that offered white children."[1] In 1965, the Coordinating Council of Community Organizations (CCCO), a coalition of civil rights, civic and religious groups, accused the Chicago Board of Education of willful segregation of its students in a compelling and detailed Title VI complaint sent to the United States Office of Education in the Department of Health, Education, and Welfare (HEW). The federal government created the 1964 Civil Rights Act to end segregation, especially in the South. Title VI of the act stipulated that programs or activities receiving federal funding could not discriminate against individuals based on race, color, or national origin. This empowered HEW to withhold federal funds from federally funded groups for noncompliance.

According to Gary Orfield, since the law was mostly designed for southern school districts, challenging a northern city with a powerful mayor was a serious miscalculation made by bureaucrats largely "insensitive" to the political ramifications of their actions.[2] HEW officials had debated about which cities to target. Detailed evidence of segregation in Chicago's schools made it seem like a suitable location. Therefore, the agency deferred Chicago's Elementary and Secondary Education Act funds. HEW took this course of action without the prior knowledge of President Lyndon B. Johnson.

This action set the stage for a classic contest between federal government policy articulation and the conflicting reactions and resistances to its implementation by the State of Illinois and the City of Chicago, the Chicago Board of Education and its superintendents, Chicago Teachers Union, and community interest groups. The multitude of reactions highlighted the politics, protests, and other processes that are ignited in utilizing policy to create social change and transform entrenched institutional interests in a democratic society.

Chicago was perhaps one of the least suitable locations for federal government action largely because Mayor Richard J. Daley's "concentrated" political power was unrivaled at the time. His biographers have called him "Boss" and "American Pharaoh" and documented his stronghold on the city. Daley was not an advocate of school desegregation but understood the importance of political symbolism. Mayor Daley often worked behind the scenes when dealing with educational issues. Members of his political machine often spoke for or against school desegregation when it suited Daley's needs.[3] No meaningful desegregation occurred in the city during his administration, which provides evidence that it was not one of his priorities. When Chicago Public Schools faced desegregation protests in the early 1960s, only limited permissive transfer plans were offered in an attempt to rebuff a more concerted effort. Permissive transfers allowed students from overcrowded schools to seek permission to transfer to other schools for the purpose of desegregation and that had limited impact in desegregating schools. More aggressive desegregation efforts would mean a lessening of Daley's support from white ethnic groups who could decide not to vote for him or leave the city altogether. Though Daley said little publically, his record on housing segregation and the lack of significant desegregation during his reign spoke volumes.

As Adam Cohen and Elizabeth Taylor argued, segregation was "an unstated foundation" on which Daley redeveloped Chicago. While segregation had long been a condition in the city, Daley's administration thrived on intensified housing segregation through the use of urban renewal. With federal funds, he revitalized downtown and solidly white neighborhoods and built high rise public housing projects to contain blacks in black communities. By constructing the Dan Ryan Expressway, he erected barriers between the dense housing projects along the State Street Corridor and white working class neighborhoods on the Southwest Side of the city. His segregation efforts helped him maintain a delicate coalition of blacks in ghettos whose votes could more easily be controlled and ethnic whites satisfied with separation from blacks.[4]

When Chicago's federal funds were deferred in 1965, Chicago politicians from the local, state, and federal levels were outraged. Some of President Johnson's political allies in Congress came from Chicago and Illinois and had helped pass the Civil Rights Act. Northern politicians supported the Civil Rights Act presuming that it would not be applied in northern states and certainly not in the City of Chicago.[5] Eventually the influential Mayor Daley met with President Johnson and the funds were released, demonstrating his political reach. This debacle exemplified the difficulty of implementing federal school desegregation policy in Chicago, and the political minefield policy enforcers had to navigate. It also served as the beginning of the federal government's involvement with desegregation in the city.

The Title VI complaint and subsequent actions provide a clear example of how politics and the actions of civil rights groups and constituents interact to influence policy in Chicago. It highlights the three important strands of analyses which are the focal point of this study: the processes and missteps involved in the formulation and implementation of desegregation policies, the politics associated with school desegregation, and the perceptions and actions of various stakeholders seeking to influence policy outcomes.

With the fiftieth anniversary of the 1964 Civil Rights Act and the sixtieth anniversary of *Brown v. Board of Education*, this study brings an important new perspective to the challenges and transformations public policy implementation undergoes and the resultant limitations and effectiveness of government legislative power in bringing about social change. The Civil Rights Act of 1964, combined with court rulings, ushered in a period of heightened school desegregation throughout the South. Chicago offers a telling example of the changing meaning of public policy and the tenuous negotiations that occurred as the 1964 Civil Rights Act was implemented in a northern city.

School desegregation was a largely conflict-ridden exercise in which federal intent was focused not on whether there should be school desegregation, but rather, on how and where it should be implemented. Desegregation policies emanated from the Civil Rights Act passed in Congress and rulings of the federal courts, but federal, state, and local officials were tasked with developing policies to articulate the intent of these laws and court rulings. The federal government, through HEW and the Department of Justice, investigated and brought cases against school districts of all sizes in the North, South, and West,[6] but the interaction between Chicago Public Schools and the federal government demonstrates that federal policy implementation is not unilateral. It often took years for federal demands to be implemented in Chicago and usually it was less ambitious than federal agencies may have liked.

Illinois state superintendents and the State Board of Education also put policies in place to achieve school desegregation, yet were unsuccessful because they did not implement sanctions for noncompliance. Chicago presented difficulties for the state because of its geographic size and the large percentage of students of color. The city's size and segregated neighborhoods would require busing students far distances. With there already being over 70 percent of black and Latino students in the district in the 1970s, ambitious enforcement of desegregation plans would lead to further loss of whites from the city. State officials lacked the political will or clout to implement the sanctions for its policies in such an atmosphere.[7]

Federal, state, and local officials interacted over the years to implement student and faculty desegregation policies with varying levels of success. Each group encountered political pressures and protest actions from stakeholders at local levels. Their political will or lack thereof, impacted their efforts to implement public policy. As federal and state officials pursued student and faculty desegregation, Chicago's school officials dragged their feet and continually issued voluntary plans calculated to stymie rather than promote desegregation. The most successful Chicago desegregation efforts occurred when federal officials applied sanctions during President Jimmy Carter's administration in the mid- to late 1970s. Unlike Johnson and other presidents, Carter did not have to deal with Mayor Daley's resistance to desegregation because Daley had passed away by December 1976, as the federal government conducted procedures to withhold federal funding for faculty desegregation and forced the city into a consent decree for student desegregation. Prior to federal government sanctions, Chicago continued to evade meaningful desegregation efforts through the administrations of three school superintendents. By the time the Justice Department filed suit against the Chicago Board of Education in 1980, the percentage of white students had decreased from to 47.7 in 1965 to 18.6. The loss of white students in the school system minimized the impact school desegregation would have had. The enforcement of policies finally occurred just as the flight of whites from the city and the school system had rendered any successful plan moot.

Generally, policy formulation and implementation are heavily influenced by politics, and the case of the development and enactment of school desegregation is no different. While school desegregation policies largely emanated from federal statutes and court cases, officials working in federal agencies were responsible for carrying out these policies. These federal officials soon found that zealous enforcement would lead to political difficulties for the administrations they served. Their actions were constrained or empowered based on the presidential administrations, their personal level of commitment to desegregation, the larger political environment in which they operated, and the resistance or support of school and political leaders in the states, cities, and districts they targeted.

Federal efforts to desegregate Chicago's schools spanned five presidential administrations from Lyndon Johnson to Ronald Reagan (1965–1983). Each president had his own personal and political philosophy about school desegregation. As presidents and federal agency leadership changed, pressure on Chicago's schools to implement desegregation policies ebbed and flowed, thus proving a lack of consistent effort in the city. The 1964 Civil Rights Act, which gave the federal government the power to enforce school desegregation, was passed during Democrat Lyndon B. Johnson's administration. Even though the mechanisms to bring about meaningful changes were established during his time in office, his administration accomplished limited results due to southern resistance. After Johnson left office, the desegregation efforts of his administration (mixed with court rulings) led to desegregation throughout the South. Republican Richard Nixon's political rhetoric signaled a departure from school desegregation as he forced the resignation of any agency personnel who moved too aggressively. Republican Gerald Ford, like Nixon before him, opposed busing and focused on faculty desegregation. Democrat Jimmy Carter, who like his two Republican predecessors disagreed with busing, had an administration committed to carrying out the law and was the most effective in Chicago school desegregation efforts. Republican Ronald Reagan's administration represented a shift in policy. He was against continued civil rights for blacks and applied more stringent justification to limit school desegregation and busing.[8]

In addition to policies and political administrations, many civil rights groups on the national and local level sought to influence desegregation outcomes in the city through use of the courts or participation in advisory committees. The National Association for the Advancement of Colored People (NAACP) stood on the front lines for desegregation nationally. Decades of their efforts led to the *Brown v. Board of Education* Supreme Court decision in 1954. When HEW was not moving fast enough to clear the backlog of cases brought to their attention, the NAACP brought *Adams v. Richardson* (1972) to court to speed up policy implementation. In Chicago, the NAACP was often disappointed by the lackluster desegregation plans the city created and the federal and state governments sanctioned. The NAACP was so strongly supportive of desegregation that the organization's leadership also spoke out against blacks who opposed desegregation. In addition, another influential organization, the Chicago Urban League, took a more moderate stance by seeking practical approaches to desegregation. Their role on the City Wide Advisory Committee in the 1970s influenced the addition of mandatory desegregation backups to the committee's plans (in case voluntary desegregation plans failed).

There were a myriad of constituencies with contrasting school desegregation views in Chicago. As indicated in map 0.1, various areas of the city were the focus of desegregation and protests. Though it may seem so, race was not the only factor in determining whether there would be support or opposition. Class, ethnicity, region of the city, ideological beliefs, and the direct impact on their children all

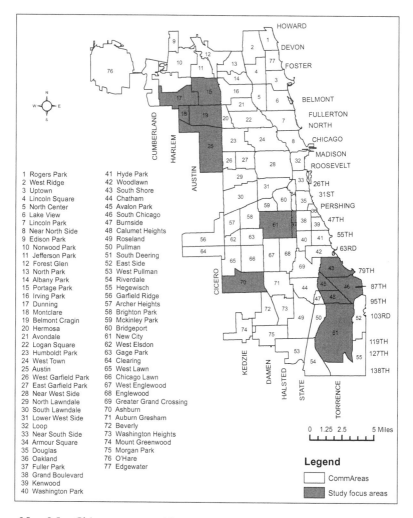

Map 0.1 Chicago communities

worked to impact how people perceived and whether they supported desegregation efforts. Blacks who lived in areas with overcrowded schools were more likely to support school desegregation whether or not their children would attend desegregated schools. They thought that movement of some students would likely lead to improvements for the children who remained. Middle-class blacks in South Shore and Avalon Park held an alternate view. They opposed desegregation because some believed the schools their children attended were better than the ones to which they would be bused. Additionally, some blacks embraced Black Power ideology which was opposed to the underlying belief that black schools were inferior.

Whites who opposed desegregation were often the most vocal when it impacted their neighborhoods. Some echoed positions with racist overtones, but others appeared to have more rational arguments against desegregation, most notably the maintenance of neighborhood schools. Although moderate whites may have favored desegregation, their voices were largely drowned out due to vigorous opposition to desegregation policies. Ethnicity and class added additional layers to the story of white resistance and support. Many Jewish and middle-class residents proposed two-way busing in South Shore. In areas on the Northwest and Southwest Sides, mostly Polish, German, Italian, Irish, Yugoslavian, Scandinavian, and Swedish working- and middle-class residents opposed desegregation.

The migration and immigration of Latinos, particularly in the 1970s and early 1980s, resulted in the expanded contentiousness of a previously black and white issue (see tables 0.1 and 0.2). Latinos were particularly concerned about how desegregation planning would impact bilingual education programs. Many Latinos also agreed with blacks and whites that school improvement was preferable to desegregation. In spite of all the varying perceptions, a late 1979 survey revealed that more than 50 percent of people from the three largest racial/ethnic groups were against busing. However, most blacks and Latinos thought desegregation would provide their children with a better education.[9]

The most popular way for people to show their discontentment, whether in support or opposition of desegregation, was in the form of protest. Every step of the process to desegregate was met with community protests either for or against desegregation. In the early 1960s, the CCCO led school boycotts and protest demonstrations to support school desegregation as part of the city's early civil rights efforts. Hundreds of thousands of students showed their support by staying out of school in 1963, 1964, and 1965. After 1967, most

Table 0.1   Student enrollments 1963–2011

Year	School percentage White	School percentage Black	School percentage Hispanic[10]	Total enrollment
1964	49.2	48.3		566,873
1965	47.7	49.5		558,491
1968	42.2	52.9	4.1	580,207
1970	34.6	54.8	9.7	577,679
1975	26.8	58.4	13.4	530,054
1980	18.6	60.8	18.4	458,497
1985	14.2	60.3	22.5	430,908
1990	11.8	58	27.1	408,714
2011	8.8	41.6	44.1	404,151

Source: Chicago Public School Racial Ethnic Surveys and Stats and Facts.

Table 0.2   City demographics 1960–2010[11]

Year	No. of Whites	Whites (%)	No. of Blacks	Blacks (%)	No. of Hispanics	Hispanics (%)	Total Population
1960	2,712,748	76.4	812,637	22.8			3,550,404
1970	2,207,767	65.5	1,102,620	32.7			3,366,957
1980	1,299,557	43.2	1,187,905	39.5	422,063	14.0	3,005,072
1990	1,263,524	45.3	1,087,711	39.0	545,852	19.6	2,783,726
2000	1,215,315	42.0	1,065,009	36.7	753,644	26.0	2,896,016
2010	1,212,835	45.0	887,608	32.9	778,862	28.9	2,695,598

Source: US census 1960–2010.

demonstrations were against desegregation. Although these protests were well organized, in some cases, it had limited power to sway school officials. In other cases, the protests impacted the scope of desegregation plans.

Many city and school leaders valued keeping white residents in the city and, therefore, opposed school desegregation efforts. The entrenched segregated housing patterns, continued loss of the white middle-class tax base, and increased influx of blacks and Latinos, collectively limited the political will of the Chicago Board of Education and its superintendents to desegregate. These demographic and economic concerns played an important role in determining the level of desegregation that could occur in the city while also tempering local political support of desegregation.

This book presents a comprehensive study of school desegregation in Chicago from 1965–1985. It seeks to add to the scholarship on desegregation in Chicago by examining several important, but under-studied areas: faculty desegregation, state involvement with student desegregation, and a detailed discussion of the federal government's role in school desegregation. This study sheds light on how political, economic, and social forces combined to make it difficult to fully desegregate the schools despite repeated efforts throughout the 1960s, 1970s, and 1980s. It chronicles the impact of demographic transition on policy implementation. It analyzes the politics and disconnection between policy formulation and policy implementation. It focuses on the conflicting perceptions about desegregation among black, white, and Latino citizens and policy makers. Finally, it highlights the dynamics of a democratic society in which a white majority sought to protect its privilege even when it involved the continued marginalization of minorities.

Northern school desegregation post-*Brown v. Board of Education* has not been fully explored. Like the South, each city or area provides a unique story. Boston is among the best known desegregation efforts because the city's protests were reminiscent of southern protests. Detroit is also well known largely because of the Supreme Court ruling in *Milliken v. Bradley*. Scholars have also documented desegregation efforts in Buffalo and New York, New York; Columbus, Ohio; Milwaukee, Wisconsin; and other cities.[12] Like Detroit, Chicago's black student population outpaced its white student population. Further, the city's sizable Latino population further complicated the desegregation efforts. New York City was the only other large northern city with a comparable Latino population at the time.

Chicago is distinctive when compared to other major cities because of the involvement of the state and federal government, and because no major court ruling came from Chicago. Other northern cities typically experienced federal and Supreme Court rulings that served as the source of desegregation policy. However, in Chicago, policy came directly from the federal and state governments. Their enforcement of the Civil Rights Act impacted both student and faculty desegregation. The courts were only used to enforce a compromise (consent decree) between the federal government and the Board of Education. This study's northern focus, policy emphasis, teacher desegregation discussion, and multiethnic demographics set it apart from other studies. Furthermore, this study's spotlight on the implementation of the Civil Rights Act makes it timely.

For this study, I use certain terminology over others. Though terms like African American and Hispanic are popular, I have consciously chosen to use black and Latino largely from personal preference. I will also use desegregation instead of integration, as it better describes the actions of the government. The Civil Rights Act used the word desegregation and defined it in Title IV in the following manner: "Desegregation means the assignment of students to public schools and within such schools without regard to their race, color, religion, or national origin."[13] The federal government favored the use of desegregation as did Chicago school officials who defined integration as something that occurred naturally. In official reports, schools were integrated when the school attendance area was already racially mixed. Desegregation referred to the changes the school board made in order for racial diversity to occur in schools.

School desegregation is often discussed without a clear numerical sense of what desegregation means. In the South, one black student attending a formerly segregated school was considered desegregation. For Chicago, the definition shifted based on who studied the city or who demanded desegregation. Some efforts for desegregation used a 90–10 definition. A school with fewer than 90 percent of one race was considered desegregated. The state's definition called for individual schools to be within 15 percent of the city's student demographics. The Chicago Board of Education eventually decided that a school with fewer than 70 percent of one race would be stably desegregated. Proponents and opponents of desegregation disliked each of these ratios, yet the definition continually varied based on who was discussing it. The changing definition was an area of conflict between the school officials and the federal and state government.

The Civil Rights Act covered more than school desegregation, yet the focus on schools as sites for transformation is fundamental to understanding the American society. As historian Tracy Steffes argues, Americans have used schooling as a "social policy choice." While European nations invested in social welfare in the progressive era, Americans funded schools in an effort to promote equal educational opportunity. Americans have had undeniable reliance on schools to solve social problems without enough consideration for the larger social, economic, and political entities that limit the transformative power of schools. Meritocratic rhetoric "about the democratic opportunity of schooling obscured these barriers and presented schooling as a project of individual effort and merit; failures were individual rather than structural."[14] Since schools have historically been an instrument for social policy and have long considered the "great equalizer," they were as logical a place as any for the federal government to focus their desegregation efforts. The *Brown v. Board* decision was a classic example of the reliance on schools as sites to solve social problems. The decision became a powerful symbol of hope and represented the nation's desire to provide equal educational opportunities when southern states refused. Yet the symbol was not enough because most southern schools remained segregated for more than a decade after its ruling, and it had a limited impact on most northern schools.[15]

As this study will show, institutional racism has had a profound impact on limiting civil rights advancement. Important laws such as the 1964 Civil Rights Act were passed to end discrimination and school segregation, but politics played a role in thwarting implementation, modifying policy, and diminishing impact. These actions occurred as an appeasement to white privilege often at the expense of the black and Latino population. In spite of the many years of negotiations between the federal government, state, city officials, and community members, very little school desegregation has occurred in Chicago. Predominantly white schools were desegregated, but the majority of black students still attended segregated schools with 95 percent or more black students. As the Latino population in the city increased, Latino students became increasingly segregated as well. These facts show that meaningful desegregation in the city is really a misnomer. Yet the minimal desegregation outcomes are an essential component for understanding policy implementation and its limitations on social change.

SETTING THE STAGE

Scholars have written extensively about Chicago's school desegregation efforts prior to 1968.[16] Chicago's housing segregation is legendary and has been well documented. Understanding the history of blacks in Chicago is essential to comprehend the significance of school desegregation. Since the first wave of the Great Migration between World War I and the Great Depression, southern blacks moved to Chicago and other northern cities by the hundreds of thousands. The first migration led to a Chicago population increase of just over 200,000 African Americans. In Chicago, blacks were limited mainly by force and real estate policies to a stretch of land on the South Side known as the Black Belt or Bronzeville. While blacks occupied smaller areas in the city, the vast majority, regardless of class, were in the Black Belt. As the second wave of the Great Migration occurred after World War II, Chicago's black population increased by over half a million in just 20 years. The substantial increase in population occurred at a time when World War II veterans returned home and were also looking for housing in an extremely tight housing market.

The competition for housing plus the fact that blacks were unwanted in new areas led to racial conflicts between the 1940s and 1960s. Blacks expanded not only into areas adjacent to the Black Belt, but also into the West Side and far South Side of Chicago. Their expansion was typically block-by-block and contiguous. Residential segregation remained for the most part with integration occurring only as neighborhoods changed quickly from white to black.[17]

The migration of black southerners to Chicago precipitated school segregation. Much of the early activism around schools was to relieve overcrowding and to have new schools built.[18] After the *Brown* decision, the NAACP immediately placed their focus on the *de facto* segregation occurring in the North. In April of 1958, *The Crisis* published "De Facto Segregation in Chicago Public Schools," which was an excerpt from the Chicago Branch of the NAACP's statement to a Chicago Board of Education meeting in December 1957.[19] The report estimated that 91 percent of Chicago's elementary schools and 71 percent of the high schools were de facto segregated. While the elementary school segregation seemed to be a factor of housing segregation, high school segregation was largely caused by policy decisions. Students coming from feeder schools in many cases were assigned to high schools based on race rather than their distance to the nearest high school. Segregated black schools tended to be more overcrowded with double shift assignments.[20] Mixed race schools did not remain mixed for long as neighborhoods transitioned from white to black. The report also highlighted the underutilization of classrooms in predominantly white schools, the concentration of inexperienced teachers in black schools, and the planned segregation based on school site selection, instruction quality, and time spent in school.[21] This and other reports highlighted the inequality in Chicago's segregated schools that resulted from official school policies.

There were a variety of desegregation initiatives that took place in the early 1960s in individual Chicago communities and citywide in an effort to desegregate schools. The NAACP was collecting data so that they could build a strong school desegregation case, but a *Chicago Defender* editorial writer and some black leaders believed that the NAACP was moving too slowly. The NAACP and the Chatham-Avalon Park Community Council, a black professional community organization, invited attorney Paul Zuber to Chicago. Zuber served as the lawyer for the plaintiffs in the *Taylor v. Board of Education* (1961) case where a judge ruled that the schools in New Rochelle, New York, had to desegregate its schools regardless of the segregation being de facto or de jure. Zuber's invitation was in hopes of pulling together a definitive Chicago case. Although the NAACP wanted to move slowly to build financial and community support, other groups wanted to press ahead with a Chicago case. Along with community, church, and civil rights organizations, the Chatham-Avalon Park Community Council planned and carried out Operation Transfer in September 1961. One hundred and sixty parents sent in requests to transfer their children to predominantly white schools, and their requests were denied. The transfer denials led to the *Webb v. Board of Education of the City of Chicago* case. The case was initially filed in September 1961 and dismissed in July 1962 because the plaintiffs had not exhausted Illinois's administrative procedures.[22] These procedures of the Illinois School Code stipulated that the county superintendent of schools had to hear complaints first, followed by the state superintendent of schools.[23] The case was reopened in June 1963, after the US Supreme Court ruled in another Illinois case that plaintiffs did not have to go through the State of Illinois's procedures to have access to federal courts. The *Webb* case was then settled out of court August 1963.[24]

Webb v. Board of Education, while failing to bring about school desegregation the plaintiffs had wished, did highlight the basic arguments for school desegregation in Chicago. The initial *Webb* case asked for a permanent injunction to keep the defendants (the Chicago Board of Education and Superintendent Benjamin C. Willis) from "maintaining and operating a racially segregated public school system." Like the NAACP report and subsequent arguments about school desegregation in future campaigns, the plaintiffs argued that school boundaries were gerrymandered, permissive transfers sent white students out of black schools, schools were constructed in black areas instead of utilizing empty seats in white schools, and junior high and high school site selections ensured racial segregation.[25] The Board of Education and Superintendent Willis denied that they had purposely segregated students.

The case was settled out of court with an agreement that a study of Chicago schools would be conducted. While some questioned the NAACP's motive for wanting to move slowly, the ineffectiveness of the case supported their reasoning. The out-of-court settlement led to the 1964 "Report to the Board of Education of the City of Chicago by the Advisory Panel on Integration of the Public School," widely known as the Hauser Report, which documented the segregation in Chicago's schools. The report found that 90 percent of Chicago's black elementary students attended segregated schools.[26] It also indicated that black segregated schools were more likely to have less qualified teachers, perform worse on standardized tests, have higher dropout and lower attendance rates, and have fewer resources than white schools.[27] Again, the Hauser Report echoed issues in earlier reports and the *Webb* case, and the findings did not surprise civil rights groups. The Hauser Report included recommendations based on the premise that racial segregation "regardless of its causes, is incompatible with the ideals of a free society and its commitment to equal educational opportunity." The authors argued, "Neither potential administrative difficulties nor limitation of existing educational policy is a morally, socially, or professionally defensible reason for failure to pursue the aims of quality education and racial integration simultaneously and with vigor, using all resource methods presently available or which reasonably can be devised for their attainment."[28]

The report's strong moral undertones did little to move the superintendent or the board. The Board of Education approved what became known as the Willis–Whiston Plan. Even though the committee recognized that "such a plan has been offered twice in Chicago with negligible results," their plan repeated earlier permissive transfer plans that were highly ineffective in desegregating Chicago schools.[29] These policies were largely unsuccessful because they did not provide transportation for transferring students. Only those who could afford the cost of commuting or had available transportation could take advantage of the plan. In sum, *Webb v. Board of Education* did not result in the major reforms that were hoped for, but showed that even solid evidence of segregation did not lead to a court ruling against Chicago Public Schools.

Webb v. Board shows that the courts were not an effective avenue for acquiring desegregation in Chicago in the early 1960s. Organizers created CCCO, which served as the catalyst for the early Civil Rights Movement in Chicago which would later become the Chicago Freedom Movement. This coalition group was responsible for organizing large scale school boycotts and negotiating with city and school officials. In 1962, CCCO included the NAACP, the Chatham-Avalon Park Community Council, the Chicago Urban League, The Woodlawn Organization (TWO), and the Englewood Council for Community Action. The group quickly expanded to include a variety of other organizations.[30] During the boycotts it organized, the group was led by organizer Rev. Arthur Brazier of TWO, and beginning in January 1964, teacher and organizer Albert Raby from Teachers for Integrated Schools served as CCCO leader.[31] Although the coalition did not always have consensus, their Freedom Day boycotts were a great show of force and the desire for changes within the schools as thousands of students stayed out of school in October 1963 (about 225,000), February 1964 (about 124,000), and June 1965 (about 100,000), in support of the CCCO's efforts. The boycotts were more a symbol of the CCCO's organizing efforts than a real source of change in the desegregation events in the city. Mayor Daley "supported" the first boycott, but was clearly opposed to the others, and black aldermen in his political machine followed his lead. The first boycott statement called for desegregation; the removal of Superintendent Willis; an integration policy for the staff and students; racial head counts of teachers, students, and administrators; the abolition of high school branches in elementary schools; availability of trade and vocational education to all children; and the utilization of all the space in school buildings before the use of mobile classrooms.[32] These and other demands again spoke to the crux of the arguments about school desegregation in Chicago, but like the *Webb* case and the subsequent Hauser Report, these efforts did little to desegregate schools.

Activists from local and national groups organized to create change in Chicago's schools. In the midst of the *Webb* court case and the CCCO boycotts, civil rights groups conducted sit-ins at the Board of Education headquarters and at sites where mobile classrooms were to be delivered.[33] In spite of their efforts, Chicago's schools remained segregated. Since local efforts to desegregate were very ineffective, the CCCO went national with their desegregation fight. A July 1965 congressional hearing brought Chicago's problems to the national spotlight. Superintendent Willis and Philip Hauser were among those testifying. Despite the effort, the hearing served more as another announcement of the problems rather than a solution.[34] Also in July 1965, the CCCO issued its Title VI complaint, which outlined the previously discussed problems in the schools with much detail and evidence. This included the gerrymandering of school boundaries and racial segregation at Washburne Trade School. It led to Chicago being under the watchful eye of the federal government for years to come, but initially it only produced more permissive transfer plans.[35] In essence, these civil rights and community groups attempted to bring real change, but their actions did not produce the desired results.

Chicago activists also had to negotiate with Superintendent Benjamin C. Willis, a known segregationist. Willis's antics included allegations of purposefully avoiding a court summons, quitting when he could not get his way, and symbolizing the segregation that many were fighting against. Willis was asked to return after his resignation and he served until his retirement in 1966. Once he retired, James F.

Redmond, who was a veteran of school desegregation in his previous role as superintendent in New Orleans, became superintendent in Chicago. Regardless of his experience, perhaps nowhere could have prepared him for Chicago politics. Redmond's reign did lead to limited desegregation, though. Even with the numbers being extremely small, this was more than his predecessor was willing to do.

Chapter 1 discusses a city on edge about desegregation, as the small scale plan Superintendent Redmond unveiled led to numerous protests within the affected Chicago communities. Redmond's plan was a direct result of the 1965 Title VI complaint fiasco and was part of the Chicago Public Schools' face-saving compromise with HEW's Office of Education. The chapter highlights the difficulty of policy implementation when necessary stakeholders are not initially involved in the decision-making process. Stakeholders' protest efforts limited, changed, and tailored desegregation plans to meet the needs of their communities.

Chapter 2 explores the federal government faculty desegregation efforts in Chicago. The Justice Department demanded the desegregation of Chicago's school faculty beginning in 1969. The federal government was able to secure faculty desegregation because, in 1976, HEW's Office of Civil Rights—which was tasked in 1966 by the House Appropriations Committee to handle Title VI compliance—began proceedings with an administrative judge who ruled that Chicago was in violation of Title VI. After negotiations, teachers and principals were desegregated in 1977 as a result of this ruling. The implementation of sanctions was the only reason Chicago Public Schools adequately desegregated its faculty.

Chapter 3 examines the state's attempts to be in compliance with federal laws and court rulings. The state took its school districts to task beginning in 1971 and demanded that they follow a set of rules and guidelines to prevent segregation in schools or face a financial penalty for noncompliance. These state policies were difficult to enforce in Chicago. The State Board of Education and its superintendent's failure to apply sanctions (withholding funds) led to Chicago school officials to blatantly ignore the state's request for a more comprehensive desegregation plan.

Chapter 4 looks closely at federal policy and politics in student desegregation. As the state failed to enforce its policies, HEW's Office of Civil Rights stepped in to demand that Chicago desegregate its students in 1979, following the dictates of the Civil Rights Act. After negotiations failed, HEW turned the case over to the Justice Department for litigation. This resulted in a consent decree, which was possible because Superintendent Joseph P. Hannon resigned, and a severe school financial crisis led to the reconstitution of the entire Board of Education. The new board negotiated the consent decree with the Justice Department.

In chapter 5, the focus is on the arduous task of desegregation policy implementation and the changing political environment as the Reagan administration attempted to reverse school desegregation trends. As the city created its desegregation plan, the Reagan administration was much more willing to accept a relatively weak plan because they were against school desegregation.

The book closes with a reexamination of challenges to school desegregation policy formulation and implementation with changing political environments, demographic shifts, and stakeholder protests. The concluding chapter reveals the limitations the federal government faced using the nation's public school system as a favored mechanism to promote desegregation and civil rights in an effort to forge a more perfect union.

CHAPTER 1

Redmond's School Desegregation Plan and Reactions

At first appearance James Redmond may not have seemed all that different from the previous Chicago superintendent Benjamin Willis, whom Redmond replaced in 1966. Both were older, white, clean-shaven men with neatly trimmed hair. But Redmond's entrance into the superintendent's office marked a symbolic shift in the handling of the city's schools—at least in regard to the city's image of desegregation. While Willis had been praised for increasing resources in some of the city's schools, his record regarding desegregation and the inequalities between black and white schools had come under vehement public attack. As black schools became increasingly over-crowded, Willis merely responded by installing mobile units, which his critics called "Willis Wagons." Willis had stubbornly maintained that outcries regarding desegregation and inequality were unwarranted—despite federal reports that acknowledged such inequalities.[1] Redmond replaced Willis upon Willis's retirement in 1966 giving civil rights activists high expectations for the city's desegregation efforts.

In January 1967, and not long after Redmond became superinten-dent, the Department of Health, Education and Welfare's (HEW) US Office of Education sent Chicago Public Schools a report that discussed concerns about faculty and student assignments, appren-ticeship programs, and vocational education. This was a direct result of the Coordinating Council of Community Organization's (CCCO) 1965 Title VI (of the 1964 Civil Rights Act) complaint that raised those very concerns. Chicago received a US Office of Education planning grant to conduct a study of segregation, and Redmond used the funding to create a school desegregation plan in conjunc-tion with expert consultants. Titled "Increasing Desegregation of Faculties, Students, and Vocational Education Programs," and also known as the Redmond Plan, it was a response to federal pressure to desegregate Chicago Public Schools. Issued in August 1967, it provided a series of recommendations; the most controversial dealt with student desegregation.[2]

The political fallout from the CCCO Title VI complaint meant that any resulting school desegregation plan would be limited and politically risky. While the federal government had to enforce the 1964 Civil Rights Act, federal officials gave the city an out by not pressing for a substantive plan. Still, some sort of plan needed to be implemented, and the superintendent, his staff, and the Board of Education were given ownership of the policy implementation process. However, Chicago residents demanded their voices be heard when the board announced its busing plan (a scaled-down version of the Redmond Plan), and these stakeholders were able to impact the scope of the plan in some notable ways. Consequently, the implementation of federal policy became hotly contested and was not simply a top-down mandate, but rather it resulted in a negotiation between federal and local officials as well as the stakeholders in the city.

After the initial Redmond Plan was issued, Superintendent Redmond and his staff created a limited desegregation busing plan announced in January 1968—which resulted in immense controversy. The busing plan caused great consternation within the white and black communities on Chicago's Southeast and Northwest Sides, and in the Austin community on the West Side. The attempt to implement the limited busing plan led to contentious white responses that clouded the lines between racism, a desire for neighborhood schools, and neighborhood stabilization. While some arguments were overtly racist, others were cloaked in the presumed cultural deprivation of blacks or the imposition of school policies on individual liberties. Some whites simply opposed the limited busing plan and favored a two-way busing plan. Black responses to Superintendent Redmond's proposal also complicated Chicago's desegregation efforts in 1968. Some questioned the underlying assumptions about black inferiority in the desegregation plans. Others pushed for desegregation as an opportunity to relieve overcrowded neighborhood schools. The varied responses to such a modest plan helped to set the stage for further desegregation in the city. Meanwhile, Mayor Daley remained relatively quiet in public about his views on the issue in order to appear neutral on such divisive school issues. However, city aldermen from his Democratic Machine publicly spoke in opposition to the plan, which strongly signified that Daley also opposed it. The development of the plan and conflicting reactions also demonstrated the challenges of policy implementation in a context in which the affected communities were not fully in favor.

HOUSING, RACIAL STABILIZATION, AND SCHOOL REALITIES ON THE WEST SIDE

One major contributor to school segregation in Chicago was residential segregation, since children were assigned to neighborhood schools.[3] However, residential segregation in Chicago was not the result of passive "choice" habitation. Residential segregation in the city had been fiercely enforced for decades through intimidation, violence, and discriminatory housing practices. A number of small housing riots broke out as blacks began migrating to Chicago from the South. In the 1910s, homes of blacks and real estate agents who served them were bombed. Deadly riots occurred in 1919, resulting in the deaths of 23 blacks, 15 whites, and one Latino—520 more were injured.[4] Smaller riots occurred in the 1940s and 1950s, illustrating the lengths white home owners were willing to go to keep their neighborhoods exclusively white.[5]

In addition, unscrupulous realtors made tremendous profit by scaring whites into selling their homes in areas surrounding expanding black areas. Once whites hurried to sell their homes at a lower price, realtors then rented to blacks or sold the homes through contract sales. Blacks often could not obtain legitimate loans from traditional mortgage lenders because of redlining policies that devalued property where blacks lived. In a contract sale, a down payment was made and money would be paid on the contract until it was all paid off. If home owners missed one month of payment, they lost all of the money they put into the home and the contract dealer would start a new contract with someone else.[6] As a result, blacks tended to pay much more for housing than whites leaving the neighborhoods, and paid, on average, higher rents as well.

The shortage of housing after World War II only exacerbated the existing problem. Black families had to work extremely hard and take on additional work shifts in order to keep homes on contract payments. Some even housed additional tenants to make ends meet. In an effort to keep their homes, maintenance was often neglected because there was no money left. As Beryl Satter indicates, whites saw the crowded homes, unsupervised children, and decaying property as a problem with blacks; others blamed economic exploitation for the home problems blacks experienced.[7]

Whites who opposed blacks moving into their neighborhoods feared the loss of neighborhood stabilization—meaning that a neighborhood would not turn over racially from white to black. In some communities, whites fought to stay in their homes in an attempt to delay black encroachment and maintain stabilization. On Chicago's West Side, home owners had fought for years to be included in the city's revitalization plans.[8] Without the power necessary to garner funds, the West Side had begun to deteriorate well before blacks moved into those neighborhoods in the 1960s. Whites sought various avenues to acquire aid to fix the crumbling infrastructure, but the city used urban renewal funds acquired from the federal government to revitalize downtown and the surrounding areas. The neighborhoods around the University of Chicago, which also received financial support, began to flourish as well. Whites on the West Side wanted to maintain their properties and stay in the city. They formed organizations to rally for neighborhood improvements as well as to keep blacks out. Beginning in the mid-1950s, residents even lobbied for the new University of Illinois Chicago campus to be placed in a park on the West Side with the hopes of improving their neighborhoods while stemming the tide of black migration into those areas. Despite community efforts, city officials used urban renewal funds for their priorities. Once the funding ran out, there was no money to improve other city areas like Austin. After a number of years of lobbying for neighborhood improvements, West Side whites eventually moved to other areas of the city or into the developing suburbs.[9]

As with other midwestern cities, Chicago's neighborhoods had a long history of concentrated ethnic enclaves and fierce contestation when neighborhood demographics transitioned from one racial group to another. Before the 1930s, Germans, Irish, Swedes, and to a lesser extent, Italians and Russian Jews dominated the Austin community on the West Side of Chicago. Italians became the largest group in 1960, followed by Irish, Germans, and Poles. The area began experiencing rapid transition from white to black. In 1960, there were only 31 blacks in Austin; but by 1970, 41,583 blacks lived in the community, making up 32.5 percent of the community population.[10] Beginning in 1961, blacks began to move into the very southeastern and poorer section of a community once settled by Italians. Although whites fought to maintain their neighborhoods, the great need for black housing meant that this area would continue to open up. Generally, blacks occupied certain census tracks as they entered the community and eventually spread to nearby tracks. By 1966, blacks began to enter even higher socioeconomic areas of Austin. Consequently, some census tracks had more middle-class blacks than others. Although middle-class blacks replaced some of the white residents, more of the new residents were below the poverty line. For example, two of the community's poorest census tracts, which were virtually all white in 1960, had 10.8 and 12.5 percent of residents living below the poverty line. By 1970, these same census tracts were over 80 percent black with 17 and 26.4 percent of residents living below the poverty line.[11] The loss of manufacturing jobs exacerbated employment opportunities for blacks. The racial and socioeconomic transitions brought additional strain to the community. City services, already lagging when whites occupied the neighborhoods, continued to deteriorate.[12]

As blacks entered the Austin area, they brought households with more children than the departing white families, and families more reliant on the public schools. The result was that some of Austin's public school populations almost doubled. Two schools in particular, May and Spencer, saw great increases in their numbers. May Elementary School had 801 students in 1963, 87.4 percent of whom were white. By 1967, there were 1,554 students, 83.9 percent of whom were black. Spencer Elementary School saw similar changes. In 1963, there were 903 pupils at Spencer, 98.7 percent of whom were white. In 1967, 82.4 percent of the 1,342 students were black. Vast overcrowding would put a strain on any school system—but the shift in the racial and socioeconomic composition imposed additional burdens on the schools as well. White teachers were at times unprepared for (or unwilling to deal with) black students. Some of these teachers quickly left for schools more to their liking. As the racial and class composition of the public school students began to change, some middle-class blacks also withdrew their children from these public schools and enrolled them in the area's two Catholic schools. This exacerbated white departure from the community because black students occupied spaces in private schools sought by whites hoping to remain in Austin. The school system was unable to immediately provide additional facilities for the community, besides mobile units.[13]

Austin High School also experienced racial transition, though not as quickly as at the May and Spencer schools. As whites with school-age children stopped moving into Austin in anticipation of black migration, the population of Austin High School began to change. With a smaller number of white school-age children, the high school enrollment began to shrink between 1960 and 1962. Black migrants eventually filled that void. Blacks comprised 25 percent of the Austin High School enrollment in 1966, and 39 percent in 1967. The increase in African Americans led to a number of racial brawls in the school. In 1965, both blacks and whites fought each other and attacked students of the other race unfortunate enough to be found alone. Police presence helped to stem the tide of violence at the

school.[14] Relative calm reigned for the remainder of the 1965–1966 school year, but the damage had been done in the minds of white parents who contemplated leaving the community.

As the conditions in Austin's schools deteriorated, both blacks and whites turned their anger on the schools. Whites, particularly those in South Austin, were concerned about the increasing numbers of blacks in their schools and the school boundary changes that helped to ensure the schools would become predominantly black. Blacks were concerned about the treatment of their children and the deteriorating conditions in the schools. The school boundaries were altered in such a way as to protect white communities in North Austin. White children were placed into a predominantly white high school beyond the Austin High School boundary. North Austin's whites were satisfied with the boundary changes because they thought the changes would be a way to stabilize their neighborhoods and limit incoming blacks. South Austin's white residents were outraged. They blamed the school's administration for damaging the schools their children attended and not doing enough to limit the proportion of blacks in those schools. Black parents were dismayed by the harsh discipline their children received. Blacks and whites in South Austin saw the worsening school conditions and the lack of Board of Education's assistance in relieving these conditions as unacceptable.[15]

The Austin community formed the militant Organization for a Better Austin (OBA) to address and resolve its problems in 1967. OBA was a biracial organization created by adherents to Saul Alinsky's organizing principles.[16] They hired white organizers, formed block clubs, and began militant action. These activities included demonstrating to improve area conditions, leafleting neighbors of block busting realtors, carrying rats from their apartments to the city's courts to emphasize landlords' neglect of housing, organizing sports leagues, and cleaning up area streets, including hauling off garbage themselves. Such collective action forced city officials to do their jobs and increase services to those areas. OBA also boycotted schools in support of busing and worked with other organizations to decrease white flight. [17] Their efforts were effective in organizing community members, but failed to push school officials to make policy changes that were satisfactory to both black and white residents.

The Redmond Plan

Superintendent Redmond's plan came as a result of federal pressure to promote school desegregation. However, because Chicago was losing white residents, the plan focused on keeping whites in the city and stabilizing neighborhoods. The plan stated: "Chicago will become a predominantly Negro city unless dramatic action is taken soon...The immediate short range goal must be to anchor the whites that still reside in the city."[18] This was certainly a concern for politicians, civic leaders, and white residents. The few desegregated schools and neighborhoods in Chicago were predominantly in transitioning neighborhoods. It was only a matter of time before those areas and their schools shifted from integrated to black. Any sufficient desegregation plan had to address the racial turnover at schools. The report suggested three types of desegregation strategies: (1) short term plans that included transferring black students from fringe and "ghetto" areas into white schools; continued use of permissive transfer plans, school attendance area adjustments; and more optimal site locations for new schools; (2) an intermediate plan that called for the creation of magnet schools; and (3) long range plans that included the creation of educational parks.[19]

After the release of the Redmond Plan, CCCO indicated that it was not happy with the proposed solutions to school segregation. CCCO members took issue with the limited discussion of school desegregation in the plan and the fact that the superintendent and school board hardly responded to the issues raised in the Title VI complaint and reiterated in HEW's US Office of Education's 1967 response. In their response called "Redmond Board Report and Its Implications," CCCO stated that "the totality of desegregation devices recommended in the Redmond Board Report, might affect, we estimate, some two percent of segregated children in Chicago's schools. Even Alabama's schools have been desegregated by more than that."[20] Furthermore, CCCO was offended by the implication that a predominantly black Chicago population and black students were somehow objectionable, stating "The thrust of the Redmond-Board Report is racist. It implies that a black Chicago would be undesirable and that Negroes will always be under-paid. It is designed to keep the whites and limit the Negroes to a quota in newly integrated schools."[21]

Underlying the structural racism that has always existed in the United States, policies and personal opinions combined to imply that the presence of blacks in certain neighborhoods meant that property values would fall.[22] Similarly, the presence of too many black students in a school automatically implied that the school was inferior. Racism has operated in such a way as to devalue black life, while at the same time, promoting the value of white life. Even well-to-do

blacks in Chicago were historically contained and violently prevented from purchasing homes in white neighborhoods.[23] While Redmond's plan highlighted the necessity of retaining white residents in Chicago, CCCO saw it as racist. The Redmond Plan recognized that "any realistic integration plan in a city as segregated as Chicago will take time, as the needs of thousands of ghetto youngsters now attending school cannot be sacrificed...Every possible effort must be made now to provide the financial and human resources necessary to ameliorate conditions and provide quality education in the inner city schools."[24] The plan acknowledged the difficulties of desegregating a segregated city, but as was the agenda of the time, suggestions were made for providing "ghetto" children extra resources so that they could achieve in spite of being in segregated schools.

Activists believed that Redmond's cautious approach was not satisfactory. CCCO asserted, "The Redmond Report is, in substance, almost entirely unresponsive to the serious matters contained in the U.S. Office of Education report."[25] Such harsh criticism was to be expected from a group of activists who had been on the front lines for desegregation of Chicago's schools. CCCO's efforts in the early 1960s, part of the larger Civil Rights Movement, were largely unsuccessful. The organization was disappointed by previous attempts at desegregation. CCCO had organized boycotts, protest demonstrations, and the Title VI complaint but acquired very little desegregation. With a new superintendent, there were higher expectations for meaningful desegregation, particularly given Redmond's past record in New Orleans. When Redmond headed the New Orleans school system, a federal court judge ordered the schools to desegregate in 1960. Redmond first attempted to desegregate the schools by enrolling four black girls into two white schools. As a result, Governor Jimmie H. Davis and the state legislature tried to take over the schools. State politicians and a federal court judge wrangled over the leadership of the schools. The girls finally entered the schools, and Redmond resigned from his New Orleans superintendent position in 1961.[26]

Redmond was in an unenviable position in both New Orleans and Chicago. In recognizing the reality of the in-migration of blacks and out-migration of whites in Chicago, Redmond believed that desegregation would be impossible without white residents. He also knew that whites were already in a mass exodus and while it was unclear how to stop it, any large-scale desegregation plan would certainly accelerate the process. He proposed cautious plans in hopes that it would be acceptable to both blacks and whites in Chicago. But as

Redmond would soon find out, any plan to desegregate in Chicago would not be easily accepted.

BUSING PLAN AND INITIAL REACTIONS

In his first plan, Redmond initially wanted to desegregate up to 10,000 students. The Chicago Board of Education approved a tentative plan for half that number by a vote of 8–2 on December 27, 1967, although some who voted for it had reservations. Margaret Wild, who later headed the committee on community hearings, believed that busing the students would be "like herding cattle."[27] Board members typically in support of desegregation included Louise Malis, Warren Bacon, Bernard Friedman, John Carey, and Harry Oliver. Board President Frank Whiston and Vice President Thomas Murray opposed desegregation and supported the neighborhood school concept. Margaret Wild and Loraine Green were less consistent in their positions. Cyrus Hall Adams often was the deciding vote when Wild and Green voted against desegregation.[28]

When the plans to bus students from the Austin community to the Northwest Side were revealed, initial reactions of some of the Northwest Side receiving schools' PTA presidents were cautiously supportive. But parents had their own ideas. One hundred and fifty parents from Bridge Elementary (one of the receiving schools) met on January 4, 1968, to plan their opposition to busing. US Representative Roman Pucinski was in attendance, and supported neighborhood schools. Well respected in the Democratic Party, Pucinski served on the House Committee on Labor and Education, was considered a liberal, and had voted for the 1964 Civil Rights Act—but northerners like Pucinski who had voted for the Civil Rights Act assumed it would not apply to their own communities. His support of those in opposition to busing, as Paul Peterson indicates, made it "abundantly clear that [Chicago's Democratic] machine was not interested in protecting the school board from white opposition to its plan."[29] Pucinski met with Redmond on January 5, 1968, and Redmond assured him that there would be public hearings on the busing plan. On January 6, 1,500 Northwest Side residents expressed their opposition to the plan in a "boisterous" gathering. Pucinski attended the meeting and passed on Redmond's assurances that public hearings would be conducted. The fervent opposition to busing was not just expressed at community meetings. Board members were inundated with letters, threats, and harassment from those in opposition to the plans. Board member Malis complained about "the gutter-type language" used by callers.[30]

Redmond and his staff, headed by assistant superintendent for facilities and planning Frances McKeag, worked to finalize the plans in two regions of the city. Redmond officially made his busing plan public on January 8, 1968. It was radically scaled down to a pilot program with the busing of 1,035 mainly black students. The school desegregation busing plan had four main goals: to relieve severe overcrowding in the sending schools, to promote community racial stabilization, to increase desegregation, and to improve the educational experiences of the students involved.[31] The plan called for busing 573 students from May and Spencer Elementary Schools in South Austin to eight schools on the Northwest Side in the Belmont Cragin, Dunning, Montclare, North Austin, and Portage Park communities. Although two of the communities with receiving schools were adjacent to Austin to the north and one school was still in Austin, the sending and receiving schools were between four and seven miles apart (see map 1.1). The distance met with the goal of sending students to schools in a noncontiguous area to promote racial stabilization. This was done to ensure that neighborhoods would not transition from white to black. The other part of the plan called for busing 462 students from three predominantly black sending schools in South Shore, Avalon Park, and South Chicago to nine receiving schools in South Chicago, South Deering, and Calumet Heights, where only one to four miles separated the schools[32] (see map 1.2).

As mentioned earlier, the Austin community was in a rapid transition from white middle and working class to black and typically less well-to-do residents. The severe overcrowding in Austin made it more likely that there would be support by both blacks and whites in Austin, although for different reasons. Blacks looked forward to a better education for the remaining pupils at the sending schools. Whites hoped that desegregation would mean that departing May and Spencer students would not end up attending Austin High School, thereby reducing the percentage of blacks at the high school.

Each of the Northwest Side communities with receiving schools was solidly white, working class and middle class. Belmont Cragin was initially settled by Germans, Scandinavians, and Irish. By 1930, one-third of the community was foreign born and new residents were Polish and German with increasing Italian settlers. Newcomers were attracted by the growing industries in the southwest corner of the community. Between 1950 and 1970, the community's residents were largely Poles, Italians, and Germans, and so 99.7 percent of the population was white in 1970. The Dunning community was mostly populated with Germans, Poles and Swedes. By 1960, Italians were

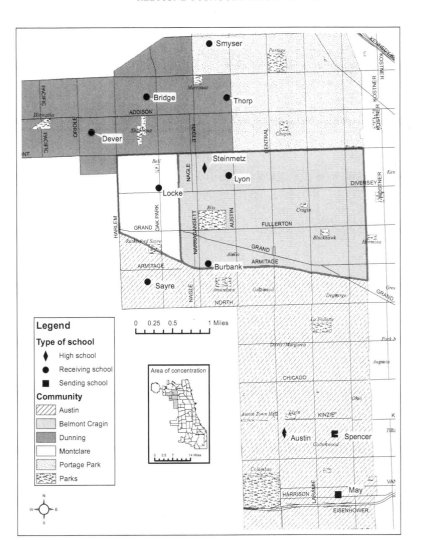

Map 1.1   Austin and Northwest Side sending and receiving schools

the third largest ethnic group. This was a largely residential community with few industries. Montclare was populated mostly by Norwegians and Germans in the 1920s. Italians and Poles increased in numbers after the 1930s and served as the areas' chief laborers. The area thrived with local retail businesses and residential stabilization in the 1960s. Portage Park, like Belmont Cragin, was populated by Poles, Germans, and Scandinavians in the 1930s. By 1970, the

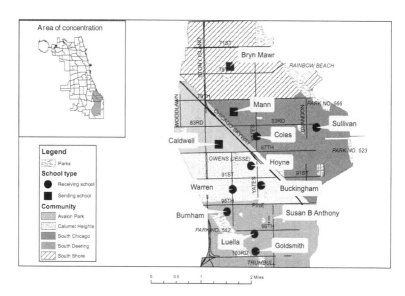

Map 1.2   Southeast Side sending and receiving schools

numbers of Italians also increased, making them the third largest group.[33] These white communities were firmly against school desegregation and busing.

On the Southeast Side, both blacks and whites also opposed busing for the most part. The South Shore community was middle and working class. South Shore was initially populated by residents with Swedish and English backgrounds in the 1920s. By 1930, Russian Jews dominated the community followed by Swedes, Germans, Irish, and English. Middle-class blacks did not gain entry into the community until the late 1950s. The South Shore community had decent housing and the areas blacks occupied were typically single-family-owned homes in the Bryn Mawr West neighborhood and apartments in the Parkside neighborhood. The South Shore Commission, a major community organization, had worked to limit the number of blacks in certain neighborhoods within the community. There were some blocks that were racially mixed and had been so for several years. However, the racial turnover in South Shore was much more acute than in Austin. Blacks were just 9.6 percent of the population in 1960; but within ten years, they were 69 percent of the population.[34]

Avalon Park, which bordered South Shore and South Chicago to the west, consisted of Irish, Germans, and Swedes in the 1920s. Blacks gained access to the community beginning in the 1960s as new black southern migrants poured into the city. By 1970, the community was already 83 percent black and the percentage expanded to 96 percent by 1980. In spite of racial turnover, the neighborhood was solidly middle class with high home values; most of the community's residents worked in government or manufacturing.[35]

South Chicago was the poorest of the five Southeast Side communities. Unlike South Shore and Avalon Park, South Chicago was a predominantly white, working-class community. However, many of the residents counted as white in the census were of Spanish-speaking, mostly Mexican, origin. By World War I, the South Chicago community was initially inhabited by Swedes, Germans, and Poles and to a far lesser extent, Mexicans and blacks working for the US Steel Corporation. After World War I, European refugees from Yugoslavia replaced earlier immigrant groups who left for the south suburbs. In 1930, Hungarians, Italians, and Croatians joined the European foreign-born population. Whites in South Chicago in the 1960s, especially those living in predominantly white neighborhoods, believed that racial stabilization would occur only if schools remained predominantly white. South Chicago saw a much smaller racial turnover from whites to blacks than South Shore and Austin. Blacks became 22.4 percent of the population in 1970, up from 4.9 in 1960. The community saw a steady increase in Mexicans and other Latinos. Their numbers went from around 4,000 in 1940 and grew to 11,915 in 1970 or 26.1 percent of the population. In spite of their long presence in the community, Mexicans were mostly relegated to four of the community's ten census tracks.[36]

Calumet Heights contained a population of Poles, Italians, and Irish by 1930. A few decades later, Russians and Germans outnumbered Italians and Irish as the community grew. The community contained the highest concentration of white-collar workers and highest home values on the South Side. Blacks in the community made up 44.9 percent of the population by 1970. The South Deering Community had the most receiving schools for the plan. Early European immigrants to the community were Yugoslavians, as well as Poles, Italians, Austrians, and Bulgarians. Mexicans began settling in the community in 1926 and blacks followed beginning in 1940. Yugoslavians were 51 percent of the foreign born population in 1930. Mexicans and blacks increased in the community and by 1970 accounted for 16.7 and 15.9 percent of the population, respectively.

Though many of the Southeast Side community members opposed busing, the South Shore Commission, one of the oldest and strongest organizations in the South Shore community, was controlled

by supporters of desegregation. The Commission developed from
the South Shore Ministerial Association and was founded in 1954
by a rabbi, minister, and priest. Believing that the South Shore
Commission was representative of the larger community's views—as
it had membership of 3,500 families in 1966—school administrators
met in secret with its leadership and agreed to a two-way busing plan
that included 3,500 students and would generate school populations
of 60–70 percent white. As information about the negotiations leaked
out, parents contacted school administrators to state their opposition. In an effort to appease white parents, Assistant Superintendent
McKeag disregarded negotiations with the South Shore Commission
and dropped two schools from the plan and decided on one-way busing of 462 black students from three predominantly black schools to
nine white schools.[37] In announcing the tentative plans, Redmond
told board members that he had the support of the South Shore and
Austin communities.[38] However, Paul Hartrich, president of the
South Shore Commission, called the superintendent's plan "tokenism at its worst." As a South Shore Commission statement explained,
"Over the last month, representatives of the South Shore Commission
and the Board of Education staff were working on alternative proposals to implement the board's decision…We were shocked to learn on
Jan. 2 that some staff members were seriously considering the token
plan."[39] In proceeding with the plan, the board continued to disap-
point the interests of various groups.

When the plan was announced on January 8, 1968, 2,000 people attended a rally on the Northwest Side to plan their strategy for
opposition to busing. They collected over 1,200 dollars to finance
transportation and flyers. The group planned to picket the Board of
Education at its next meeting.[40] Before and after that meeting was
held, there were several negotiations between politicians and board
members. In one meeting, board president Frank M. Whiston allegedly told politicians that he would work to prevent busing. He later
denied the allegations. At another meeting between board members and politicians, board members agreed to hold hearings in the
affected communities instead of downtown as long as the politicians
would promise to keep the meetings peaceful.[41]

Mayor Daley did not attend the meetings with other politicians,
but still weighed in with views about the busing plans. He thought
that a plan should be decided by the people. He was also opposed to
Illinois state politicians who threatened to veto the board's request
for additional funds if busing proceeded.[42] Daley could be perceived
as respectful of the democratic process by remaining quiet on these

mayor - not thinking busing would [pass]

issues—but in fact he had appointed all of the Board of Education members, and so he knew most were likely to vote his views. With the aldermen from his machine publically speaking out, Daley did not need to express his opposition or appear in meetings with disgruntled residents. This way he could appear politically neutral in order to maintain votes from various constituencies on different sides of the issue.[43]

On January 10, 1968, as the Chicago Board of Education held a meeting to discuss the busing plans, groups of anti-busing protestors descended on the building. As promised, busloads of Northwest Side residents came out in protest. About 1,500 people crowded the meeting room, hallways, and first floor lobby. Some wore signs that read "Parent Power," and others carried signs that said, "Put Redmond on the Bus and Leave the Driving to Us." OBA also sent two busloads of blacks and whites to the board meeting to support the busing proposal. One woman from Austin said, "We feel busing is the answer to the overcrowded situation at this moment." She also stated that integration was not the main goal, but an "irrelevant by-product" of busing. Her statement provides evidence that busing was a strategy some people were willing to try in an effort to achieve better education for students. Still, the number of anti-busing protestors far outnumbered those in favor. Both the *Chicago Daily News* and the *Chicago Sun-Times* reported that the number of people in attendance exceeded those at meetings in support of school desegregation earlier in the decade. While Chicagoans had become accustomed to uproar at school board meetings by desegregation proponents in the early to mid-1960s, the ruckus created by opponents of desegregation at January 10 and other meetings in late 1960s over one small school busing plan was rambunctious and made the previous protests seem tame by comparison. Outside the meeting, protestors hung Redmond in effigy. The boisterous meetings and subsequent hearings provided an uncivil atmosphere where racial animosity was publicly showcased. Once Superintendent James Redmond arrived at the January 10 board meeting, he received both cheers and jeers with protesters yelling "Down with busing." Redmond, in an attempt to appease the crowds, read a statement emphasizing that the busing plans could be modified. The board voted to delay its decision until February 28, despite board president Whiston's efforts to prevent setting a date. It also decided community hearings about Redmond's plan would be held.[44]

Before the February hearings occurred, those opposing and supporting busing engaged in rallies, letter writing campaigns, petitions, and political posturing. Politicians at all levels of government expressed their support or opposition to the plans. Peter Libassi, director of the US Office of Civil Rights in HEW, added federal pressure for Chicago to carry out its busing plans. He indicated that the overcrowding at black schools, the underutilization of white schools, and the gerrymandering of school boundaries could cause the federal government to withhold funding.[45] State politicians who were against busing threatened to oppose a June tax increase referendum if busing was successful. Additionally, two Chicago city aldermen held up the passage of the school budget because they were opposed to financing busing. The budget was passed late January 1968 (a few weeks later) by a vote of 41–5.[46]

Newspaper coverage at the time revealed the reasons why some board members were concerned about busing. Board member Jack Carey was quoted in the *Chicago American* saying, "We are facing a crisis in education…a crisis in the city. Chicago is rapidly becoming a Negro city. I don't think either whites or Negroes want this. I don't know if busing is going to help, but the board has a responsibility to try and do something to prevent this from happening."[47] Cyrus Hall Adams said the plan was an effort to keep middle-class people in the city.[48] The maintenance of white middle-class families in the city was certainly one of major priorities in the initial Redmond Plan. Interestingly, neither board member mentioned anything about desegregation. This observation was not lost on black Southeast Side residents as will be discussed later.

In February 1968, the board held six hearings—one in Austin, two on the Northwest Side, and three on the Southeast Side—to give the affected communities a voice in the process. There were also two citywide hearings held at Jones Commercial High School on February 26 and 27.[49] The only community mostly supportive of the busing plan was Austin. The other communities expressed limited support but mainly opposition, the reasons for which ranged from racist to practical.

SOUTHEAST SIDE AND BLACK RESPONSES TO THE BUSING PLAN

Some of South Shore's community leaders were committed to stable integration. The South Shore Commission was a powerful organization and its leadership worked to maintain racial stability in the community through neighborhood crime prevention, screening potential residents, and demanding that the city enforce building codes. The

→ keep white from leaving

Commission wanted to maintain the community's conditions to attract more white residents. Other Southeast Side residents were highly skeptical of the busing plan's ability to stabilize their neighborhoods. Three differing views about school desegregation existed on the Southeast Side. The first group, many of whom were associated with the South Shore Commission, agreed with the Commission that two-way busing would be the best way to stabilize the area. A second group consisting of whites, particularly those in neighborhoods with fewer black residents, thought that keeping their schools predominantly white would be best in maintaining stabilization. The third group comprising black residents saw the South Shore Commission's stabilization plans and Redmond's busing plans as favorable to whites. The South Shore Commission's plans, these black residents thought, aimed to attract a new white population and to satisfy current white residents. These three competing interests were expressed at the busing hearings.[50] The combined black and white opposition to the proposed school desegregation plan served to alter the outcome of the busing plan in this community.

As noted before, these Southeast Side communities were largely opposed to the superintendent's busing plans. At the first hearing held at South Shore High School on February 5, 1968, one of Redmond's staff members, Walter Pildtich, gave the opening remarks and argued that the schools could not solve the problems caused by housing. However, schools could play a role in helping to stem the tide of racial change by stabilizing racially integrated schools in fringe neighborhoods, which was essential to housing stabilization. Pildtich reiterated the points of board members who believed that whites needed to remain in the city to avoid "a predominately Negro city with an accompanying decline in its tax base and resources and, therefore, in the quality of education it can provide."[51] These remarks angered many middle-class blacks because it assumed that blacks did not provide financial resources and depended on whites to pay their way.[52]

Many of the schools' PTAs conducted surveys that showed that the majority of members favored neighborhood schools over the Commission's two-way busing or the Redmond one-way busing plans. The racial makeup of the PTAs varied, and at times, more than one organization represented a school. For example, concerned parent groups had formed with parents who were not associated with PTAs. Mrs. Chatman Wailes, a member of Concern Parents of Bryn Mawr (one of the South Shore sending schools) and the only black person to speak at the February 5 meeting, recited the group's objection to one-way busing at the hearing.

The using of Negro children to maintain a racial balance in Bryn Mawr or any school is total racism and a lack of respect for black people as human beings! It is racism to do things to people without consulting them and working with them! The manipulation of black pupils has been easy for the white power structure—(applause)—because it seems that they feel that minority groups have no feelings and that they are to be pawns. Stabilization should not be placed as a burden on the backs of Negroes. It should be a total community, understanding the solution does not mean a containment of minority groups. South Shore bigotry wants to sacrifice this generation of Negro pupils to keep white families here. If there are whites who want to leave let them go.

This kind of approach for stabilization only substantiates the lie that black schools and communities are no good...Why is it necessary for Bryn Mawr to have a greater percentage of whites for pupils to receive quality education as many of the whites feel?

We feel that there has not been the equal educational opportunity for the black pupils in Bryn Mawr. In this desegregated school the white pupil is deprived because he is constantly being given the misconception that he is better because of his color. We, the Concerned Parents of Bryn Mawr, will settle for no less than a system where quality education is maintained, not just to keep white children in Bryn Mawr School but to provide equal educational opportunities for all children.[53]

The arguments of Mrs. Wailes's group did not represent the views of all black people or even the views of all Bryn Mawr parents. It is, however, an example of a black interest group that questioned the goal of racial stabilization and school desegregation. The statement gets to the heart of some of the assumptions that undergird school desegregation in general and Superintendent Redmond's plan in particular. As noted earlier, the very presence of too many black students in a school often generated the opinion that the school is automatically inferior. This parent disagreed with this assumption that served as part of the rationale for the *Brown v. Board of Education* decision, namely that segregated education was inferior and segregation damaged the psyche of black students.[54] A number of blacks disagreed with the belief that black segregated schools had a deleterious effect on black students. Historians have argued that some segregated schools often provided a buffer against racism; had caring, devoted, and highly educated teachers and school leaders; and gave black students the training necessary to overturn Jim Crow in the South.[55]

However, the circumstances surrounding Bryn Mawr Elementary School was not like those in many of the underfunded schools in the

South. The idea of containing black students was not only insulting to Mrs. Wailes, but she believed it was also racist. She touched directly on the assumed inferiority of blacks, as well as the "misconception" that whites were superior. Racism in American society has always held these notions to be true. The structural nature of racism allows those in a dominant position, in this case whites, to create arrangements and practices that help to maintain racial stratification and the continued privilege of those in power.[56] Structurally, Chicago's city and school officials valued the presence of whites in the city not only for what they represent financially, but for the superior status their presence in the city implied. Mrs. Wailes likely lived in the neighborhood around Bryn Mawr School. This neighborhood was among the most well-to-do areas in the South Shore community. Residents had high rates of education, higher incomes, white-collar jobs, and higher home values.[57] Part of her response was as a middle-class black woman who lived in a neighborhood with other successful blacks. Her class status as well as race directly impacted her reaction to the busing plan.

black teacher view

At another Southeast Side hearing on February 12, 1968, a black parent echoed the sentiments of Mrs. Wailes. Mrs. William Howard of the Concerned Parents of the Caldwell-McDowell Schools listed three objections to the busing plan: "1. Removal of students from an existing integrated school to one where there is a greater racial imbalance does not foster integration nor quality education. 2. Removal of Caldwell students to a school with fewer facilities and programs is not integration nor quality education. 3. Subjecting children to the trauma of howling mobs, hostile teachers, and threatening fellow students is not integration nor quality education."[58] Mrs. Howard went on to say, "We reject the outright idiotic contention that black children must be in classrooms with whites to learn." She faulted the inadequate education blacks received on "the absolute refusal of teachers and administrators to educate them. The standard of practice in Chicago and elsewhere has been that whenever a school becomes more than half black, the good, experienced teachers are replaced by untried or incompetent ones, and services deteriorate, making the school's decline into mediocrity a near certainty." She requested changes in curriculum, teacher assignments, and textbooks.[59]

Mrs. Wailes and Mrs. Howard's responses indicated the radicalized era of the late 1960s when Black Power dominated. Militant black leaders spoke out against busing for the same reasons listed above: the assumption that quality education could occur only in desegregated schools. Those with a black nationalist ideological orientation could not understand why blacks would continually want to be educated with people who did not want them. For nationalists, it was almost admission of their own inferiority. Commenting about busing in an article in the *West Side Torch,* one leader wondered why students should go to school in a community where they could not live. Another thought the busing plan was a "humiliating pittance to the Black community" and did not deal with "the root problems of miseducation, of white-dominated ciricula [*sic*] and white dominated stewardship of the minds of Black children."[60]

These arguments focused on two things. First, they examined the neighborhood school concept from the black perspective. Many black parents were as satisfied with their neighborhood schools as many white parents and when schools were predominantly black, they were not automatically viewed as inferior. Second, associating quality education with the education of whites did not consider curricula that ignored the contributions of blacks. As Carter G. Woodson stated in 1933, the educational process that makes whites believe that they are "everything and [have] accomplished everything worthwhile, depresses and crushes at the same time the spark of genius in the Negro by making him feel that his race does not amount to much and never will measure up to the standards of other peoples."[61] For parents and community leaders, quality education would require a fundamental change in the curriculum and not black children simply sitting in classes with whites.

As the fight over Redmond's busing plan was occurring, the consciousness raising that accompanied the Black Power Movement[62] affected black teachers, community leaders, and students. Although organizing around Black Power had been occurring in the city prior to the late 1960s, 1968 was a pivotal year in Chicago for activism around school reform. A number of student protests at individual schools occurred in 1968. By October, students organized citywide and demanded more black history classes, black school leadership, and greater input of community members in school decision making. Black teachers were also involved and were among the first to issue manifestos with similar demands as the students. While some black people did not support the demands or the tactics, this activism that led to walkouts and school boycotts was part of a national effort by students to make their schools and universities more accommodating of their needs. Students of all races protested and demonstrated for their rights and for a system that was more reflective of the true meaning of democracy. For many students, teachers, and community leaders in Chicago, community control of schools appeared to be a more viable option for quality education than school desegregation.[63]

However, black parents in the Austin community with children at the overcrowded May and Spencer schools saw desegregation as a viable option for students who were to be bused as well as for those left behind. The busing of students meant that average class sizes would decline. Jesse D. Madison of the Austin Tenants and Owners Association put it this way, "To us, integration is a secondary by-product. May and Spencer are incomparably, and almost irreparably, overcrowded. There are empty classrooms on the Northwest Side of Chicago. WE WANT THOSE CLASSROOMS FILLED!"[64] Madison made it clear that overcrowding was the biggest issue and the reason for supporting the plan. It is debatable whether black people in the Austin community would have been as supportive of the desegregation plan if their schools were not overcrowded. Prior to the hearings, black parents from Austin held a rally at Resurrection Church to support busing. The president of Spencer PTA shared complaints about the conditions of Spencer school. Students had to share books, class sizes were over 40, and some classrooms were leaking.[65] These complaints were not about segregation, but were a protest against the inferior conditions at that school. White speakers at the Board of Education hearing also reiterated this point.

No racial or ethnic group is monolithic. Blacks viewed desegregation with both suspicion and enthusiasm. They have been historically split on this issue since the mid-nineteenth century as seen in the *Roberts v. The City of Boston* case in 1849, and a host of cases both in the North and South where blacks disagreed about having black schools with black teachers or having desegregated schools. A 1935 W. E. B. Du Bois article illustrated the dilemma over school desegregation as he argued that both types of schools had their benefits and detriments, but he concluded that with all things being equal, a mixed school would be the best way to educate all children.[66] Just as blacks quarreled over the pros and cons of school desegregation, not all whites opposed desegregation. Yet large numbers voted with their feet by moving from cities to suburbs, demonstrated, wrote petitions, and held rallies to show their disapproval of school desegregation. There were some whites in South Shore who supported two-way busing. However, school board member Cyrus Hall Adams received letters from the Southeast Side, and many were opposed to two-way busing. Most who wrote Adams were also not supportive of Redmond's busing plan and preferred that children attend neighborhood schools.[67]

For some Southeast Side whites, like their black counterparts, the disagreement was primarily about Redmond's plan rather than desegregation per se. At a South Shore hearing, Mrs. Norman Katz stated the problem this way: "The racial balance in all our schools would be 70% white, 30% Negro. An immediate commitment to equalizing instructional programs, changing certification proce- dures for competent teachers and social workers, reducing class size throughout the area, and providing special services for children with social and emotional problems must be part of the plan. Anything short of this is truly 'much ado about nothing.'"[68]

Mrs. Katz mentioned the benefits of school desegregation, but saw Redmond's plan for the community as little more than "tokenism." The South Shore Commission president Paul Hartrich argued that the superintendent's proposal would not "equalize and stabilize inte- gration, and it would not help quality education materially."[69] After the plan was announced, Hartrich had met with black and white par- ents and both groups wanting to know how their children would be affected by his plan. Hartrich stated, "If the Superintendent's staff had deliberately set out to kill the busing program we have to say it would not have done a better job."[70]

A number of representatives from various Southeast Side organi- zations spoke at the hearing which indicated that the South Shore Commission was not representative of everyone on that side of town. Many of these groups were neighborhood improvement and hom- eowner associations. Groups such as the Fair Elms Civic League and South Shore Community Valley Association were organized to maintain Southeast Side neighborhoods. These groups worked on environmental issues caused by landfills, improvement of streets and alleys, and to lobby for new schools and other essential community facilities.[71]

Some representatives of these Southeast Side organizations said they supported integration but not the Redmond plan, and they sug- gested the creation of magnet schools and gifted education programs. Mrs. Carl Lerner of the South Shore Community Valley Association said her group supported busing, but not the Redmond Plan in its present form. She would support busing if it provided clear educational advantages, including facility and teacher upgrades, if it reduced class size and if it would make a "significant contribution toward commu- nity stabilization…We can see no educational advantages resulting from the execution of this plan because of its limitations."[72]

Others argued that there were no educational upgrades in the receiving schools, the schools were being used as a sociological exper- iment, and schools with white student bodies were simply assumed to provide a higher quality education. Some parents wanted quality education before desegregation and said the program would not stabilize the neighborhood, but would lead to a rapid departure of whites.[73] Mr. James Belew, president of Fair Elms Civic League, who opposed busing, argued that children were used as pawns to solve a housing problem, that the plan probably underestimated the real costs, and that it took the youngest students away from their familiar surroundings.[74] Mrs. Roberto Francisco of Clay PTA stated, "When a school board declares that children in receiving schools will make higher academic achievement than those in sending schools the teaching policies of that board are to be questioned...The manner and the curriculum which children are to be taught should not be dependent upon the locality of the school or its racial head count...Quality education must be offered in all schools."[75] Mrs. Francisco opposed one-way busing and felt it was unfair and would eventually lead to two-way busing. She also believed that stabilization of the community should be the responsibility of the residents, not the Board of Education.

The South Shore community presented interesting class and racial dynamics as some radicalized, middle-class blacks opposed Redmond's school desegregation plans, and some middle-class whites supported an alternative desegregation plan. While they disagreed with Redmond's busing plan for different reasons, most agreed that quality education should be the goal and not busing. Those who agreed with the South Shore Commission's two-way busing plan were outraged that school officials with whom they had been in communication had dismissed their ideas in favor of such a token busing plan. Whites, who opposed busing all together, made it clear that the South Shore Commission did not speak for the entire Southeast Side. However, the presence of the South Shore Commission's plans, the vocal opposition of blacks, and the lack of extensive community protests, at times prevented the entire community from being labeled racist, even if many held opinions that were racist and often the same as those on the Northwest Side.

Events on the Southeast Side demonstrated the role constituents could play in limiting or rejecting the scope of a school desegregation plan. Redmond's staff mishandled community involvement in the initial stages of the plan, incurring massive popular outrage. In an attempt to appease the communities, his staff dramatically scaled down the scope of the busing plan—which in turn also created opposition, as many saw the new, compromised version as severely lacking in the areas of both integration and quality education. This made it easier for the Board of Education to back away from this portion of the plan in ways that would not occur in other parts of the city. Constituents in this instance were successful in eliminating a desegregation plan that did not meet their needs. The board eventually had to focus on quality education with desegregation for the South Shore community through the use of a voluntary busing project at Robert A. Black Mini-Magnet School starting September 1968. Students were randomly selected to participate in the program. The goal of this small-scale desegregation project was to maintain 40 percent white enrollment at this school. However, over the six years of the project, white enrollment dropped to less that 30 percent.[76]

Northwest Side Resistance to Redmond's Busing Plan

White Northwest Side residents had some of the same complaints as white residents on the Southeast Side. However, their community's rational arguments became quickly tainted by many vocal, overtly racist agitators. Since participation in the busing plan was initially mandatory, many whites assumed that it was a slippery slope—if black students were to be bused, how long before their children would be bused? The more practical objections were gradually obscured by increasing threats of violence, expressions of anger, and the disruption of board meetings and hearings. The busloads of demonstrators also were cause for alarm. Some city officials wondered if there would be a race riot if things were not calmed. Alderman William Cousins Jr. of Chicago's 8th Ward spoke at the second Southeast Side meeting about the anger he witnessed: "I attended the Board of Education hearing last month and what I saw there shook me because I have been around the country and I have been on the battlefield and I have never seen what I saw on the faces of some of those people there. This mob was very substantial and I moved about and I talked to people and I know the attitudes of the people. It disturbs me."[77] Alderman Cousins supported Redmond's busing plan, although he had hoped for a better alternative. But he and others at the hearings were disturbed by the rage expressed by Northwest Side and some Southeast Side residents.

Some of the responses from Northwest Side residents were decidedly racist in tone and sometimes in substance. The overtly racist comments typically appeared more in letters to board members than at the board hearings. One letter to board member Cyrus Hall Adams stated: "Some of these people worked hard for many years to choose their neighbors and environment. Now you want the Negroes to have the right to choose their neighbors but not the whites who pay most of the tax dollars in Chicago. Our forefathers had to work hard when they came to this country. The Negroes have jobs handed to them and they loaf on the jobs, stay home from work, rob & steal, because they know they have civil rights groups protecting them charging discrimination."[78] The letter also acknowledged that the writer's son was robbed and beaten by blacks downtown. A second letter echoed the stereotypical beliefs about blacks: "The colored trouble makers—to realize that it takes STUDY and ATTENTION in school to gain knowledge and not attending another school or getting another teacher. Colored have freedom of speech all of a sudden. Jews made progress, Polish [were]...looked at as inferior. No one owes you anything, work hard."[79] The writers of these letters assumed that blacks had the opportunity to choose their neighbors, when the forced containment of blacks in Chicago provides evidence of something quite different.

The issues over busing, especially on the Northwest Side where relatively few blacks lived, have to be viewed within the larger context of the city's history and whites' defense of their neighborhoods. In that instance, even sensible concerns about the school desegregation plan can reasonably be seen as a defense of the status quo: white privilege, white neighborhoods, and all white schools. Since Chicago's black population increased at the turn of the twentieth century, it was typically a violent and uneasy endeavor for them to move into surrounding areas where whites lived.[80] For whites on the Southeast Side, their communities for the most part were not all white, and some of their organizations had made efforts at interracial cooperation. Little if any such efforts existed on the Northwest Side.

Gregory S. Jacobs eloquently captured the use of busing as a way to "compress legitimate concerns and irrational fears into a single word whose racial neutrality lent it public legitimacy." He argued that support for integration but opposition to busing meant that whites could support the ideal of racial equality but not the "means to achieve it." Jacobs noted that whites "were able to mask profound racial fear, resentment, and disdain with exaggerated arguments about a mode of transportation never questioned when it was used to facilitate rather than eliminate segregation." Moreover, the debate about busing shifted attention away from past policies and actions that led to segregation and toward demonizing courts and school boards, thereby "transforming white guilt into white victimhood."[81]

As previously mentioned, the Northwest Side was populated by mostly working-class and middle-class whites.[82] However, this area was unique in Chicago as its citizens were largely Republican. For those whites who had moved there from other areas of the city to escape black encroachment, the idea that the Chicago Board of Education could impose such a policy without their approval was incomprehensible. According to Anton Vrame, some of the community's ethnic groups saw the plan as "an act of collusion between Redmond and the Democratic Mayor Daley" as all the receiving schools chosen were in Republican wards.[83]

The Northwest Side hearings really brought to life the assumptions of many vocal whites in the community. While arguing for the benefits of the neighborhood schools and the lack of community involvement in decision making, whites also feared that blacks would eventually move into their neighborhoods and believed that blacks in Austin were culturally deprived and lacked parents who valued education. They argued for their rights to freedom as tax payers in a noncommunist society. While speakers represented different community groups or political entities, there were many similarities in their arguments against the busing plan. Like their Southeast Side counterparts, a number of different Northwest Side neighborhood improvement and school organizations were represented.

The Northwest Side hearings occurred on February 15 and February 19, 1968. The overwhelming argument in the hearings, letters, and newspaper articles and editorials was the call for neighborhood schools. These arguments were usually well articulated and spoke to the desire to maintain close-knit families and communities. Many of these arguments sounded like that of Mrs. Joseph Johnson of the Smyser PTA:

> What right does anyone have to snatch a young child from his mother, his neighborhood and familiar surroundings, force him on a bus and take him miles away? Every mother and child deserves the right to remain close together for as long as possible...Children who must stay for lunch would rather come home to eat a warm meal and visit with someone in the family, even if for just a few minutes, at times to be reassured and made to feel secure about problems which may arise at school, or even boast about some achievement. Mayor Daley himself was quoted in the *Chicago Tribune* on January 30, 1968 as saying, "I may be old-fashioned. It used to be that people wanted to see their children home for lunch and discuss what happened in school with them."[84]

Many speakers at the hearings, while speaking glowingly about their own neighborhoods, harbored deeply stereotypical assumptions about blacks living in Austin. One of the popular arguments at the time was that black youth were culturally deprived and that was why they did not do well in school. While this argument may have been well-intentioned liberal belief,[85] it was nonetheless inaccurate and damaging. The 1960s was a time of fundamental struggles over schooling and quality education. Prior to the 1960s, blacks in the North and South had long fought to acquire an education equal to that of whites. Southern blacks, both educated and uneducated, had risked their livelihoods so that their children could get a better education. Many had joined desegregation lawsuits or signed their children up to attend desegregated schools at risk of economic reprisal. Northern blacks fought for their children as well. Community members and leaders, teachers and students, consistently pushed for improved education. Although they did not always agree on the tactics or the solutions, they agreed that they were often not getting the type of education they deserved or wanted.

In the midst of these struggles, scholars began writing about the pathology of black families and the cultural deprivation that kept blacks from reaching their potential. Unfortunately, while such scholarly efforts may have sought to legitimize the plight of blacks through sociocultural analysis, their work was easily misconstrued to place the blame on blacks themselves rather than a racist system. For example, in 1965, Daniel Patrick Moynihan issued a report titled *The Negro Family: The Case for National Action*, arguing that female-headed black family structures led to pathology within inner city communities. While the legacy of slavery was blamed for these problems and while the report recognized the structural issues that disadvantaged blacks, the Moynihan Report was highly problematic. The report perpetuated the blame associated with single parenthood and influenced social and educational policy around such "family" issues, rather than systemic racism.[86] This report occurred at the same time that blacks in the Civil Rights Movement were fighting against the injustices that had held them back for generations by calling for massive structural change in the United States. The Moynihan Report undercut their cause. James Farmer, the leader of Congress of Racial Equality (CORE), called the Moynihan Report a "massive copout for the white conscience. We are sick to death of being analyzed, mesmerized, bought, sold, and slobbered over, while the same evils that are the ingredients of our oppression go unattended."[87]

While the arguments about black pathology ensued, some argued against the misuse of such terms as cultural deprivation particularly if it suggested that such children do not want to be educated.[88] Akin to cultural capital arguments today, scholars in the 1960s wrote that cultural deprivation "refers to those aspects of middle-class culture—such as education, books, formal language—from which these groups have not benefited."[89] Cultural deprivation became the educational buzzword used to describe black youth and to explain their presumed low educational aspirations.

William Kolling, representing the Dever Community Organization, discussed culturally deprived students at one of the hearings. "If Negro children are culturally deprived and the Chicago schools have had many of these children in attendance, what has the Board of Education done to overcome the cultural deprivation?...You wouldn't want us to believe that the only single way to offset cultural deprivation is to have children, Negro and White, attend schools together."[90] Similarly, Mrs. Karen Schreiber from Mothers for Better Education made use of such buzzword terminology in order to justify her stance against busing. Mrs. Schreiber was troubled by the proposal to move "children block by block, including the severely culturally deprived, emotionally disturbed, and socially maladjusted into stable, middle class schools is unwise educationally and socially. These are the social factors not considered by Dr. Redmond and his staff." She asked, "How many children who are to be bused to our neighborhood school come from home-owning families? How many are on public assistance and from broken homes?"[91]

One frequent assumption of the cultural deprivation arguments was that children were deprived because of the failings of their parents. Many at the hearings expressed these views. Mrs. Lyle Johannsen of the Thorp PTA commented on parental responsibility for education. "Teachers have the responsibility to further the character and education of a child only 30 hours per week and the parents have the responsibility to further their children's character and education the remainder of 138 hours per week. Will busing be a solution to improve their education?"[92] State Representative Henry J. Hyde also blamed the lack community and black families for their disadvantages in education. He asserted:

> The real heart of the matter, and we all know it, is that the family as a unit has no effective existence in the inner city. The destruction of the neighborhood school system further removes the family unit from any effective impact on the young plastic lives being shuttled around the city.

> Taking children out of the ghetto for a few short envious hours a day does not take the ghetto out of the children. They must get up in and

return to a ghetto environment that has far more effect on that young life than a daily bus trip to a strange school can have. Maybe we're looking in the wrong direction. Perhaps if we can devise a welfare system that doesn't make it profitable to split up a family, the family concept can have some viability in the inner city.[93]

State Representative William M. Zachacki, who was also quite critical of busing as a viable solution and used the family unit argument as well, claimed that "Busing of students will not solve educational problems. The foundation of a good education begins in the home and in far too many families, this foundation is seriously deficient." He continued, "The thought disturbs me very much that busing will create a chaotic condition in the area of receiving schools as a result of children arriving from a different environment and family structure. We must make the neighborhood school system a bastion of each local community. We must have each community get at the roots of the real problem—home environment."[94] Zachacki stated that he did not believe that the two different groups of children should be mixed because of their "different…family structure." He, like others, suggested that more schools be constructed and teachers be paid higher salaries.

People in the Austin community supported the busing plan because they were well aware that the overcrowded conditions at the school prevented their children from having quality education. But this concern was lost on Hyde and others like him who believed that these students had inferior parenting and not inferior schooling. There was also an assumption that all blacks in the Austin community were on welfare and lacked a traditional, nuclear family unit. According to census data, the Belmont Cragin, Dunning, Montclare, and Portage Park communities had an average of 10.9 percent female-headed households, a 3.9 percent poverty rate, and 2.9 percent unemployment rate. The female-headed households in Austin were 15.9 percent overall with a poverty rate of 8.1 and 4.1 percent unemployed. Austin's predominantly black census tracks had 20.4 percent female-headed households and 15 percent below the poverty with a 5 percent unemployment rate. In spite of higher rates of female-headed households and families below poverty, most Austin blacks were from nuclear family units and were not on welfare. Furthermore, blacks in Austin had higher levels of schooling than the Northwest Side receiving area residents.[95] Underlying the speakers' assumptions at the hearings was a belief that tied race and class together. Sociologist Kevin Fox Gotham argued that whites attempting to preserve certain neighborhoods for themselves perpetuated segregation with negative images and stereotypes about black communities as dangerous, deteriorating, and pathological.[96] Their assumptions were often incorrect and did not focus on the structural issues that led blacks with higher levels of education to have fewer high quality job opportunities than whites with less education.

While cultural deprivation became the major focus of the perceived failure of black families, other arguments focused on individual liberties of whites threatened by the busing plans. Opponents of school desegregation nationwide crafted arguments supporting segregated schools and neighborhoods in terms of freedom.[97] According to historian Kevin Kruse, those opposed to desegregation fought for "the 'right' to select their neighbors, their employees, and their children's classmates...and perhaps most importantly, the 'right' to do what they pleased to remain free from what they saw as dangerous encroachments of the federal government."[98] Many argued that they were taxpayers and consequently had a say in how their taxes were being spent. They opposed the imposition of school desegregation policies. Congressman Roman Pucinski discussed the fears of the taxpayer who wonders "where all the money will come from for these elaborate plans. His fears are legitimate and have nothing to do with either racism or bigotry." Mr. Steven Telow representing the North West Polish Homeowners and Taxpayers Council brought Redmond in effigy since Redmond would not appear at the hearings. His reasoning for this act was that "We Poles like to see our enemy even in effigy, when we address them." He went on to say, "Mr. Effigy Redmond...you are wet behind the ears if you think that the 250,000 Polish homeowners would allow you to take over one of our northwest side schools for integrated schooling. After all, our tax dollars are divided to take care of local improvements and one of our local improvements is the neighborhood schools—and this we aim to keep."[99]

Cold War rhetoric was also capitalized upon in order to argue against busing. In Chicago, these arguments took the form of the rights of taxpayers and American freedoms in comparison to communist societies. Many opponents argued that because they were not living in a communist society, they therefore had rights against busing. Mrs. Virginia Strugalski of Locke PTA commented, "It seems the main idea is to break up family unity and indoctrinate an education program fashioned more in line with education in Soviet Russia...This is a democratic society where majority rules, and as part of the majority we oppose the Redmond Plan—and we must protect individual rights and freedom of future generations."[100] Hyde stated, "To turn our public schools into social laboratories may be suitable under a more authoritarian form of government, say, Cuba or East Germany, but not in America."[101] As far as these speakers were concerned, their democratic rights and individual freedoms were violated with the busing plan.

Of all the speakers at the Northwest Side hearings, only one person, Mr. Frank Hilkin, president of the Northwest Chicago Human Relations Council, supported desegregation and the audience kept interrupting him. Hilkin began his statement by saying, "Busing school children is as American as apple pie." After interruptions, he continued, "Much of the response to the proposal is based on genuine concern, unreasoned fear and emotion. The main opposition, however, appears to be triggered by deep-seated racist feelings. Factual information on school busing is almost completely ignored and the approaches in the Northwest area uncover the depth of the problem of the white community in the matter of interracial relationships."[102] After hisses from the crowd, Hilkin continued, "The issue [of] whether or not children are to be afforded the best educational opportunity possible [should] have been clear in the minds of all. But because the children are Negro, we must deal with an unreasonable and dangerous menace, racism. Racism has not been purged from our society by the passage of Civil Rights Legislation nor by strong words of prominent political and religious leaders. Racism still exists in our society."[103] Hilkin spoke for those he believed were fearful of speaking out, and because of the continued disruptions from the audience, it is understandable why people who supported busing did not want to speak at the Northwest Side hearings.

There undoubtedly were Northwest Side community members who either supported the busing plan or had moderate views about it, though they were not typically represented at the hearings. Their voices remained muted, much in the same way as the moderate voices of people in places like Little Rock, Arkansas; Boston, Massachusetts; and Prince Edward County, Virginia. Many moderates feared retribution and intimidation. Little Rock moderates were typically silenced by the "coercion" of business leaders and the "bullying tactics used by segregationists." In Boston, moderates who cooperated with busing or joined on councils to work for peaceful desegregation faced violence, harassment, and threats. Similarly in Prince Edward County, those opposed to the closing of public schools to avoid desegregation were largely kept in check by business leaders and the fear of harassment and loss of friends.[104]

While Chicago moderates remained silent, the vocal opponents on the Northwest Side had no problems expressing their disdain for what they believed were black failures. Their responses were tinged with racist assumptions, mixed the seemingly logical arguments for neighborhood schools and personal liberties. Missing from their inaccurate assumptions was the devastating economic market and housing policies that undermined the development of some black communities and as a result neighborhood schools.

Like their Southeast Side counterparts, Northwest Side residents were concerned with neighborhood transition. However, the Northwest Side communities did not experience the rapid racial turnover that occurred in Austin and the Southeast Side. In 1980, Belmont Cragin was still 96.3 percent white, Dunning 98.2 percent, Montclare 98.7 percent, and Portage Park 97.5 percent. At the same time, Austin was only 20.8 percent white. South Deering and South Chicago had 27.5 and 31.2 percent whites, respectively, and the other Southeast Side communities had only between 2.7 to 7.7 percent whites remaining.[105] Northwest Side residents could not eliminate the school desegregation plan, but were able to keep their communities predominantly white. Southeast Side residents eliminated the plan for their communities but were unable to maintain community stabilization in spite of a neighborhood organization working for school desegregation.

The school desegregation plan fostered by the federal government and designed by the superintendent and his staff caused Chicago's Northwest Side residents to react in similar ways as others around the country. They were intent on resistance. However, federal pressure, though muted, meant the board still had to implement some aspect of the policy. Overcrowding in Austin made this portion of the plan much more likely to be enforced. The plan also did not destabilize the Northwest Side communities.

RESULTS OF THE BUSING PLAN

A Chicago Board of Education meeting was held February 28, 1968, to discuss the findings from the hearings. The meeting was described as emotionally charged as protesters against busing marched outside and filled the board meeting room. The busing dialog lasted two hours.[106] Chairwoman Margaret Wild talked about the findings and noted that the committee had heard from 164 community organizations, of which 106 disapproved of the busing proposal, 11 wanted the plans to be refined, and 47 approved of the busing plans. Wild made a motion to have Redmond and his staff reexamine the Southeast Side plan and work with the community to revise the proposal. The motion passed 9–1. As far as the Austin plan was concerned, Cyrus Hall Adams moved first that the plan be approved, and second that stipulations be added that gave parents a right to refuse to send their children. The vote was 5–5, and Adams's motions were not passed.[107] Since the plan was not dealt with at the February 28 meeting, both supporters and opponents were dissatisfied.[108]

Board members held a special meeting on March 4, 1968, to deal again with Adams's motions. Before the vote was cast, Superintendent Redmond—inspired by his meetings with the May and Spencer groups who criticized him for not exerting his leadership—rose to speak. While he acknowledged that he had no right to ask board members to change their minds, he stated, "I urge your favorable consideration of the amendment of the Board report, I leave to you Board members and your individual consciences the reconsideration of the proposal which has brought us together again in this special meeting."[109] Redmond then went on to evoke the recent findings of the Kerner Report, which suggested that both blacks and whites needed to be assimilated into America. The board voted to approve the plan 8–1. The only dissenting vote came from a black board member, Loraine Green, who thought the quotas in the plan were racist.[110]

The amended plan allowed parents the right to refuse to have their children transported, prohibited transferring children with disabilities, and increased the number of city blocks in the sending area in order to reach the goal of 573 students. The revised plan meant that busing was no longer mandatory and students would not be bused from the receiving area,[111] giving a sense of comfort to parents in both the sending and receiving areas. Parents in the sending school areas could refuse to send their children into hostile areas, and parents in the receiving areas were assured that their children would not be bused. The massive neighborhood protests had decidedly altered the busing plan. While the initial protests did not prevent busing to Northwest Side communities, it was doubtful whether informed school officials would create desegregation plans in the future without allowing more meaningful participation of the communities affected.

Despite the many compromises made by the board, neighborhood discontent remained. Before the students were bused, white parents had their children boycott all eight receiving schools. On the weekend before the busing was to take place, some opposition leaders allegedly recruited volunteers to assault the bused children. Rumors circulated that black parents would be arming their children for protection. Since police and school officials believed the rumors from both communities to be credible, they reacted by adding security at the receiving schools during the day and appointing a night watchman in the hopes of preventing school bombings. The Board of Education also adopted safety precautions to protect black children, and bus supervisors would remain with the students throughout the day.[112]

On the first day of busing, March 11, 1968, just 280 of the 330 children who initially signed up arrived at school. Many parents were rightfully afraid for their children's safety. Angry residents had gathered at all the receiving schools. While police presence was significant, some clashes with angry demonstrators broke out. Whites cursed, spat, and threw rocks at children proceeding to the school buildings. There were a number of people arrested attempting to pass police barricades to attack the children. Luckily, no child was injured. There were some disagreements between black and white students, but nothing that security guards could not handle. White protesters continued to show up at the receiving schools throughout the first week.[113]

In order to assess the implementation of the busing plan, the Chicago Public Schools issued a status report titled "The Austin Area Project" every year between 1968 and 1974. The first report stipulated that the most difficult issue was the continued reorganization of the schools as more students were added to the receiving schools until April. These reorganizations received the most complaints because they affected students in both the sending and receiving schools. Students were shifted to different classrooms to accommodate the increasing or decreasing numbers of bused students. Other issues involved a lack of consistent bus drivers which was a result of the late start of the program. Child Welfare attendants assigned to each bus helped to provide a sense of stability for the students. One of the reported successes of the program was that some parents of bused students attended PTA and room meetings at the receiving school and interacted with white parents. The Northwest Clergy Association also orchestrated community meetings to help residents better understand busing[114] illustrating that not all Northwest Side residents were unsupportive.

Principals from the receiving schools were surveyed. In 1968, one principal's comment effectively summarized the overall experience for the first year: "Considering that this was a completely new experience for all groups concerned, and being cognizant of the bitter defeat which the adults took when the busing program was implemented in spite of their dramatic efforts to oppose the proposal, the progress made has been better than we had a right to expect. Under more normal conditions greater improvements should be apparent next year."[115]

Most consistently, the seven reports showed continuing opposition for busing by parents and increasingly by principals and teachers in the receiving areas. Comments were still largely disapproving of the program in 1974. Of the eight receiving school principals surveyed that year, five believed that the program was harmful for all children and should be phased out. Some principals wanted a more selective process in the recruitment of students, and one suggested that the program begin with first graders. Another principal commented that "this school is not equipped (staffed) to handle the bused children" who had social and academic problems.[116] A third argued that race and socioeconomic differences were too difficult to overcome. The 1974 report surmised that, "It can be safely observed that a consensus of receiving school parents, teachers, and principals, relative to academic achievement is a resounding negative, whereas a consensus of parents of the bused children indicates an overwhelming opinion of positive academic achievement (of the bused children) and strong approval and support of the program."[117]

Like the principals, teachers surveyed at the receiving schools had negative attitudes about busing and the impact it had on the students. Of 123 respondents, 47 believed busing had a negative effect or had no purpose, 31 believed it was positive for all children, and 22 believed it had no scholastic effect on bused children.[118] Again, this was in 1974, seven years after the program had started. It is unclear how many of the teachers and principals had been around since the beginning, but as mentioned before, the responses became more critical as the years went on, which begs the question: how did teacher and principal attitudes affect the children bused into these schools? Ray Rist asked a similar question of integration as it was occurring in Portland, Oregon. In Rist's study, *Invisible Children*, he examined the classroom experiences of students at a desegregated school and found that black students who had difficulty adjusting to norms of the school were often viewed as troublemakers and were marginalized academically because teachers focused on behavior modification over teaching curricular content. Rist did not view the inability of teachers to respond to students outside the norm as conscious teacher racism, but he attributes it to the "'business as usual' approach which almost invariably results in the tracking of the black students into the low group."[119] Although Rist's study did not address Chicago, it provides some insight about aspects of desegregation that may impact teacher and administrator interactions and perceptions.

One of the program's goals was to increase desegregation in District Four. The sending and receiving schools were all a part of administrative District Four. According to table 1.1, increased desegregation was certainly accomplished at the eight receiving schools, although

Table 1.1 Racial change in school membership 1967–1970

	1967		1968		1969		1970	
	White	Black	White	Black	White	Black	White	Black
Receiving schools								
Bridge	99.5	0	89.6	10.4	86.6	11.4	91.8	8.1
Burbank	99.2	0	87.3	12.7	87.6	12.4	86.2	11.3
Dever	99.6	0	90.3	9.6	91.3	8.7	91.7	7.9
Locke	99.8	0	89.7	10.1	87.9	11.9	89.7	9.9
Lyon	99.0	0	89.3	9.8	89.1	10.5	89.5	9
Sayre	100	0	89.8	10	90	10	87	12.2
Smyser	99.3	0	89.9	9.4	89	10	90.4	9.1
Thorp	99.6	0	90.4	9.2	91.4	8.3	90.3	9
Sending schools								
May	13	83.9	2.8	95.9	0.8	99.2	0.3	99.7
Spencer	11.9	82.4	7.4	90.8	3	97	0.8	98.8

Source: Austin Area Project Reports.

0 to 9 %

some would argue that the desegregation that was achieved was insignificant. Each receiving school gained over 9 percent black students when there had been no or very few black students prior to the plan. May and Spencer schools over time became 99 percent black. Thus, while the district overall was more desegregated, the desegregation improvements mainly occurred in the receiving schools.[120]

While the program was far from perfect, it did manage to desegregate the receiving schools, and some students increasingly went on to Steinmetz High School over the years. Although it was unclear what the students' experiences were like in those schools, many remained from the time they were first transferred until they graduated from high school. Nevertheless, the busing plan had a miniscule impact on the school system as a whole. Fewer than 600 students annually participated in the program (in a school system that had over 580,000 students in 1968). Overall, it meant the desegregation of only a couple thousand students.

*   *   *

In spite of all the controversies this plan caused, it was an extremely limited attempt at school desegregation. While the CCCO'S Title VI complaint and federal government pressure meant that some sort of plan had to be created, the federal government did not determine how school desegregation policy would be implemented, instead allowing Chicago Public School officials to guide the process. As a result, the newly appointed superintendent Redmond and the board were left to navigate hostile political waters. Stakeholders demanded democratic participation in the policy formulation and implementation, and ultimately the various stakeholders were able to alter the scale of school desegregation in their communities. Meanwhile, the more politically savvy and calculating Mayor Daley limited his public views of the plan by allowing his machine politicians to participate in the dialog, while reaping the results from a Board of Education he chose. The next decade would bring about the involvement of the federal government and the State of Illinois to force Chicago to do more to desegregate its students and teachers.

CHAPTER 2

Faculty Desegregation, 1969–1981

A myriad of interlocking conflicts emanated from efforts to enforce the policies of faculty[1] desegregation in the City of Chicago. These conflicts stemmed from the actions of federal agencies seeking to enforce the Civil Rights Act in a climate of both militant resistance and support. Federal agencies such as the Department of Justice and the Department of Health, Education, and Welfare (HEW) disagreed with the Chicago Board of Education as the agencies worked to implement teacher desegregation. The Chicago Board of Education at times conflicted with the Chicago Teachers Union (CTU) as they negotiated a number of limited faculty desegregation plans as a result of federal inducement. Still, these plans did not satisfy federal agencies. Ultimately, it was the threat to withhold funds resulting from administrative court proceedings that yielded success.

The role the CTU played in faculty desegregation efforts was viewed by some as obstructionist and by others as protectors of teacher's rights. On the one hand, the CTU argued that it was in support of desegregation, but not at the expense of teachers' rights. The federal government, on the other hand, perceived teachers' rights to be in conflict with the enforcement of the Civil Rights Act. As faculty desegregation eventually occurred, many teachers were uprooted from schools they had served for many years. Even if teachers had not been fully committed to the schools where they had previously worked, some were nevertheless mistrustful and fearful of the new schools and communities where they were moved, exposing the deeply entrenched racial divides in the city. Their mandatory movement was viewed as a blow to their rights as teachers and an impingement on their contracts.

Desegregation of school faculty became an initiative primarily because segregated faculties helped to make schools racially identifiable. The Supreme Court in *Swann v. Charlotte-Mecklenburg* (1971) ruled, "Independent of student assignment, where it is possible to identify a 'white school' or a 'Negro school' simply by reference to the racial composition of teachers and staff...a prima facie case of violation of substantive constitutional rights under the Equal Protection Clause is shown."[2] The process, which eventually led to teacher transfers in Chicago, began in December 1966 when Howard Howe II, the United States Commissioner of Education, issued the "Revised Statement of Policies for School Desegregation Plans Under Title VI of the Civil Rights Act of 1964," which provided guidelines for faculty desegregation.[3] The guidelines authorized districts to desegregate teachers and professional staff to correct past discrimination, end dismissals of teachers based on race, and assign new teachers in a desegregated manner.

In the 1970s, the federal government, through the Department of Justice and HEW, began to focus more on teacher desegregation and slowed their emphasis on student desegregation. According to Michael Rebell and Arthur Block, "Compared with the administrative complexities and political confrontation involved in attempts to integrate students, the process of faculty integration is relatively straightforward: racial imbalance patterns are easier to identify, harder to justify and are more readily remedied through the application of numerical guidelines and quotas."[4] Faculty desegregation remained stable over time and often alleviated worries of white flight that occur with student desegregation. It became easier for federal officials to demonstrate success with faculty desegregation, unlike the politically tenuous results with student desegregation and busing. Much of the early teacher desegregation initiatives were aimed at the South. By the end of the 1960s, it was becoming evident that northern cities such as Chicago were lagging behind in regards to faculty desegregation. The problems HEW incurred in their initial interactions in Chicago with the Title VI (1964 Civil Rights Act) Complaint and resulting withholding and releasing of federal funds certainly made Chicago a prime target for faculty desegregation. Since the initial complaint, Chicago was still under the watchful eye of the federal government. As a result, faculty desegregation gave the government an opportunity to enforce some form of school desegregation in a less controversial manner.

When HEW's Office of Civil Rights (OCR) began enforcement of faculty desegregation, the staff targeted big cities where there were no court orders to desegregate or court findings of purposeful segregation. OCR acted strongly during Richard Nixon's administration, when politicians wanted to slow school desegregation in the South and limit busing. Because the majority of the Title VI enforcement was aimed at the South, southern politicians added legal provisions to the Civil Rights Act that would ensure equal enforcement in the North and South. OCR's staff had been successful in desegregating southern school districts but soon shifted their focus to also include northern and western districts to implement faculty desegregation. The staff had to be equally divided between the regions. OCR had been successful in creating voluntary desegregation in a number of cities largely because it threatened to withhold federal funding.[5] Once the Emergency School Aid Act (ESAA) was passed in 1972, it provided an immediate way to withhold funding and granted some leverage for voluntary cooperation. ESAA was designed to provide funding to eliminate faculty and student segregation, encourage voluntary desegregation, and aid minority children in overcoming educational disadvantages.[6]

As part of the 1964 Civil Rights Act, Title IV and Title VI provided the enforcement mechanisms for desegregation. Title VI allowed HEW to withhold funds, and Title IV, which dealt directly with the desegregation of public education, permitted the Justice Department to file suit. The threat of withholding funds had forced southern school districts to desegregate. However, on July 3, 1969, the Justice Department and HEW issued a joint statement announcing a preference for Justice Department law suits rather than HEW withholding funds from recalcitrant school districts.[7] The Nixon administration and southern politicians were successful in limiting HEW's power to withhold funds just as the agency was beginning to be successful in desegregating schools.[8] Eliminating that threat in exchange for law suits from an under-resourced Justice Department meant a possible slowdown in school desegregation, as it was much easier to threaten a district's funding rather than to bring a law suit against it.

With the shifting federal priorities, the Justice Department, not HEW, was the first agency demanding faculty desegregation when the federal government approached Chicago. This was an important move as the consequences for withholding funds in a city controlled by Mayor Richard J. Daley had already proven to be unwise in the CCCO Title VI complaint incident. Just six days after the joint statement, the Justice Department sent the Chicago Board of Education a letter demanding faculty desegregation.

As the federal government targeted Daley's city for faculty desegregation, cracks in Daley's unlimited power continued to widen. The city was reeling from the police assassinations of Black Panther leader Fred Hampton and Mark Clark in the early morning of December 4,

1969. The police claimed that they responded to shots fired from inside Hampton's apartment, but evidence later revealed that several dozen shots came from the police firing into the house and directly at Fred Hampton who had been drugged and had not gotten out of bed. The Federal Bureau of Investigation's (FBI) confidential informant William O'Neal had provided the floor plan of Hampton's apartment to the police and had drugged Hampton.[9] States Attorney Edward V. Hanrahan then attempted to coverup the assassination. When he came to office in 1968, Hanrahan had declared war on the street gangs and the Black Panther Party. Black Panthers were being targeted and killed nationwide by the FBI's Counter Intelligence Program. Scholar Paul Kleppner argued that, "Hanrahan at once became a loathsome symbol within the black community, a living reminder of how lightly white leaders valued black lives and how cavalierly and unapologetically they violated the civil and human rights of black citizens." Hampton's and Clark's assassinations were just two of 39 police murders of black Chicagoans in 1969, for which police faced no indictments. The murders of Hampton and Clark were a "more wanton gross abuse of the civil rights of blacks than even the Daley Machine normally tolerated." [10] In the 1971 mayoral elections, Daley lost much of his black support, although he was still elected to his fifth term.[11] These murders and the subsequent election highlighted a city with a continued racial divide and mistrust. But it also impacted the context in which faculty desegregation was to occur, making it much more difficult than federal officials had hoped.

Faculty Segregation Background

As with housing, access to jobs for blacks in Chicago has been historically limited and difficult to secure; acquiring teaching positions was no exception. Black teachers throughout the North had difficulties being assigned to permanent positions at the turn of the twentieth century. In 1908, prior to the Great Migration, few black teachers were hired in major northern cities. New York had the highest with 43 teachers and Chicago just had 16. By 1930, after thousands of blacks moved north as a result of the Great Migration, New York had 500 black teachers and Chicago had approximately 300. Despite the increased number of teachers, both cities still had fewer than three percent black teachers. In cities like Indianapolis and Cincinnati, the proportion of black teachers was higher, but black teachers were limited to segregated institutions. Other cities like Buffalo, Milwaukee, and Pittsburgh had a miniscule number of black teachers, if any.[12]

In Chicago, many black teachers spent years on substitute lists until a position opened at a black school. Blacks also tended to be on substitute lists longer than whites, as they were identified and intentionally sent to black schools.[13] The *Chicago Defender* noted in 1916 that such a policy would limit job opportunities for black teachers.[14] Black teachers remained on the substitute rolls longer than white teachers as white teachers were assigned to both black and white schools. Like teachers, black principals were also assigned to all or predominantly black schools. The first black principal in Chicago, Maudelle Bousfield, was assigned successively to three black schools throughout her career.[15] As the city's schools become more segregated, the assignment of teachers and principals made schools more racially identifiable.

While black teachers were seeking positions at black schools, white teachers tended to transfer out of those schools as soon as they could. According to school policy, teachers were allowed to transfer after just one year of teaching, and many white teachers at black schools took advantage of this policy. Some transferred to be closer to home or into white middle-class areas with less population turnovers. The transfers were considered a sign of seniority and upward mobility. The transfer policy often meant that the most experienced white teachers taught at white schools and schools with students from higher socioeconomic statuses. As a result, there was high teacher turnover in predominantly black schools, which some believed led to inferior training of black children, as black schools tended to have less experienced teachers.[16]

These trends continued into the late 1960s. A sizable number of black teachers often held Full Time Basis (FTB) substitute status for a number of years. FTBs often taught their own classrooms; however, they were uncertified new teachers or had not taken or had not passed Chicago's written and/or oral teacher certification exam. One black teacher who had a master's degree still took three attempts to pass the certification exam. He believed the test was racist because large numbers of black teachers failed the exam.[17] Some teachers who passed the written exam failed the oral exam. The oral exam was a subjective judgment of the southern dialect of individual test takers.[18] If one failed the oral exam, he/she would then have to retake both exams.

The certification process became a contentious issue since FTBs' jobs were not secure. FTBs could be reassigned with little recourse because of their political beliefs or if principals did not like them. CTU represented certified members as well as FTBs. However, FTBs were not given the rights and privileges of full members. Between

November 1967 and January 1968, many FTBs, particularly black FTBs, held various strikes to oppose the Board of Education's "backward" certification exam.[19] One strike lasted ten days. In August 1968, the *Chicago Daily News* reported that a certification exam was given with the oral portion eliminated. This was likely as a result of the ten-day strike. Of the 2,381 people who took the written exam, only 725 (30 percent) passed.[20]

The issues with black teachers finding permanent teaching positions persisted in the 1960s. While some teachers continued to fight for certification, black teachers continued to be placed at all black or predominantly black schools and many white teachers continued to transfer out of black schools. By the late 1960s, some black teachers and black community members became more militant, with many favoring Black Power and community control of schools over desegregation. Teachers had far less concern about only being placed at black schools as job opportunities increased and because many felt an obligation and responsibility to the black community. As black teachers congregated at black schools, some began to consider their ability to use these schools as centers of power. When the CTU held a strike in May 1969 to increase teachers' pay raises, black teachers kept many black schools open. They opposed the strike, arguing that instead of pay raises, money should go to improving inner city schools. In addition, there were a number of calls for the removal of ineffective or insensitive white principals at black schools. In several cases, those principals were removed and replaced with black principals. There were also manifestos issued by several teachers groups demanding more community control of schools because they believed that they could better cure the ills of black schools than a system they perceived as racist.[21] Like their colleagues in New York's Ocean Hill-Brownville and Harlem experimental districts, many black teachers firmly believed that their commitment was to their students, and saw the school system as an impediment to their success.[22] There were certainly white principals and teachers who were just as dedicated as black teachers, and some joined with black teachers to fight for improved conditions.[23]

The concern black teachers have had for black students has historically been a part of the African American educational experience. In early desegregation arguments in Boston in the mid-1800s, black advocates for segregated education wanted to hire black teachers who would show more care and concern for black students.[24] W. E. B. Du Bois had also expressed that sympathetic teachers were an asset of segregated schools although he believed that mixed schools would be the most natural way to educate students.[25] Southern educators have demonstrated care and concern for black students beyond just emotional feelings. According to Vanessa Siddle Walker, "Teachers were increasingly well-trained educators who worked in concert with their leaders to implement a collective vision of how to educate African American children in a Jim Crow society."[26] In the North, racial uplift also undergirded much of the educational philosophies of black teachers. However, northern black teachers were not usually capable of working on a collective vision with school leaders, as few schools had all black teachers and administrators. Still, schools such as Crispus Attucks in Indianapolis were able to accomplish such collective visions as black teachers and school leadership provided excellent training for black students.[27] The community control efforts of teachers in the 1960s in places like Chicago and New York were similar attempts to provide the essence of a collective concept for the education of black youth.

REDMOND PLAN AND TEACHERS

HEW originally became involved in Chicago in 1965 when the Coordinating Council of Community Organizations (CCCO) issued a Title VI complaint against the Board of Education for the purposeful segregation of schools. While mostly documenting incidents of student segregation, the complaint also called attention to the number of uncertified teachers concentrated at black schools. It showed that 12 percent of uncertified teachers were at white schools compared to 27 percent at black schools. The 1964 Hauser Report, which came as a result of an out of court settlement in the *Webb v. Board of Education* (1963) case, indicated that "It is apparent that teachers in Negro schools are younger and have less formal education and that the teaching staff in these schools has a much higher turnover."[28] The Hauser Report also noted the segregation of black teachers since most worked at black schools. According to school data for the 1965–1966 school year, 88 percent of black teachers worked in schools with 90 percent or more black students. Moreover, 51 percent of white teachers worked at schools with 90–100 percent white students.[29] It is evident from these numbers that many schools were racially identifiable.

While black FTBs fought for certification, they were not the only uncertified teachers at black schools. There was also a number of uncertified, typically first-year white teachers at black schools as well. As noted earlier, some of these white teachers would transfer as soon as possible, which led to the high teacher turnover rates that black schools experienced. Black parents had been complaining about these trends since the 1930s.[30] Teachers with less experience, whether certified or not, were often perceived as providing a lower quality of education for students, particularly when those teachers were often concentrated at certain schools.

What CCCO and HEW saw as segregation, black radicals viewed as an opportunity to provide black students with teachers who were interested in their educational and social advancement. They viewed their control of the public schools as essential to that process. Concerned FTBs also believed that they were capable of providing a good education for black students and recognized their inability to be certified as a systemic problem rather than a measure of their abilities. The previous example of the one highly educated black teacher who had difficulty with the certification test seemed to provide some anecdotal evidence of their claim.

Although the federal funds were released after the Title VI complaint, Chicago still had to respond to CCCO's allegations. In January 1967, the US Office of Education in HEW sent Chicago a report with four areas that needed attention. One area was faculty assignment patterns. The Redmond Plan, which was the response to the US Office of Education, also addressed faculty segregation. The report acknowledged faculty segregation and the concentration of inexperienced and uncertified teachers at black and low socioeconomic schools, indicating, "We have started from the conviction that significantly more integration of school faculties than now exists will be desirable throughout the system, that it is necessary to build stability and reduce turnover of the staffs of all central city schools and that significant numbers of more experienced and better qualified teachers are needed now to balance staffs in most central city schools."[31] Starting from that premise, the Redmond Plan then focused on four areas: climate of inner city schools; teacher assignment and transfer policies; new teacher recruitment, preparation and training; and integration efforts.[32] In order to improve school climate, the report recommended the formation of teaching groups, principal training in inner city schools, better community relations, beefing up security, shoring up shortages in substitute teachers, and provisions to deal with students with severe discipline problems. Real and perceived issues of student discipline and security were some of the reasons white teachers gave for not remaining in inner city schools. At times, cultural misunderstandings and racist assumptions led to those beliefs. Redmond did not address the possible problems that black teachers could have in white schools and communities.

Investigating the assignment and transfer patterns of Chicago Public Schools, the Redmond Plan contradicted the beliefs held by black teachers, particularly black FTBs' leadership. The writers of the Redmond Plan thought that the FTB status was more an issue of youth rather than intellectual quality. However, the writers differed with the FTBs because the writers believed that the written and oral certification exam, additional professional course hours, and student teaching made for better teachers. FTBs, particularly those who had been teaching more than one year, were not against professional development, but believed the test was the problem. According to the Redmond Plan, a second area of difference was that, "The percentage of regularly certified teachers in a school correlates highly and positively with the length of experience, advanced degrees held, lower turnover, and, to some extent, the existence of a predominantly white teaching staff. Inversely, where the percentage of regularly certified teachers is low, we find less experience, higher turnover, fewer advanced degrees held, and the greater likelihood of a predominantly Negro teaching staff."[33] Furthermore, the Redmond Plan indicated that the changes in the certification standards would further devalue the quality of teachers. Again, these findings contradict concerned FTBs' assumptions because they believed that they were more than qualified and certainly capable of being effective teachers. Despite the report's findings, in June 1969, the Board of Education approved automatic certification for FTBs who had three or more years of satisfactory teaching.[34]

In an administrative hearing discussed later, a judge balked at the assumption that black teachers "do not provide minority students with the same educational opportunities as a white teacher would. Such a proposition is untenable. The ability of an educator is not dependent upon his or her race." Furthermore, years of experience did not necessarily correlate to quality. He stated that, "In many instances, young teachers with only one to five years of experience and fresh new ideas might prove to be better teachers."[35] Judge Everett J. Hammarstrom effectively captured the underlying assumptions held by school officials and HEW that black and new teachers were less capable teachers. Scholarship on effective teaching practices for African American students indicates that a holistic teaching approach serves as best practice. While the knowledge base of a teacher is certainly essential, their cultural competency builds an important bridge between content knowledge and the ability to inspire students to achieve in spite of racism or poverty. Black teachers' care for the students means that they can reach students, set high expectations, and often identify with their experiences.[36] Still, the concentration of so many uncertified and inexperienced teachers at predominantly black schools was unsettling.

The Redmond Plan also indicated that the Board of Education should adopt transfer policies that would assist with schools having the same number of certified teachers. The importance of an even number of certified teachers at various schools was so that teachers who had passed the certification exam and probationary period could be evenly distributed at all of the schools. In a case where a school has certified teachers higher than the city average, certified teachers could not transfer into those schools. An exception would be made in the case where a certified black teacher wanted to transfer. Movement of certified black teachers would essentially defeat the issue of lack of certified teachers in black schools and would serve as a further benefit for white schools. The report recommended changing policies to allow for integration while acknowledging the activities the Board of Education was already pursuing. Certified teachers would no longer be placed in schools with 95 percent or more certified teachers. FTBs would be assigned to those schools instead. Also, newly certified teachers would be assigned to schools, instead of having a choice.[37] These new policies led to some desegregation of faculties, although not nearly enough to produce meaningful desegregation.

JUSTICE DEPARTMENT DEMANDS TEACHER DESEGREGATION

On July 9, 1969, school officials received a letter from the United States Department of Justice demanding that they desegregate their faculty. According to the letter written by US attorney general Thomas A. Foran and assistant attorney general Jerris Leonard, black parents in Chicago had complained that their children were deprived of "equal protection of the laws." Moreover, "In accordance with our responsibilities under Title VI of the Civil Rights Act of 1964, we have completed an examination of the Chicago Board's policies and practices of faculty and staff assignments...This examination compels the conclusion that the school system's practices with respect to the assignment and transfer of faculty have had the effect of denying Negro students the equal protection of the laws in violation of the Civil Rights Act of 1964 and the Fourteenth Amendment of the U.S. Constitution."[38] The letter gave the Board of Education two weeks to respond with a plan to implement faculty desegregation (by September 1969). If such plans were not implemented, the Justice

Department threatened to sue Chicago schools in federal court and cut off federal funding to the schools. This was the seventh such letter the Nixon administration had sent to school systems in both the North and South in an effort to implement faculty desegregation.[39]

A 1969 Justice Department study noted that 215 of the 578 Chicago schools had all white or all black faculties. It also indicated that 93 percent of the black elementary and junior high teachers were in schools with 90 percent or more black students.[40] The Chicago Board of Education released its own figures on teacher segregation. It defined integration as schools having fewer than 90 percent teachers of one race. According to that standard, Chicago schools had 35 percent of its faculties integrated in 1966. In 1967, 43 percent were integrated but the number of schools with integrated faculty dropped to 41 percent in 1968. More than one in three schools still had all white faculties in 1968.[41]

In response to the Justice Department letter, Superintendent James Redmond and Board of Education president Frank Whiston issued a statement saying, "We have never practiced segregation of faculty in Chicago, but we have permitted seniority choice of schools by teachers. Race has never been a basis of assignment or transfer."[42] CTU president John E. Desmond insisted that "many teachers, both black and white, will not accept a forcible transfer."[43] Desmond had been a part of the union's executive board since 1947 and had been a physical education teacher at three elementary schools. He became CTU president in May 1966 and during his presidency, the CTU became the sole collective bargaining agency for the city's teachers.[44] Desmond blamed the city's segregated housing patterns for the choice teachers made in transferring, noting that many simply wanted to teach closer to where they lived. Desmond also said, "The union has always believed in integration, but we will have to uphold our present contract with the Board of Education." Mayor Daley also denied intentional segregation, chiming in to say that teaching assignments were done according to seniority rather than race.[45]

In July 1968, Superintendent Redmond reported that there were a number of issues preventing the desegregation of the faculty. First was the contract with the union. The CTU had opposed the proposal to lower the number of certified teachers from 95 percent to 90 percent. Second, Redmond, agreeing with CTU president Desmond, determined that housing patterns also served as a deterrent as teachers did not want to travel far from home to teach. Third, racial isolation hindered the experiences teachers needed to move beyond their stereotypical ideas about people of other racial groups. Fourth, the growing black consciousness of black teachers meant that desegregation was no longer desirable. Fifth, the riots, demonstrations, and boycotts that occurred sometimes deterred the progress of racial integration. Black demands and protests for black school leadership, black teachers, and control of black schools mixed with white protests against busing heightened racial tensions. Last, Illinois School Code prevented the assignment of staff by race.[46]

Redmond had long been aware of the issues surrounding faculty desegregation. His concerns regarding the fallout of demonstrations were particularly pertinent by the late 1960s in Chicago. The city had experienced a multitude of public actions over the past decade, ranging from peaceful to riotous. In many ways, Chicago was as a microcosm of increasing racial tensions throughout the country. Since 1963, blacks had been demonstrating in large numbers for desegregation in Chicago. By 1968, many whites were also demonstrating in large numbers against desegregation policies. Years of protest ranged widely in both purpose and tactics: some fought for community control while others fought for and against school desegregation. Groups utilized actions ranging from boycotts, to marches, to riots. There had been a number of riots in black communities nationwide throughout the 1960s. One of the most well known was the Watts Riot in Los Angeles in 1965. While Watts has become one of the more notorious riots of this era, Chicago had its own rebellion in 1965. It began when West Side residents protested at a fire house demanding that a black firefighter be hired. During this initial protest, a fire truck knocked over a light pole and killed a black woman, sparking a riot that lasted for four days. In July 1966, another riot occurred when the police turned off a fire hydrant black youth used to cool themselves in the summer. The uprisings represented a display of deep social, political, and economic dissatisfaction, and symbolized the entrenched divide between blacks and whites. After Martin Luther King Jr. was assassinated on April 4, 1968, riots broke out across the nation. Chicagoans rebelled until the National Guard was called to quell the disruption.[47] These rebellions have shown a spotlight on the deeper structural injustices that continued to oppress a number of urban blacks that were not being remedied simply with changes in laws. While Redmond correctly articulated the obstacles for teacher desegregation, the Department of Justice was responsible for carrying out the law in spite of these very real impediments. This represented an instance where policy articulation and implementation were not readily aligned.

On July 14, 1969, Illinois governor Richard B. Ogilvie wrote a letter to US Attorney General John Mitchell asking the Justice

Department to withdraw its ultimatum. Ogilvie stated, "Arbitrary deadlines and hasty decrees, which must be modified later by the dictates of common sense to achieve effective solutions, do a disservice to all concerned." The governor admonished the intervention of the federal government in a local matter. He also asserted that there needed to be mutual cooperation among the groups involved. He said the 14-day deadline "is wholly inadequate to permit a meaningful effort toward mutual cooperation or real communication, much less a settlement negotiated with local support and with a realistic financial base."[48]

Redmond did not wait for a response to Governor Ogilvie's letter, but continued working to meet the Justice Department's deadline. Redmond and Board of Education officials met with CTU representatives on July 22, 1969, in a four-hour closed-door meeting to discuss teacher desegregation.[49] The next day, the Board of Education approved a 15-point program as an answer to the Justice Department's demands for desegregation. The response came in the form of a letter from Board President Frank Whiston. The letter indicated that the board and CTU had made an agreement on May 10, 1967, in which both groups would encourage regularly certified teachers to transfer in order to promote desegregation.[50] However, the CTU would have to approve any changes that did not meet their contract. In spite of the meeting with CTU officials, some union leaders were not happy with the transfer policy changes. They had their own plans for faculty desegregation and wanted to meet with the board and Justice Department.

Redmond told newspaper reporters that, "The plan of action which we are proposing is designed to bring about in each…school a city-wide ratio of experienced and inexperienced teachers thereby modifying the pattern of faculty assignment." This would be done with voluntary transfers. The integration plan included the following: (1) increase the number of uncertified teachers from 10 percent to 15 percent by September 1969 and to 20 percent by September 1970; (2) transfer temporarily certified black teachers to white schools and temporarily certified white teachers to black schools; (3) in order to transfer, certified teachers would need two years' experience instead of one; and (4) create incentive pay and security improvements to inner city schools in order to attract more experienced teachers. The incentive pay would be a $1000 salary bonus to 204 teachers who transferred to increase integration. Redmond requested $5,600,000 in federal aid to accomplish his plan. The funding would be used for incentives, instructional teams to aid with in-service training, and security for faculty parking lots.[51]

The CTU received dozens of calls from concerned teachers complaining about the faculty desegregation plan. CTU vice president Vivian Gallagher argued that many teachers were concerned about the incentive pay being offered in the plan. "The teachers would rather have working conditions cleaned up...They don't want to be paid an extra $1000 to work in deplorable conditions." A union field representative, Ed Powell, said it would be unfair to white teachers currently working in black schools and black teachers currently working in white schools to suddenly offer incentive pay for other teachers. "What about the teachers who have been sticking it out all of these years? Why don't they get incentive pay too?"[52] The Justice Department met with board members on July 28, 1969, to discuss their response, but the CTU was left out of the meeting, even though CTU had asked to be a part of the negotiations. Foran said the union was excluded because, "By law, the responsibility for the proper conduct of the school system is with the Board of Education...The union doesn't run the school Board."[53]

Perhaps Foran did not have the insight to see that excluding the union could cause problems for any plan approved. The union's exclusion from talks would make it more likely that CTU members would oppose the efforts of the Board of Education. Furthermore, the May 1969 teachers' strike served as proof that teachers were more than willing to strike. Likely, Foran was under the impression that he had the power of the federal government behind him and the threat of court action which would negate the opposition efforts of the teachers' union. If the teachers' contract was impeding the law, Foran saw the need to bypass it. But unions have historically been established to ensure the rights of teachers by allowing their collective voices to be heard; and Foran's disregard for the union contract and denial of their participation in negotiations directly challenged this.

Negotiations between Foran and the board were unsuccessful. On October 20, 1969, the Board of Education received official word from the Justice Department that their plan was rejected. Now the board had not only failed to satisfy the federal government, but had created tensions with the CTU in the process. The Justice Department said that it would not file suit, but would give the board another chance to desegregate. In its letter, Justice Department officials highlighted the main points of contention: the purposeful segregation of faculty, and whether the CTU's needed to approve plans the board created.[54]

The first reason outlined for the rejections of the board's plan was that it would only lead to token desegregation. The plan still allowed teachers to transfer out of schools where they were the minority;

they would just have to wait an additional year to make that transfer. Second, in terms of equalization of faculties, the board's plan called for movement of teachers when vacancies occurred; but some schools were stable, and it could take years for vacancies to occur. Furthermore, the board's concern about uncertified teachers was negated when it certified FTBs after three years of satisfactory service. The letter stated: "To a large extent, the board's plan calls for correcting the equalization problems by certifying many of the teachers in the inner city schools who have heretofore been unable to meet the certification requirements." The Justice Department expressed, "serious reservations concerning the validity of the board's standard for determining who the better qualified teachers are." Third, no provisions were made to distribute substitutes equitably throughout the schools. Inner city classes go without substitute teachers on a daily basis, and the board's plan did not mention this at all. Fourth, the board's request for over $5.3 million was also rejected because Chicago's schools already received $21 million in federal aid. The letter stated, "The school board's duty under such circumstances is not merely to refrain from continuing with the policies which have led to segregated faculties, but also to take affirmative steps to overcome the effects of its past racially discriminatory policies, including, if necessary, the reassignment of incumbent personnel."[55]

In regards to the involvement of the CTU, the Justice Department suggested that the board continue to proceed without appeasing the CTU. The desegregation of faculty and the equal distribution of certified and substitute teachers were a "fulfillment of this constitutional obligation [which] cannot be made contingent on approval of the union."[56] It ordered the board to complete the following steps: allow HEW to prepare a faculty desegregation plan; agree that the implementation of a plan would not need the CTU's approval; and compile a list of the entire faculty and professional staff's names, addresses, race, and school. The board's records were not centrally compiled making it difficult to implement and evaluate the progress of faculty desegregation.

Reactions from Board of Education members varied. Louise Malis thought that CTU leaders needed to be in on future negotiations saying, "After all, we need the full cooperation and understanding of the union to make teacher integration work, and we can't get it if the union is left out of discussions because of legal technicalities." Carey B. Preston suggested that the Justice Department should sue the board because "a court order is the only way to settle all the legal points we disagree on."[57] The board postponed a decision on whether

policy hard to make into practice

union inclusion in discussion

to obey the Justice Department's new requests until it could meet with US officials to discuss details of the new demands.

On November 19, 1969, the board voted to comply with the Justice Department's demand to allow the HEW to help create the faculty desegregation plan. It also decided to ignore the other two orders that involved not allowing the CTU to veto any plan created and compiling a list of teachers by race. Both of these orders involved legalities with the state and teacher contracts.[58] Prior to the board's response, their racial head counts revealed that there was an increase in faculty desegregation. In 1969, 48 percent of city's schools had integrated staffs, up from 41 percent in 1968. Schools with one race teaching staffs decreased from 36 percent in 1968 to 29 percent in 1969. Because the Board of Education started to assign new and uncertified teachers to limit segregation in January 1968, an increase in desegregation had occurred. Although 28 white schools on the North and Southwest Sides received their first black teachers, close to 27 percent of the schools still had all white faculties.[59] Table 2.1 shows minor improvements in faculty desegregation although it was far from what the Justice Department would consider equitable.

During the 1970 contract negotiations with the CTU, the board asked for the authority to make compulsory transfers of certified teachers. This would make it easier to distribute experienced teachers throughout the system. The CTU refused. However, the union did agree to work with the board and federal officials to create a teacher desegregation plan.[60] In order to reach an agreement and avoid a strike, the board dropped the demand for mandatory transfers and a contract agreement was made in January 1970.

On July 1, 1970, almost a year after the Justice Department initially demanded faculty desegregation, HEW sent the Board of Education a recommended plan. The plan was created by educational

Table 2.1 Faculty desegregation

Faculty makeup	Schools	
	1968	1969
All black	13	7
90–99% black	40	24
Integrated	239	282
90–99% white	91	113
All white	196	161

Source: Chicago Sun-Times, November 18, 1969.

consultants hired by the US Office of Education, but was sure to be opposed by the CTU and had set no deadline for implementation. The recommendations called for major changes in teacher assignments, including (1) the number of black teachers to be placed at each school would be set at 24–44 percent; (2) teachers could transfer only if it promoted desegregation; (3) mandatory lottery transfers were to be made for 1,000 teachers with at least three years experience and not more than 50 years of age; and (4) black principals were to be promoted and assigned to desegregated schools. Although there was recognition of the importance blacks placed on having black teachers and principals at black schools, the consultants agreed that, "it should be noted that the panel's role is to recommend a plan that meets constitutional requirements."[61]

CTU president Desmond dismissed the plan and responded to HEW's recommendations with sarcasm, calling it "a good ivory tower report with a lot of nice-sounding words and a lot of double-talk in between." Desmond thought that moving experienced teachers to inner city classrooms with 40 students would not change the quality of education one bit. Instead, he insisted that lower class sizes, better security, and more supplies were the only changes that would lead to better education. While Desmond agreed with faculty desegregation in principle and the assignment of new teachers to promote desegregation, he again reiterated the importance of honoring the CTU contract.[62]

Although union officials speculated about the difficulties of carrying out the HEW plan, the board remained relatively quiet on the issue until its July 16, 1970, meeting. At that meeting, it decided to do a racial census of the teachers. Redmond was given permission to negotiate with federal officials and CTU leaders to work out a more realistic plan. He could also continue to assign new teachers and newly certified teachers to engender desegregation. There was concern about randomly choosing 1,000 teachers to desegregate, and thus Redmond would chose teachers from schools that were above average in the number of experienced teachers.[63] As the 1970–1971 school year was about to begin, Redmond announced that 920 new and newly certified teachers would be assigned based on race. He also worked with HEW to negotiate a smaller percentage of teachers who would be affected by reassignments. The negotiations did not alter the demand for mandatory transfers. As a result, 750 certified teachers would still subject to mandatory transfers.[64] However, it is unclear whether the certified teachers were ever transferred because of CTU resistance.

The CTU House of Representatives voted unanimously to strike if the Board of Education forced teachers to transfer. Desmond reiterated it was really the new teachers who would move the desegregation process forward. The union believed that if all teachers were subject to forced transfers, the plan would cause more harm than good as experienced teachers may leave the school system altogether. In a counterproposal to the board's plan, the CTU continued to refuse the transfer of any certified teachers. It believed that desegregation could be accomplished with new teachers alone—a stance which indicated that the union was more concerned with protecting the teachers' contracts than desegregation.[65]

Jesse Jackson, a longtime community activist who had been an associate of Martin Luther King Jr., also spoke in opposition to the plan. Jackson and his organization Operation Breadbasket (later renamed Operation Push) was actively involved in supporting teacher and student organizing around community control in the 1960s. The organization wanted to help black youth achieve middle-class status and believed school desegregation was a worthwhile cause.[66] But Jackson argued that the desegregation plan would only take experienced black teachers out of black schools and replace them with white teachers "incapable of inspiring black students." He stated that, "If we have 54 percent of the school population, we should have 54 percent of the power to run the schools…All four levels within the school system—school Board, budgeting powers, curriculum, and student enrollment—should be controlled by a more integrated school power structure."[67] Some of his concerns mirrored the Black Power and community control position. Moving black teachers from black schools was certainly viewed as harmful by black community members and leaders. But Jackson was not against school desegregation. He opposed the lack of Black Power within the system. Oftentimes school desegregation occurred without the input of the black community and left the same power structures in place after desegregation occurred. Therefore, the very people who held power over segregated systems were then held responsible for desegregating those systems. Some people, such as Jackson, questioned whose interests those power brokers would have.[68]

In the summer of 1970, Chicago schools' Department of Personnel processed the assignments of 4,363 new or uncertified teachers. Of those assigned, 3,603 teachers accepted their assignments. However, 600 teachers who accepted assignments either did not report to the assigned school or reported only for a few days and then did not return. As a result, 480 positions were still left unfilled.[69] On September 29,

1970, Superintendent Redmond transferred 480 substitute teachers to increase faculty desegregation. The CTU's contract stipulated that day-to-day substitutes could not be transferred after working at a school for 20 consecutive days. In order to avoid breaking the contract, Redmond transferred the 480 substitutes prior to their 20 days. Some principals were upset with the decision because of the potential disruptions to classes.[70] In this instance, though, the CTU allowed the changes to occur in order to assist the board. It agreed to allow the board to withhold FTB status from substitute teachers who refused a full-time assignment at a school that they disliked. The CTU still would not budge on transferring certified teachers, but this new modification would be helpful to the board's desegregation attempts.[71]

When the 1970 racial head counts were released, the board still failed to meet desegregation guidelines set up by HEW, even though the city's school teachers were more desegregated than in 1969. The biggest decrease in segregation occurred at all white elementary schools. In 1969, there were initially 156 schools with all white faculties. By 1970, that number had decreased to 83. Still, after a year and a half of negotiations, the Justice Department and HEW had failed to force the type of faculty desegregation it wanted in Chicago.[72]

In June 1971, the Justice Department Communications and the Employee Relations Committee met with school staff and CTU representatives to hammer out a desegregation plan, and the Board of Education and the CTU came to a tentative agreement regarding faculty desegregation. The plan's goal was to have no more than 50–75 percent teachers of one race at each school. The board planned to achieve desegregation through the recruitment of more black and minority teachers, the careful assignment of new teachers to achieve desegregation, and the reappointment of certified teachers returning from resignation. [73] The mandatory transfer provisions for certified teachers remained elusive. Redmond noted, "It is one thing for consultants to suggest something and quite another to develop a practical program...We are not buying the consultants' concept of bouncing experienced teachers because we do not think it is practical."[74]

The CTU House of Representatives voted to approve the plan, as did the Board of Education. They then turned to a teacher referendum for final approval. Although 95 percent of teachers surveyed said they favored integration, teachers across the city only voted to approve the faculty desegregation plan by 2–1, illustrating that they remained uncertain about the plan and that they were concerned about how it would impact them individually.[75] In early 1972, Redmond reported that 298 schools had faculties with 75 percent or fewer one race up from 223 the previous year.[76] The voluntary transfers were making some headway with faculty desegregation.

In April 1972, the Justice Department yet again rejected the city's teacher desegregation plan because it did not go far enough to achieve the desired level of desegregation. The board was given 30 days to come up with a stronger plan and to implement it by the time school began in September.[77] Although the deadline was extended to June 26, 1972, the Justice Department rejected the board's third plan. Officials stated that the board's plan did not work because "It does not offer a realistic prospect for eliminating the existing patterns of segregation and disparities in the future."[78]

Chicago's schools continually failed to meet HEW and Justice Department requirements of demands for school desegregation. However, the federal pressure the Chicago Board of Education received from 1969 to 1972 waned for a few years. In those years, the board and CTU continued to try to acquire faculty desegregation, but without the movement of certified teachers. In June 1973, the Chicago Board of Education was denied $2.3 million in ESAA funds. The rejection letter indicated that Chicago had not done enough to desegregate its teachers.[79] That same month, the Justice Department decided to drop its plans to sue Chicago over teacher desegregation primarily because of HEW's denial of ESAA funding. The Justice Department's Civil Rights Division did not have the resources to file suit, having already brought teacher discrimination suits in Baltimore, suburban St. Louis, and Kansas City, Kansas.[80]

The 1974–1975 school racial census showed a continued increase in black and Latino teachers and a decrease in the percentage of white teachers. Of the total 26,695 teachers, blacks represented 40.1 percent of the teaching force with 10,798 teachers; Latinos were 2.2 percent

Table 2.2 Teacher demographics 1970–2012

Year	Percentage white	Percentage black	Percentage Hispanic	Total population
1970	64.2	34.5	0.1	24,516
1975	55.8	40.7	2.7	27,003
1980	50.7	43.6	4.3	23,714
1984	46.1	47.3	5	22,930
2009	49.7	29.7	16.1	21,230
2012	49.3	25.1	18.3	23,290

Source: Chicago public school racial ethnic surveys and stats and facts.

with 589 teachers; and whites were 56.8 percent with 15,308 teachers. Despite the increase in black and Latino teachers, the district lost
ground on its desegregation guidelines (See table 2.2). In 1973, 55.3
percent of schools met the board's standards, but that number decreased
to 53 percent in 1974. The board's goal was to come into compliance
with its standards by 1976. Almost 13 percent of the schools still had
90 percent or more teachers of one race and 3.6 percent all white or all
black faculties. Seeking better results through different tactics, the federal government stopped threatening the schools with a suit and instead
resorted to withholding the much needed federal funding.[81]

HEW Takes over Negotiations

On October 6, 1975, HEW threatened Chicago with the possible
loss of $147 million in federal funding in the 1977–1978 school year
if the board did not submit a new faculty desegregation plan, evenly
distribute teachers with experience and education among all schools,
and improve services to bilingual education. HEW gave the Board
60 days to create plans dealing with the three issues. The department was under pressure to enforce its own policies since the National
Association for the Advancement of Colored People (NAACP) filed a
suit against them. The NAACP targeted HEW in 1973 over its poor
record of enforcing desegregation nationwide in the case *Adams v.
Richardson*. Deciding in favor of the NAACP, Judge John H. Pratt
ordered HEW to quickly enforce school desegregation in 125 districts in border and southern states.[82]

Meanwhile, Chicago Public Schools appointed a new superintendent, Joseph P. Hannon, in September 1975. Hannon had been the
assistant superintendent for facilities planning under James Redmond
who had hired Hannon to the position in 1970 after Hannon had
completed his doctorate in education from the University of Northern
Colorado. Prior to his position in Chicago, Hannon had been a teacher,
assistant principal, and education consultant. He had beaten out the
school system's number two man, Deputy Superintendent Manford
Byrd, for the general superintendent position. Jesse Jackson and other
blacks and Latinos had wanted Byrd for the position because he was
black and experienced. In protest of Hannon's appointment, Jackson
organized a demonstration outside the Board of Education offices.[83]
The protest had no impact.

Once HEW made its demands on the city, Hannon accused HEW
of playing politics. In January 1976, he told the *Chicago Sun-Times*
that President Gerald Ford's administration was picking on big cities

where Democrats had power, but backing off of suburbs and rural areas, presumably as a result of upcoming elections. Cities like Detroit, St. Louis, Boston, Seattle, Los Angeles, and Baltimore, all faced pressure to desegregate their school faculties. However, Richard E. Friedman, HEW's general administrator, said that far more suburbs and rural areas had experienced HEW pressure. Friedman also refuted the claims of politics stating, "What we are doing here is enforcing the law as described under two controlling U.S. Supreme Court cases over the last five years. There's been a need to take action over the last few years and that's been our motivation."[84]

Kenneth Mines of HEW's local Office of Civil Rights (OCR), the enforcement arm of HEW, sent Superintendent Hannon a letter in January 1976 indicating that the faculty assignments made it so that certain schools were considered racially identifiable.[85] Mines wrote, "The assignment of teachers should not further identify schools as racially isolated...Each and every school should reflect the racial composition of the district in the assignment of teachers."[86] Chicago schools were given until February 8, 1976, to come up with a satisfactory plan.[87] In response to OCR's demands, Hannon stated that "Large cities and large city school systems need assistance in the implementation of plans for integration...Assistance—not mandates—not threats—not ultimatums. They lead only to further flight from cities trying to build restoration and revival."[88] Superintendent Hannon predicted that close to 11,000 of the board's 27,000 teachers would have to be moved to meet OCR's requirements and to avoid an administrative review, which was similar to a court action.

Hannon proposed a faculty desegregation plan that would assign 1,000 new teachers and transfer 2,200 of the almost 3,000 FTBs within 18 months. Like plans in the past, Hannon did not include certified teachers. The plan called for 80–85 percent of the city's schools to have faculties with no more than 70 percent or fewer than 30 percent of one racial group by September 1977. Certified teachers would also not be allowed to transfer until 1979.[89] The Board of Education voted to approve the plan 6–3 on February 11, 1976. The CTU's House of Delegates also overwhelmingly approved the plan.[90] As the dissenting board members expected, HEW rejected the teacher desegregation plan. At a press conference on March 30, 1976, an OCR official said the plan did little to end the "racial identifiability of a substantial number of schools...thus denying (students) the right to be educated in an atmosphere free from unlawful segregation." However, room was left for a compromise as the funds were not immediately withheld.[91]

With the school board unable to provide a plan in sufficient time, HEW turned the case over to an administrative review in June 1976. HEW accused the Board of Education of creating, sustaining, and exacerbating the racial identifiability of faculty and staff; keeping inexperienced teachers at predominantly minority schools; and not providing adequate bilingual education programs for non-English-speaking students. The racial identifiability of the schools was done through allowing teachers and principals to pick their own assignment, acquiescing to community pressures for teachers and principals based on race, creating teachers' contracts with the union giving teachers flexibility in assignments, assigning minority teachers to minority schools with discipline problems, and limiting the job opportunities of minority teachers and principals. HEW provided unrebutted evidence from Otho M. Robinson, former assistant superintendent of personnel. According to Robinson, there were numerous cases where teachers and professional staff were assigned based on race. He stated, "We generally agreed that Black persons would be sent only to Black schools. What existed in assignment procedures in effect resulted in Blacks working in schools that were predominantly or totally Black."[92]

Judge Everett J. Hammarstrom of HEW handled the hearing which was to decide whether Chicago would receive $150 million in federal funds. On February 15, 1977, Judge Hammarstrom ruled that Chicago schools violated the 1964 Civil Rights Act and ordered that most of the district's federal funds be cut off. This included Elementary and Secondary Education Act (ESEA) funding. Chicago schools were ruled to have discriminated in their teacher assignments and to have failed to provide bilingual education services. Federal officials had not proven that Chicago assigned less experienced teachers to minority schools. Judge Hammarstrom ruled that "the School District's consciously consummated actions or omissions in regard to the assignment of teachers and professional staff which has resulted in racially identifiable faculties, raised a normal inference of intent to separate the faculties on the basis of race." Additionally, Hammarstrom insisted that "The cumulative effect of the actions or omissions of the Chicago Public School officials has been to isolate black administrators, black teachers and black students in a limited number of schools and increasingly to isolate another number of schools with almost exclusively white administrators, white teachers and white students."[93]

This ruling came about during the second time that Chicago had its federal funding revoked, but Chicago still had an opportunity to appeal the withholding of the funds. The bureaucracy created after the first time Chicago's funds were deferred led to a lengthy federal fund termination process where negotiations between HEW lasted up to 115 days before a termination hearing could be established. Yet, unlike the first time in 1965 when political pressure caused the quick release of funding, the administrative judge's ruling—backed by court cases like *Adams v. Richardson*, which forced HEW to expediently follow through on school districts found guilty—led to Chicago Public Schools moving quickly to resolve a desegregation issue that would have devastated their school funding. Furthermore, Mayor Richard J. Daley had passed away and the weakened Democratic Machine he left behind could not amass power to thwart federal plans.

After a series of meetings between OCR officials and the Committee on Faculty Integration (a joint Board-staff committee), a plan that differed from previously rejected ones was developed. For the first time, certified teachers were included in the transfers, as were principals. The percentage set for desegregation also shifted. HEW would continue to press forth with procedures to cut Chicago's funds until all of the schools had no more than 65 and no fewer than 40 percent white teachers and no more than 60 and no fewer than 35 percent minority teachers at all the schools as the board's plan suggested. Also, 28 percent of minority principals needed to be assigned to predominantly white schools to correspond with their percentage in the system.

On May 25, 1977, the Board of Education approved the transfer of 2,212 teachers and 80 principals by September. Of the 2,212 teachers to be transferred, 1,686 would be certified teachers and 526 would be FTBs. FTBs would be moved first, followed by teachers with increasing years of experience. Teachers with more seniority would be moved only if there was no match for teachers in the lower group and teachers 55 years of age and older would be exempt from transfers.[94] Robert M. Healey, CTU's new president since 1972, said that although the union did not agree with the movement of certified teachers, "we felt that within the law this is the best we can come up with...It's acceptable because we have no choice."[95] Almost eight years of previous negotiations had failed to successfully desegregate schools, but the sudden threat of losing millions of dollars in federal funds led to meaningful desegregation of teachers and principals within a matter of months.

Still, tensions between the board and CTU remained high. As the school board notified teachers of their transfers, CTU president Healey accused the board of not notifying teachers of transfers before school ended; not providing enough time for teachers to appeal their transfers; not processing over 200 teachers who volunteered to be transferred; and violating an agreement not to transfer teachers who worked at schools with declining enrollment. The board did admit mistakenly transferring 298 teachers because of errors in race or subjects they taught (such as accidentally transferring a history teacher in exchange for an English teacher). Healey announced that CTU lawyers would petition a federal judge to stop the transfers.[96]

The CTU sued on behalf of 270 senior teachers who, according to their contracts, were exempt from the transfers. These supernumeraries had special seniority rights that gave them priority in choosing a school in case of vacancies. They could only be transferred if they were allowed to pick their new school.[97] Circuit Court judge Francis T. Delaney decided in favor of the union and stopped the transfer of the 270 teachers on September 14, 1977. He believed that the board did not handle the situation well, and criticized the board for taking so long to notify the teachers of transfers.[98]

On October 12, 1977, HEW agreed not to require any more teacher transfers. It also decided not to cut off funds in spite of the fact that the board fell short in transferring the planned number of teachers. They had hoped to transfer 2,212 teachers, but ended up moving 1,800 teachers and 100 principals. HEW and the board compromised on the desegregation guidelines that limited the number of minority teachers for each school to between 35 and 65 percent (up from 35 to 60 percent). The board also compromised with the teachers union to gain the power to make future teacher assignments with the goal of desegregation in mind. In order to receive ESAA funding, the board would still have to create three new bilingual education programs within two years.[99]

HEW secretary Joseph A. Califano Jr. suggested that "the [Chicago faculty desegregation] plan can become a model for the nation and serve as proof that men and women of reason can sit down and resolve long-standing civil rights controversies in a manner that is equitable to students and teachers."[100] OCR officials accused Califano and other HEW officials of not wanting to withhold funds. One federal official claimed that "Keep the money flowing is the dominant philosophy here at HEW. Needless to say, this philosophy has been adopted and strongly supported by the Secretary and program officials." When there were attempts to withhold funds from recalcitrant districts, this official stated that the secretary would step in to resolve the issue.[101] This suggests that Califano may have been involved in behind-the-scene negotiations in Chicago after the funds were to be withheld. Simple negotiations prior to the government actually withholding funds through the administrative hearing had failed to sufficiently pressure an otherwise defiant school administration. Acquiring desegregation of certified teachers resulted from strong enforcement that provided the necessary leverage for what Califano referred to as negotiations among "men and women of reason." The school board and superintendent only became reasonable once they were faced with the loss of millions of federal dollars.

Faculty desegregation efforts were reported in January 1978. According to the racial census done in October 1977, 69 percent of schools met the teacher desegregation guidelines that no more than 65 percent and no less than 35 percent of teachers be minority (up from 38.4 percent in April 1977). The percentage of schools in compliance had actually been as high as 88 percent until the court ruling ended the transfer of the 270 supernumeraries. Hannon called the improvement significant, stating, "We are pleased with the efforts that have been made and we will continue to work toward further integration of our faculties."[102]

Further desegregation was again impacted in November 1978, when US District Court Judge John Powers Crowley ruled that the Board of Education's faculty desegregation plan was unconstitutional because it discriminated against younger teachers. The board's plan had exempted teachers 55 years and older. The ruling did not attack the faculty desegregation, just the exemption of older teachers. The board's attorneys had argued that older employees were more likely to quit or retire if moved, and that they were more valuable at the schools they served because of their long years of experience. Judge Crowley disagreed and determined that the board had not provided "a scintilla of substantiation" in what was a clear issue of age discrimination.[103] The court ruling in this case as well as the case involving supernumeraries gave teachers some semblance of power over their own careers. The supernumeraries' case protected the teachers' contract while the age discrimination case ensured a level of fairness in the involuntary reassignments of teachers regardless of age.

Still, the court rulings did not deter the efforts to desegregate. The Board of Education announced in February 1979 that 76 percent of their schools met the faculty desegregation goals in 1978 (up from 69 percent in 1977). Another 7 percent of the schools were within 2 percent of reaching the goal of having 35–65 percent minority teachers. HEW maintained watch over faculty desegregation, and by September 1981, approximately 150 more teachers were transferred to maintain compliance.[104]

HUMAN COSTS OF TRANSFERS

The wrangling with the federal government through the Justice Department and HEW's Office of Civil Rights was difficult for Chicago's superintendents and their staffs, the Board of Education, and the CTU. Faculty desegregation was finally accomplished in some meaningful way, but not without tremendous cost to individual teachers and principals. While voluntary transfers had been a part of the city's system for decades, involuntary transfers were new and incurred resistance. Once the Board of Education approved the first round of transfers in June 1977, Superintendent Hannon sent a letter to the principals of schools where teachers were affected. The letter discussed the delicate nature of the situation and stated, "Please remember the teachers who have not been selected for transfer are equally anxious, and after your official notification to those transferred, it will be necessary for you to inform all the teachers that notification has been completed."[105] Principals were given an integral role in the transfers. Hannon's letter to the teachers indicated the goal to comply with the Title VI of the 1964 Civil Rights Act. The letter explained the actions the teachers needed to follow and ended with, "You have our deep appreciation for your service, and best wishes in your new assignment. You also have my sincere hope that you will derive many additional years of professional and personal satisfaction from your career in Chicago Public Schools."[106]

Although faculty desegregation rarely led to massive protest and demonstrations, on Chicago's predominantly white Southwest Side, parents and students picketed the transfer of teachers. Teacher transfer orders had been issued to 550 teachers on June 14, 1977, and protests erupted the very next day at Hubbard and Bogan High Schools, and Dawes Elementary. At Hubbard, 95 percent of students boycotted classes.

As schools closed for the summer, teachers felt as if they were being uprooted from their schools and communities. One teacher told the *Chicago Sun-Times*, "I guess we got our report cards today, four D's: depression, discouragement, dismay, and dejection." Another said, "It was like someone dropped a bomb on us." A third teacher revealed, "We're all upset because we get the feeling we've lost control of our own destiny. This was done with a total disregard for the stability and morale of the teachers." One principal was concerned about the impact this would have on the community. He commented, "They have given service to the community. I can't visualize (incoming) teachers having the same commitment."[107]

Some of the distraught teachers decided to sue. In July 1977, 36 teachers filed suit claiming that "there has not been a judicial determination that the faculty is segregated," or that the board had practiced racial discrimination. This statement was actually misleading as the administrative judge had found the board guilty of both. The teachers believed the transfers to be arbitrary and "not based on an effort to improve education but [are] aimed solely at modifying teaching staffs on the basis of racial or national origin." The teachers came from predominantly white schools including Taft, Schurz, Steinmetz, and Jones Commercial high schools along with some elementary schools. The suit also charged Superintendent Hannon and HEW secretary Califano of violating the board's contract with the CTU. The teachers wanted their transfers declared unlawful and be returned to their former teaching assignments. They also wanted the court to block the implementation of the teacher desegregation plan.[108] However, US district court chief James B. Parsons would not grant the temporary injunction to prevent the transfer of teachers.[109]

Many of the teachers who received transfers in June were able to appeal because of personal hardship, program need, or error. Principals could not participate in the personal hardship appeals because of their potential bias. They were, however, essential in determining if transfers would disrupt or end programs. If so, they could discuss the matter with the district superintendent and then appeal to the Special Monitoring Committee with a detailed explanation. A similar process was created in the case of data error. In those situations, there were mistakes made with the race or specialty of the teachers transferred.[110]

Teachers who were transferred managed to create their own recourses. Some teachers refused to show up to the new school. Others took a leave of absence while their transfers were being appealed. Still, some teachers left the system altogether. Since the school system operated on a seniority basis, forcibly transferred teachers could try to take positions at other schools. This rifting process sometimes meant that they bumped FTBs. FTBs with seniority could then bump FTBs with less seniority. The entire process led to classrooms that experienced up to three transferred teachers over the course of a few months, at the detriment of the students, teachers, schools, and the community.[111]

There were also problems among teachers at individual schools. An example of the agony faced by a school and community involved a music teacher who was transferred and took a leave of absence. Once a leave of absence was granted, a permanent replacement could not be given for five months. While the old teacher was gone, a new music teacher took over and became a favorite among the students. Then the older teacher won his appeal and returned to the school, much to the dismay of the students. The new teacher was then forced to serve as a substitute and continued to work with one of the school's orchestras. Still, the older teacher was jealous of the popularity of the newer teacher and retired in the spring. Once he retired, he was replaced by yet another teacher, instead of the teacher the students wanted. Similar disruptions occurred at several other Chicago schools, leaving young FTBs uncertain about their teaching situation.[112]

Teachers who had been forcibly transferred often had difficulties dealing with students, parents, and communities due to cultural and class differences. Teachers moving from middle-class white schools to schools with poorer black students faced challenges based on a lack of understanding or lack of respect for the new environment. Black teachers who ended up at white schools also confronted issues with parents, students, teachers, and administrators. However, teachers who loved their jobs, had strong personal fortitude, and had supportive colleagues or administrators were able to overcome many of the challenges they faced. One white teacher, Constance Putney, began her career at Austin High School in 1968 when the school was transitioning from white to black. Putney stated that it was "absolutely the worst situation to work in because every fall the place would erupt" as a result of racial fights. Five years later, Putney went on to Taft High School which was over 95 percent white. She was then transferred to Farragut High School, with a predominantly black and growing Latino student body, as a result of mandated faculty desegregation. When Putney arrived at Farragut, the neighborhood was largely low income and the students were severely undereducated. While Putney prided herself on eventually helping her students to improve two grade levels in reading each year, the students still lagged behind grade level. While many other white teachers said they were concerned about their safety in black, low income schools and neighborhoods, Putney said she was never afraid while at the school. "My kids loved me. However, the reality was at three o'clock that neighborhood changed, and it wasn't going to be safe in that neighborhood anymore. I was safe in the building. I would be away from the neighborhood as soon as school was out." Putney finished her career at Von Steuben High School, a specialized science school, which was desegregated even prior to student desegregation in the 1980s.[113]

Kimberly Muhammad, a black teacher, had a different experience. She was teaching at a school that was 100 percent black with majority black teachers and was transferred to Oscar DePriest Elementary

School in the Austin community. When Muhammad heard about her transfer, she cried.

> I worked on the South Side of Chicago in the inner city with children and staff my own [race] and I was very comfortable and complacent. And when I got the letter, it sent me to the West Side of Chicago, a place that I was totally unfamiliar with. I remember taking a ride out there prior to the opening of school with my son who probably was about two or three at the time. And by the time I got off the expressway at Central Avenue and headed north to look for the school, I literally was in tears.

The students at the school were mostly black, but the teachers were desegregated after Muhammad and several other black teachers transferred in. Muhammad was later transferred to Patrick Henry Elementary School, a predominantly white school, on the North Side, after another teacher with more seniority took her position at DePriest.[114] Just a handful of black teachers were at Patrick Henry, most of whom were from the South Side of Chicago. Muhammad had no problems with students as she was commended for being an excellent teacher. However, parents complained that she was hollering at their children. As part of her teaching style, she raised her voice to project. The parents misinterpreted her projections as yelling, illustrating the types of cultural differences and misunderstandings that occurred often during the transfer process. Another example of cultural differences displaying itself in the classroom occurred with Muhammad's student teacher who was from the South:

> I remember I had a student teacher who was African American and one specific incident. She was giving a spelling test. And she would call out the words and the kids were to write the words down. And one of the words that she...enunciated was "yella" and the children all stared and looked and were like "okay, we don't recognize that." And the student teacher kept saying 'yella' and I recognized what the word was because I know what the spelling words were, and I had to intercede and say "yellow." And then of course they knew what the word was. But it just happened that her diction where instead of saying the word yellow, she said "yella" which is a southern type of accent more so than anything.

Muhammad recalled another incident that spoke about the community opposition she experienced. Early in her tenure at Patrick Henry, Muhammad was a single parent raising her young son alone. She recalled that her son had not started school yet, and the distance she had to travel to and from home was difficult. The 45 minutes to an hour commute made her have to leave home early in the morning and caused her to get home late in the afternoon. When Muhammad first arrived at the school, her principal was white, but because of desegregation he was replaced with a black principal. She asked the black principal if her son could attend the preschool at Patrick Henry. She remembered that the principal had agreed. "I think my son was there for about three or four days when the principal informed me that he had to be removed. The community had gotten together and had a meeting." According to Muhammad, community members made up of policemen and firemen told the principal "'correct your mistake.' And he was very apologetic. I'm a very feisty person and I was like 'oh no they not going to kick my child out. I'm going to go to, you know, the mayor of the city, whatever, whatever.' And you know he literally begged me. You know he said, 'Because I let [your son] in, they're blaming me and you can make the ruckus if you want to make the ruckus, but it's still going to fall back on me.'"

As a result of the principal's request and the fact that she did not want to keep her son where he was unwanted, Muhammad took her son out of the school. While the community members said that they had made their decision because her son did not live in the community, Muhammad knew it was most likely because he was black. She recalls, "Back then, true enough, you had to live in the community to attend a community school. But you know in retrospect, a preschool kid wouldn't disrupt the education of what's going on in a school. So it was more of a racial thing than anything. I removed my son…And I determined that if they didn't want him there, then I didn't want him there. That wasn't a pleasant place for him to be. And I made other arrangements for him to go to preschool."

What Putney and Muhammad had in common was their commitment to teaching, but just as Putney left immediately after school for her safety, so did Muhammad. The race of the community around the school mattered. Muhammad did not want to be North Side any more than Putney wanted to be on the West Side. As a matter of fact, Muhammad was reprimanded by the initial white principal at Patrick Henry for not following dismissal procedures. She would walk her class down to the office, sign out, walk her students out, and immediately go home. However, the principal reminded her that she was to wait for the bell, walk the students out, and then sign out.

Still, Putney and Muhammad were exceptional teachers. Some of their colleagues did not adjust as well as they did. A study conducted on the teachers' and principals' reactions to desegregation indicated that both transferred teachers and principals were less satisfied with their new positions than the ones they had the previous year. However, minority principals and teachers were not as dissatisfied as white teachers and principals. Teachers who had four or fewer years' experience were also less dissatisfied than their colleagues who had more years of experience. This occurred primarily because white and experienced teachers often were transferred from more affluent schools and had been highly satisfied with their positions prior to transfers. Minority teachers were more likely moving from schools with students from lower incomes, while less experienced teachers may have also been more flexible. The study found that there were very few transitional programs implemented to assist teachers with their new placement. Up to a third of the teachers surveyed said that there were no transitional programs at all. About half had no formal support or very little from the administration and the holdover staff. In terms of transfers adversely affecting student achievement, 40 percent of transferred teachers thought there would be an adverse affect. The majority of transferred principals (73 percent) believed that transfers would not affect student achievement.[115]

Chicago teachers were not the first to experience desegregation. In southern areas in the late 1960s and early 1970s, teachers participated in crossover experiences where black teachers were sent to white schools and vice versa. Although the southern context is different, teachers faced similar issues. In studies on teachers in Austin, Texas; Atlanta, Georgia; and East Baton Rouge, Louisiana, teachers who were highly competent, hard working, with inner fortitude, were more able to withstand any difficulties that came up. Beyond personality, teachers were also successful when they had the support of administrators and colleagues. A combination of these factors allowed some teachers to withstand challenges from students and disrespect from administrators and other teachers. Other teachers who were not as successful internalized their experiences or did not have the adequate support of their superiors and peers.[116] This in no way belittles the hostile experiences some teachers experienced. Their lack of support as well as their lack of preparation to deal with continual racist hostilities they faced made them cope in the best way they could. What it illustrated was the importance of a supportive school environment and prior training. That helped to ease the transition of teachers in desegregated teaching environments.

Change is often difficult, but it was particularly difficult for experienced teachers who were forcibly reassigned. Their seniority rights were impacted. While the changes increased desegregation and the level of experienced teachers at a number of schools, as the study indicated, it was difficult to tell what the impact may have been for students. One of the complaints opponents of desegregation had was the loss of community associated with desegregation. Losing teachers who had come to know the children, their parents, and the community was certainly one of the shortcomings of desegregation. In addition, long commutes added to this dilemma.

*   *   *

The desegregation of faculty was not quite as difficult as desegregating students. While the community weighed in their opinions heavily on student desegregation, outside of the protests at some Southwest Side schools, few spoke up about faculty desegregation except the CTU whose job it was to lobby on behalf of teachers. The absence of a more substantial outcry made it politically easier to target faculty desegregation. However, as has been shown, implementing faculty desegregation was not easy. Rebell and Block indicated that faculty desegregation in Los Angeles and Philadelphia successfully came as a result of similar mandatory transfers. OCR's dealings in New York, on the other hand, led to political controversy and teacher union resistance. The strength of the teachers union in New York limited the impact of faculty desegregation in that city. [117]

The most significant reason Chicago was able to desegregate its faculty was because the judge in the administrative hearing ruled that the schools could have their federal funds withheld. As HEW began the process to withhold the much needed funds, Chicago's superintendent, board, and even the CTU responded relatively quickly to avoid financial devastation. The implementation of the carrot-and-stick approach made the faculty desegregation agreements occur quicker than with just federal negotiations alone. Ultimately, however, neither the federal government nor the State of Illinois were willing to move as decisively to withhold funds for student desegregation as will be seen in chapter 3.

threat vs. actually taking the $ away

State Involvement with Student Desegregation, 1971–1979

In 1977, Illinois state superintendent Joseph M. Cronin published a controversial 'dream' in *Phi Delta Kappa* describing how Chicago desegregated its schools. In his dream, the city lost a court case, which proved that it had intentionally segregated its schools, and the courts ordered "metropolitan desegregation" through the creation and pairing of township districts with Chicago's segregated areas. Chicago closed several segregated schools, increased its magnet schools, and eliminated its mobile units. The sun beaming through his window caused Cronin to awake from his dream.[1]

Although a metropolitan desegregation plan would have been difficult and heavily protested, it was an easy scenario for Cronin to imagine. It took the responsibility of desegregation out of his and the state's hands and eliminated much of the back and forth jockeying with the Chicago Board of Education and its superintendent for compliance. In a 1978 article, Cronin also provided much more realistic suggestions about how states could assist with desegregation. The significance of his suggestions was that he was actually in a position to enforce them. Cronin thought state boards of education were central to desegregation efforts and needed to have members supportive of desegregation. However, in order to be effective, Cronin suggested that the state board of education should announce their desegregation policies, the state superintendent selected should be supportive of desegregation, and sanctions should be attached to these efforts. New York, Massachusetts, New Jersey, and Illinois had implemented some of these suggestions as a result of having desegregation experts in place on their state boards.[2]

In 1971, the State of Illinois demanded that its school districts follow a set of rules and guidelines to prevent segregation or face a financial penalty for noncompliance. Cronin's predecessor Michael

Bakalis led the state's charge. The policies were created as federal courts began to hold states accountable for the desegregation of local schools because of segregative statutes or de facto segregative practices.[3] Such pressure, coupled with the threat of withholding funding (through Title VI of the Civil Rights Act), spurred many of the state's districts to desegregate their schools. Chicago, however, provided a unique challenge. The student population was well over 500,000 with 71 percent of students being of color in the early 1970s. To put the challenge into perspective, a report to the State Board of Education indicated that Chicago had more black students than 42 states and more Latino students than 41 states.[4]

An overwhelming population of black and Latino students, coupled with the lack of political will on the part of the Chicago Board of Education made it extremely difficult for the state to force Chicago to fully desegregate, in spite of the fact that the state had the desegregation policies and supportive people in place. The efforts were further hampered because the Illinois State Board of Education and Superintendent Cronin were extremely hesitant to withhold funding, and would not enforce the sanctions for noncompliance beyond "the stigma of probationary recognition."[5] In a 1976 interview, Cronin admitted that he would withhold state and federal aid only "as a last resort." Further stating his caution, he continued, "I would favor a court case in most situations prior to the actual shutting off of aid—that's a nuclear weapon. First, I would favor a probationary status, with a warning of possible loss of state and federal aid. It just would be hard for some school districts to make the necessary changes fast enough."[6] His admittance that he was tentative about withholding funds undermined his ability to force Chicago school officials to act. Without a clear indication that the state would hold Chicago Public Schools financially accountable, school officials continued to evade the state's demands. As the federal government pursued faculty desegregation, the state took the responsibility of student desegregation policy implementation. However, because of the state's overall unwillingness to enforce harsh penalties, it faced similar resistance from school officials and local constituents.

BACKGROUND ON STATE RESPONSIBILITY

Beginning in the mid-nineteenth century, states began to take control of much of the policy and financing of local public schools.[7] Northern and southern states had de jure segregation as part of their school policies and practices, although northern states had eliminated most of those statues by 1949. Southern states continued their seg-regative policies and practices in a strict manner. The cultural and social nature of the Jim Crow southern society meant that there was a certain place blacks occupied within the society that left them com-pletely subordinated to whites. Once the *Brown v. Board of Education* Supreme Court decision was ruled in 1954, southern governments had to decide how they would respond to the new legal mandates. Few southern districts attempted to desegregate and some south-ern governors became the symbols of resistance to school desegrega-tion. Governor Orval Faubus used the Arkansas National Guard to prevent desegregation at Little Rock High School, until President Dwight Eisenhower sent in the 101st Airborne Division to enforce the law of the land. While the move by Faubus and other governors was the public height of state sponsored and endorsed segregation, his southern colleagues also used state laws to delay or limit school desegregation. Georgia, Mississippi, Louisiana, and other states made it illegal to desegregate schools or fund desegregated schools, while Virginia closed public schools and created and funded private white academies. South Carolina used standardized tests to limit black students from entering formerly all white schools.[8] These were among the some of the variety "massive resistance" tactics against desegregation.

In the early desegregation cases, state governments were only defendants when they disregarded court-ordered desegregation. These cases in the 1950s and 1960s focused mostly on the South. In the 1970s and 1980s, as cases had also shifted to northern dis-tricts, states were defendants in court cases and were ordered to pro-vide funding for school desegregation. States were held responsible for segregation: if they impeded local desegregation efforts; if they knew of intentional segregation and did nothing to stop it, or pro-vided funding to support those actions; and if their actions indirectly impacted school desegregation with, for example, the support of seg-regated housing.[9] According to David S. Tatel et al., the courts began to better understand "the deep-seated and pervasive nature of the ves-tiges of state-imposed segregation." Therefore, federal courts devel-oped "more extensive and sophisticated remedies to alleviate those vestiges."[10] School districts had to go beyond mere reassignment of students in metropolitan areas and large cities where racial segre-gation was entrenched. Courts ordered the use of magnet schools and other educational improvements to help desegregate. They also ordered compensatory funding to promote better education for stu-dents where desegregation was difficult to achieve. In sum, states had to take a more proactive role in desegregation to avoid court decisions against them and to be in line with federal policy.

Illinois State Pressure to Desegregate Begins

Seven years prior to Cronin's "dream," another state superintendent attempted to desegregate Chicago's schools. On November 17, 1971, State Superintendent of Public Instruction Michael J. Bakalis, announced a plan to desegregate the schools in the State of Illinois. Bakalis had been a high school and junior high school teacher and became a professor at Northern Illinois University after receiving his PhD in history from Northwestern University (where he had received his two previous degrees). He also served as assistant dean of the School of Liberal Arts at Northern Illinois University. Elected in 1970, he became the superintendent of public instruction in 1971, and from that position was able to exert considerable influence over desegregation efforts.[11] The 1963 Armstrong Law granted the superintendent of public instruction the power to act on behalf of desegregation, and because state and federal aid was channeled through his office, Bakalis had the ability to withhold funds.[12]

Bakalis announced that 44 school districts, including Chicago, would be affected. The other approximately 1,100 districts would not be impacted because they either were already desegregated or contained only one race.[13] According to Bakalis, the rules and procedures he created for desegregation had to match court requirements that included desegregation of students, elimination of inequities in facilities and programs in minority schools, and the desegregation of faculties. However, he also wanted to avoid major interruptions in schools and communities and sought school desegregation plans that would provide quality and integrated education for all children.[14] School districts would be given until January 1, 1972 to submit a report about their desegregation efforts since 1963 and to submit their racial headcounts. Those schools determined to be noncompliant would be notified and would have to create a desegregation plan within 90 days. The plan needed to be "within the constraints of economic and administrative feasibility and educational soundness."[15] Although there would be some leeway, Bakalis wanted schools to be within 15 percent of the black enrollment in their district. (For instance, if a district was 30 percent black, its schools should have 15–45 percent black enrollments.) Bakalis insisted that the requirements "do not advocate a single method for desegregation. I recognize, as the Supreme Court has, that 'there is no single universal answer to the complex problems of desegregation. There is obviously no one plan that will do the job in every case.' Chicago, Springfield, and Cairo each present a particular set of problems and variables. These rules will permit us to deal with each of these systems separately and differently." He acknowledged that "Desegregation is a process. It is not an event which must occur on a given day and hour for all school districts. It will occur in different places at different times under widely different plans."[16]

If a district's plan was found unacceptable, Bakalis could propose a new plan or add amendments. Districts would then be given 240 days to comply before Bakalis would withdraw state recognition of that district, seek court order to force compliance, or withhold state and federal funds.[17] The superintendent's guidelines provided much flexibility for individual districts. Since Chicago was also by far the largest district in the state, Chicago Public Schools were given an extra month to submit its plan because of the deep financial problems it was facing.

As required, Chicago Board of Education officials submitted a report about its desegregation efforts to the state by the February 2, 1972 deadline. Since 1963, Chicago's plans for desegregating schools included permissive transfer plans, the creation of two magnet schools, the busing of 500 black students, and attempts at faculty desegregation.[18] In September 1972, Bakalis notified 21 Illinois school districts, including Chicago, that they were not in compliance with his desegregation guidelines. He called Chicago's efforts to desegregate its faculties commendable. However, he faulted the city for not having any plans to desegregate its students.[19] Bakalis did not expect each system to be within the 15 percentage points of black enrollment, but did want "a carefully planned program" in reasonable time. He also announced that, "In no way are we requiring the transportation of any students."[20] Eighteen of the 21 districts were given three months to create desegregation plans. Bakalis offered to pay for experts to assist Chicago and Rockford school districts with their plans, as they constituted the two largest cities in the state. Chicago was found to have 501 of 656 schools not in compliance with his guidelines, which would mean that between 52.2 and 82.2 percent of each school's enrollment would have to be students of color.

A new state constitution was created in 1970 to replace the archaic 1870 constitution. One of the changes in the constitution eliminated Bakalis's elected position as state superintendent of public instruction (once his term was up) and established a state superintendent of education and a State Board of Education based on appointment. The board was created in order to remove the leading educational officials out of politics.[21] The *Chicago Daily News* reported Bakalis's warnings about the potential takeover of the State Board of Education by the then governor, Dan Walker. According to Bakalis, "It was the intent of the framers of the 1970 Constitution and general assembly that the State Board of Education be an independent spokesman for education, not an arm of the governor's office...The State Board of Education should be free from political influences of all kinds and should be a spokesman for no politician."[22] Yet appointing candidates for various state positions could also lead to the same type of political influence as an elected official.

Cronin became the state's first superintendent of education in 1975 under the new state constitution. Cronin, like Bakalis, was among the educated elite with two degrees from Harvard and a PhD from Stanford. He had been a teacher, principal, and was a professor and associate dean at Harvard before being tapped as secretary of educational affairs for Massachusetts.[23] By the time the State of Illinois got around to requiring enforcement of desegregation, it was May 1975, and Cronin was serving as the new state education superintendent. Cronin placed six districts on notice for not complying with desegregation rules and because their segregation had worsened since 1971. Chicago was among those six. Cronin threatened to withhold federal funds if the districts did not comply.[24]

The Chicago Board of Education had begun to desegregate some of its schools, including vocational and technical schools. It set up racial quotas at Gage Park High School which helped Gage Park to remain desegregated for a number of years. There were also racial quotas at the newly created magnet, Whitney Young High School, which opened its doors in September 1975. Similarly, the new Cooley Vocational High School also had racial quotas. The board also used permissive transfers to allow students to move from overcrowded schools to those with more space available. The intent was for students to request a transfer to a school to increase desegregation at the new school. The use of these transfers had begun in 1963 in an attempt to placate civil rights activists leading school desegregation protests. In spite of these efforts, school segregation increased in the city as the white student population continued to shrink, the Latino student population continued to increase, and the black student population remained the majority.[25]

Chicago schools, along with eight other districts, were formally accused of noncompliance with the state's recently revised desegregation guidelines on February 26, 1976.[26] Chicago school superintendent

Joseph P. Hannon called the state's demands unrealistic for Chicago. Of the 667 Chicago schools, only 81 met with the state standard of being within 15 percent of the district's racial makeup. Hannon deflected the schools segregation problems on the housing problems that existed in the city. In a staff report, he insisted that attempts to desegregate would "trigger population shifts that may not be desirable in the city in the long run." The superintendent feared further white flight and the loss of the middle-class tax base although white flight occurred in spite of school desegregation efforts. He preferred voluntary forms of desegregation.[27]

Chicago failed to get a desegregation plan to the state in a timely manner. Superintendent Hannon asked Cronin for an extension, but was denied. Cronin told Hannon that Chicago had been given four years to develop a comprehensive plan and had failed to do so. In April 1976, Chicago was placed on probation along with two other districts.[28] Cronin recognized the difficulty in desegregating Chicago schools and suggested that perhaps voluntary metropolitan desegregation could be a solution, since the suburbs surrounding the city had predominantly white schools.[29]

The state created a mechanism for districts to be accountable for desegregation and had leadership from the State Board of Education, and the state superintendent was largely supportive of desegregation. Nonetheless, the initial interactions with Chicago were not effective in bringing about any more desegregation than the city already had in place. Further pressure mixed with economic support would be needed to assist Chicago with the development of a school desegregation plan.

CHICAGO BEGINS DESEGREGATION PLANNING

In November 1976, Hannon announced the goal to implement desegregation by September 1978. He wanted to bring together a citywide advisory committee consisting of various community constituents to assist with the planning. Three Board of Education members, Margaret Wild, Edgar E. Epps, and Carmen Velasquez, would also be included. The board also hired Edward A. Welling Jr., a consultant of the Illinois Office of Education, to assist with the plans. Welling had helped plan desegregation in Peoria, Illinois; Philadelphia, Pennsylvania; and a number of other cities, and had a history as an educator on several fronts. He started his career as a math and science teacher, was appointed to the Venezuelan Ministry of Education, and had served as a superintendent in several districts, including Freeport, New York, where he desegregated their schools. His employment with Chicago began in December 1976.[30]

Not satisfied with Hannon's timetable, the State Board of Education pressed Chicago to have a desegregation plan by March 1977 and implement it by the end of 1977, as opposed to Hannon's September 1978 deadline.[31] Hannon responded that he was more concerned with the "substance" of the desegregation plan than the time it took to create, and the newly hired Welling agreed that Hannon's time table "permits sufficient time to involve everyone in this city that wants to be involved." Chicago received a $127,000 state grant for desegregation planning, providing funding for Welling to hire staff to assist with the planning and to get the advisory committee started.[32]

Consultant Welling worked with the Chicago Board of Education to organize the City-Wide Advisory Committee (CWAC). The CWAC would consist of 40 members to include the 10 elected representatives, three high school students, business leaders, civil rights leaders, Chicago Teachers Union representatives, religious leaders, and senior citizens. January 1978 was chosen as the target date for the committee to create a comprehensive student desegregation plan.[33]

To begin the process of meeting the 1978 deadline, Chicago submitted its CWAC-created integration report to the state in April 1977, which outlined why it was so difficult to desegregate Chicago's schools. The report titled, "Equalizing Educational Opportunities in the New Chicago: Student Desegregation Planning Process and Progress Report," served more as a progress report than a planning process. The vastly shifting population had led to a loss of 57,527 white students between 1971 and 1976. There were also 9,536 fewer black students. Asian student populations had risen to 3,005, and Hispanic student numbers increased to 14,054. The report stated, "The Chicago public schools presently have 83 racially balanced schools which represent 12.5% of total number of schools in the District. These schools have a total enrollment of 66,362 which is 12.7% of the total enrollment of the district…The Chicago public schools have more students attending more racially balanced schools than the total combined enrollment of the Peoria, Rockford, and Springfield, Illinois public school systems."[34] This quote explicitly argues both the difficulty in desegregating and the progress Chicago had already made. The problem was that desegregation of 12.7 percent of the students was extremely limited since the Chicago schools had an enrollment of 524,221 in the 1976–1977 school year.[35]

Cronin did not find the city's report sufficient because it lacked "enough specific details or new measures, including voluntary programs scheduled for next September [1977]."[36] Cronin was also concerned about the six new neighborhood schools Chicago was planning to build, which would certainly lead to majority black or Latino schools—even though Hannon insisted that five of the six schools to be built would have integrated academic centers.[37]

Despite having a member on the CWAC, the Urban League also criticized "Equalizing Educational Opportunities in the New Chicago." The Chicago Branch of the Urban League was a moderate organization run by professionals interested in desegregation. Throughout their history, education and employment had been at the thrust of their work. They saw school desegregation as an avenue for enhancing the education of black youth so that they could be prepared to join the professional and middle-class ranks. Their role on the CWAC served as an intermediary between the education establishment and the community.[38] The Urban League had also organized a multiethnic coalition called Citizens Coalition on School Desegregation and held a desegregation conference in June 1977.[39] In their report submitted to the CWAC, the Urban League accused the CWAC of avoiding its responsibility. According to the Urban League, "The City-Wide Advisory Committee for 'Equalizing Educational Opportunity in the New Chicago,' even by acceptance of this euphemistic title, has for several weeks been maneuvering around its principal responsibility, rather than meeting it head on. Perhaps it is for avoidance of our primary purpose that the committee has produced nearly nothing of substance to date."[40] The Urban League wanted assurances that the CWAC would not continue to propose vague ideas and evade desegregation.

The criticisms of the CWAC and its shaky start were highlighted in the city's newspapers. The first meeting of all the CWAC representatives, held May 6, 1977, dissolved quickly into disagreements and shouting among whites, blacks, and Latinos after Welling gave a speech and initially refused to answer questions. Once Welling changed his mind, Board of Education member Edgar Epps could no longer control the meeting and had to adjourn. Epps realized that perhaps the group was too large for a productive meeting; but according the *Chicago Sun-Times* it was more of speech making by Welling than an actual meeting.[41] The rough start for the CWAC led many to question their ability to create a plan in their stated time.

In May 1977, Chicago was given its first extension on its probationary status from the state to create a substantive desegregation plan. The new extended deadline was June 3, 1977.[42] In that time, the Chicago Board of Education approved a permissive transfer plan that involved both elementary and high schools. While this plan was used to try to increase desegregation, some argued that permissive transfers were used to avoid more comprehensive desegregation. Because previous plans did not provide transportation to students, the impact was limited. At its height in 1966, only 1,500 students participated; but by 1975, only 115 participated. From 1963 to 1975, a total of only 7,345 high school students had participated.[43] The low level of participation demonstrated the inability of permissive transfer plans to be effective—especially when they lacked transportation.

The new transfer plan did include transportation as it allowed elementary students to be bused from their original schools to the receiving schools. The plan also provided public transportation tokens for high school students. Parents with children in overcrowded schools were notified by letter and were sent a pamphlet from the superintendent in July indicating the receiving schools which their children were eligible to attend. The purpose of the plan was to "relieve overcrowding, to more effectively utilize facilities, to enhance racial integration on a voluntary basis, and to improve quality educational opportunity for all children."[44] Hannon was a firm believer in voluntary desegregation and each of his plans put emphasis on the voluntary movement of students no matter how much the state and the federal government tried to push him.

For a second time, the state extended Chicago's probationary status—this time to March 15, 1978. The city had to meet certain provisions to end their probation. Chicago school officials had to involve the community in the creation of a comprehensive plan, which was already underway with the CWAC. The permissive transfer plans had to involve at least 65,000 students, 350 mobile units which were used for additional classroom space had to be eliminated, and the city had to carry out the faculty desegregation as HEW required.[45]

Despite the fact that state officials could have withheld over $500 million in state and federal aid, Hannon was still annoyed with their decision to continue the probation. He expressed his concern in a statement released to the media saying, "I am deeply distressed and disappointed at the action of the State Board of Education in not lifting the probationary status of the Chicago Board of Education...We have every reason to expect that the probationary status would be lifted. By our positive and tangible actions, we have verified our commitment to desegregation and we continue to fulfill this pledge."[46]

The Chicago executive secretary of the NAACP, William Hardy, thought the state had not gone far enough. He declared that, "Certainly *worried that the [delay]* ✱

it means that the state board has joined with the rest of the criminals who continue to perpetuate an injustice on our young people. They are not abiding by the law. The law of the land says we must have an integrated school system."[47] Despite the NAACP's harsh criticism, it was apparent that the expectations for major desegregation seemed unrealistic to a Board of Education that had never made considerable efforts to desegregate its students. Moreover, the dwindling number of white students in the city's schools meant full-scale desegregation would be impractical. Hannon thought his permissive transfer plan along with his previous plans would be enough to evade any type of sanctions. Yet he and the Board of Education were still accused of not doing enough. As far as Hannon and some board members were concerned, whatever they did came with consequences to the number of white students who would remain in the city's public schools, and they were concerned that aggressive school desegregation plans would lead to further white flight.

At the Urban League's June 1977 desegregation conference, Hannon assured the audience of his and the board's commitment to desegregation, stating, "It is the law. It is just. It must be done." While veterans of the desegregation movement in Chicago were skeptical, Hannon insisted that, "it will be done." Hannon also met with people from the Ashburn community on the Southwest Side, a predominantly white and working-class neighborhood. There had been continual protest demonstrations and boycotts as a result of permissive transfers in the past, and the residents from Ashburn did not want Hannon to carry out the permissive plan at all, or to at least put a three-year moratorium on the plan for their community. According to a spokesman, Hannon told the group, "I am truly committed to the total permissive transfer program which was recommended to the Board of Education on May 25 and I am not recommending any changes or adjustments."[48] It is clear from the statements that Hannon was firmly committed to his view of what school desegregation should look like. Groups that wanted more or less desegregation were unable to move him.

Aside from Hannon's stubborn vision of desegregation, the CWAC had gotten off to a poor start, which did not seem to instill confidence in observers. The CWAC was to be the mechanism for which a comprehensive school desegregation plan would be developed. As the state placed the district on probation for its limited desegregation efforts, neighborhoods effected by permissive transfer plans still believed that those efforts were too much.

Buses Roll, Protests Follow

The permissive transfer of students to desegregate previously white schools was set for the beginning of the 1977–1978 school year. There was a lot of concern about the safety of black students to be bused to white schools. This was occurring at a time when disagreements over busing were at a fever pitch throughout the nation.[49] Chicagoans had expressed their dismay over busing since 1968 with a variety of protests and demonstrations. Before the first buses could roll in September 1977, city officials, including the police department, pledged to protect bused students. Uproar had already been in progress, particularly by Southwest Side residents in the area near Bogan High School who did not want black students in their schools (see map 3.1). Like the opposition to busing black students from Austin schools to Northwest Side schools in 1968, Ashburn residents were fearful of their communities turning over racially from white to black.

The residents met with Superintendent Hannon and Mayor Michael A. Bilandic. Bilandic had succeeded Mayor Richard J. Daley upon his death in December 1976. Ashburn community residents had enjoyed previous success negotiating school boundaries with Mayor Daley and Superintendent Benjamin C. Willis in the early 1960s and

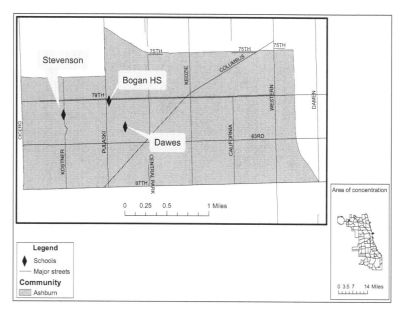

Map 3.1 Ashburn community

were able to thwart the transfer of black students to Bogan High School.[50] This time around, however, Southwest Side residents did not have much luck. Hannon refused to budge. Meanwhile, Bilandic had told a group of Southwest Side residents that he would use his influence to get a three-year moratorium for the plans involving their community—but he could not deliver. When Southwest Side residents attempted to picket Bilandic's home, police cordoned off the streets. The unsuccessful attempts to negotiate with city and school officials did not deter them, however, and Ashburn residents held a two-day boycott at Bogan High School and surrounding elementary schools to protest faculty desegregation in June 1977; 80 percent of Bogan students did not show up for classes.[51]

When the fall semester began, Southwest Side residents decided to hold another boycott on the first day of school. The boycott at Bogan was highly successful: only 350 of 2,300 students showed up, and other schools in the area reported 75 to 80 percent absences related to the boycott. The first day was peaceful, which could probably be attributed to the lack of picketing.[52] On the second day, protests escalated. According to news reports, 50 demonstrators protested outside Stevenson School and yelled racial epithets at black students as they left school for the day. The demonstrators charged the buses and attempted to sit down on the school lawn, sidewalk, and streets, but they moved when police threatened to arrest them.[53]

On Sunday, September 11, 1977, 1,000 adults and teens gathered in Bogan Park for a rally. Police arrested the rally leaders and the crowd tussled with police officers.[54] On Monday, September 12, protesters blocked students from entering the Stevenson School for 15 minutes. They had arrived before school started with placards saying "Bus them back to Africa." Police did nothing to move them until reinforcements arrived. Once back-up came, the police moved the protesters and arrested two people.[55] On Tuesday, September 13, Bogan students conducted a walkout and 300 of them were suspended. When students did not disperse, 27 were arrested. Police superintendent James M. Rochford announced that the police would change standards for protesters. No parking signs would go up around the schools and protesters would have to remain across the street from schools. More plain-clothed police officers would also assist with arrests. Rochford stated, "I want to warn parents that if they are not responsible for their children, they (the children) will be processed as criminals." That day four people were arrested outside of Stevenson school.[56] On Thursday, September 15, protests continued outside Bogan and Stevenson schools. Six people were arrested in separate incidents.[57]

The protests kept some transfer students away as parents were concerned for their children's safety, yet the number of participants increased in other parts of the city. Close to 500 students utilized the transfers on the first day of school. A week later, more than 800 students participated citywide. By October, 1,003 students participated, and the heavily picketed Stevenson school reached its maximum with 90 students transferring.[58] Nevertheless, the overall transfer numbers were far below expectations of 2,180, and did very little to effectively desegregate the city's schools.

Like the 1968 demonstrations, the boycotts and picketing were symbolic of the disdain Southwest Side whites had with busing and with blacks in their schools. Southwest Side resident, Betty Bonow, a recent attendee of the Boston convention of the National Association of Neighborhood Schools who would later become a Chicago Board of Education member, best expressed the protesters' sentiment: "I learned two words in Boston. One is resist and the other is never."[59] While South Boston became the symbol of white racism as a result of the resistance to court-ordered desegregation, cities like Chicago proved equally defiant, and conventions such as the one held in Boston helped to nationalize resistance.[60]

CWAC Finishes Desegregation Planning

Julia Dempsey, a lawyer for the Illinois State Board of Education, warned CWAC members at their meeting in October 1977 that voluntary desegregation efforts would not be enough. She insisted, "A totally voluntary plan is not going to be found acceptable by the Illinois Board of Education." Dempsey said that the busing initiated in September was just a beginning, and urged that mandatory provisions were necessary. State Superintendent Cronin also insisted that voluntary measures for desegregation would be acceptable only if there were mandatory backups.[61]

In October 1977, Welling released a delayed proposal that was more theoretical than specific. The Illinois Advisory Committee to the US Commission on Civil Rights' Midwestern Regional Office did an analysis of Welling's paper. Without mincing words, the advisory committee said the paper,

> constitutes another disappointing setback in the struggle to deseg-
> regate the Chicago schools. Besides proposing an all volunteer plan,
> which would violate Illinois Board of Education regulations according
> to that board's legal counsel, and proposing a ten-year timetable which

Illinois Education Superintendent Joseph M. Cronin said would be "too leisurely a pace," the process Welling offers for evaluating alternative desegregation program is totally inadequate. It raises serious questions about his familiarity with the Chicago schools and the regulation under which they operate, and about his overall expertise as an educational desegregation consultant.[62]

This stinging attack exposed Welling's poor record with desegregation efforts in Chicago. In an attempt to apply for a grant from the federal government to study desegregation, Welling called for the use of media technologies for students of different races to talk to each other via television. The Chicago Board of Education refused to approve the plan. This was one of the first missteps Welling made. His inability to be timely with reports was another problem. And this latest disappointing proposal further shook confidence in his abilities. According to the *Chicago Sun-Times*, CWAC's steering committee "questions both the commitment and ability of Welling to draft the initial desegregation plan." The committee had gone through 17 position papers from the community before Welling submitted his.[63] The steering committee minutes read, "The major concern . . . was that (the delay) would increase the credibility gap with the Chicago community with respect to CWAC's efforts . . . CWAC's timelines are severe and the community has responded with numerous papers of widely varying opinions. On the other hand, deadlines for receiving papers from Dr. Welling have been regularly missed."[64]

An October 30, 1977, *Chicago Tribune* editorial sided with Welling's slow desegregation pace. The editorial discussed the conflicting positions between Welling and Cronin. It insisted that "if Welling had proposed a massive desegregation plan that would call for minority majority schools in two-thirds of Chicago's elementary schools, presumably Dr. Cronin would be pleased. But who else would be?" The editorial continued, "Would the effect on learning in Chicago schools be good? Could the costs of a huge busing program be met out of available revenue?"[65] The editorial addressed the reasons Welling moved slowly, but not the fact that his paper failed to really address desegregation efforts in a specific or timely manner. Welling's paper offered a ten-year implementation plan for desegregation. He later admitted the ten-year provision was a mistake.[66] The *Tribune* editorial highlighted the trepidation many Chicagoans had with school desegregation. With whites in the minority, the editorial noted that a comprehensive, citywide plan would be a mistake that could further intensify segregation in the city's schools. A school desegregation plan for Chicago had to account for these demographic realities.

The Chicago Urban League submitted their proposal to the CWAC which expressed that a realistic desegregation plan did not have to be wedded to the State Board of Education goals for racial balance. They saw desegregation as a way to acquire quality education for students in racially isolated schools. They considered the state's "racial balance" to be ignoring the fact that it was usually easier to establish racial balance than to maintain it in Chicago schools. Once racially mixed schools reached a tipping point they would eventually become black schools.[67] The League believed the systemic separation of black and white students needed to be corrected, not the racial balance. According to the League:

> School segregation in Chicago is a function of non-black groups avoiding black people. We do not think it results from a primary intention to isolate black pupils so that they...may be purposefully given inferior instruction. Instead we regard it as determined by wider social, political, and economic interests in the containment of Chicago's black population. At bottom, these interests are respectful of social antipathies and other fears held by non-black residents of the city, which are based on prejudicial, derogatory notions about social and cultural traits of the black population.[68]

The Urban League's proposal highlighted the racist policies that led to the isolation of blacks in inner cities and segregated schools. Recognizing that total desegregation was not possible, they suggested that students spend a portion of their education in desegregated schools and stated: "A desegregation plan should restructure the system and assign students in such a way as to assure them and to make them expect that significant periods in their schooling shall interact in racially mixed groups."[69]

As the proposals came in, the CWAC, divided on mandatory provisions, voted 17–5 to accept the idea of mandatory provisions in the plan they would create. This idea was tied to the Chicago Urban League's proposal to "decide openly and immediately" whether to recommend mandatory desegregation transfers.[70] CWAC's division over mandatory desegregation did not go unnoticed. In November 1977, the US Commission on Civil Rights sent a report to the state, disparaging the CWAC and calling it "self-destructive, [with] in-fighting and leaden 'grass-roots bureaucracy.'"[71] The report also discussed the tension that existed between the Board of Education and CWAC. The Commission doubted that CWAC would meet its January 1978 deadline to create a desegregation proposal and called for federal pressure to force Chicago to comply. "The Committee believes that Board

staff—from Dr. Hannon on down—will continue to avoid and thwart all efforts toward [conformity] with the State desegregation guidelines until the Chicago Board of Education publicly and unequivocally directs the Superintendent to fully comply with the State law." The Commission suggested replacing Welling as project manager.[72]

Just days after the harsh report from the US Commission on Civil Rights was sent to the state, Welling produced a more detailed plan that called for desegregation within a five-year period.[73] The plan offered the specifics Cronin was calling for all along. According to Welling, the proposed plan offered "a logical extension of some of the emotional debates, rationales, plus specific actions, while…responding to the stated positions and beliefs of those who contributed their individual and collective ideas to the City-Wide Advisory Committee."[74]

The CWAC took Welling's plan under advisement as it had the other approximately 100 proposals they had received. CWAC met 13 times in December and once in January to finalize the plans for their proposal to Superintendent Hannon. Voluntary verses mandatory provisions remained the sticking point for the committee. As the Plan Development Committee met to create the plan, the Urban League expressed concern that the committee gave Welling's plan "preferential treatment" because it called for voluntary desegregation. James Compton accused CWAC of violating procedures because they used Welling's plan as a framework without a committee vote. Welling insisted his plan was built on the suggestions received from various groups and included voluntary and mandatory provisions.[75]

In spite of all the doubts about the CWAC's ability to complete a plan, at the beginning of January 1978 and on schedule, CWAC finished "Equalizing Educational Opportunities: Proposed Plan." The group was well aware that modifications would be made to the plan and encouraged citizens to let their voices be heard by contacting the board and superintendent prior to a vote on the plan. The goals of the plan were first to "significantly reduce racial isolation in the schools of Chicago through voluntary programs providing maximum mobility of students throughout the City of Chicago." The second goal was "to increase programs at every level of student involvement throughout the City of Chicago." The plan's key elements included a commitment to voluntary desegregation, consideration of the needs of individual students, the design of a variety of options to increase desegregation, and a provision for mandatory desegregation as a backup.[76]

Just as CWAC was handing its report to Hannon in January 1978, Kane County Circuit Court judge Ernest W. Akemann ruled that the Illinois State Board of Education's desegregation guidelines were both

illegal and unenforceable. East Aurora School District 131 brought the case to court. Judge Akemann thought the rigid 15 percent quota was illegal. Furthermore, the state board's ability to cut off funding without due process for local district appeals was unconstitutional. The judge's ruling declared, "Rules prescribed by the State Board of Education for the establishment and requirement of procedures for the elimination and prevention of racial segregation in schools are hereby declared void and of no force and effect whatsoever...The board may not require any strict mathematical quota for racial balance." In discussing the 15 percent requirement, Judge Akemann ruled, "To set up such a standard and bless it as an end in itself, whatever the consequences, in face of the statutory admonition against required busing, was bureaucracy at its worst." However, the 15 percent quota was part of the rules originally created by Superintendent of Public Instruction Michael Bakalis and was not created for strict adherence.[77] Nonetheless, while the Armstrong Law required school districts to adjust attendance boundaries over time to prevent racial isolation, it did not call for a quota. The state went beyond what the Armstrong Law required. The Illinois Supreme Court rejected the state's appeal to Judge Akemann's decision in March 1978.[78] However, the Illinois Appellate Court overturned Judge Akemann's decision in May 1979, because the State Board of Education was not given an opportunity to answer District 131's allegations or have a hearing. Still, the state was not granted a rehearing in 1981 because the Illinois Appellate Court ruled that the state had gone beyond its authority in setting up a strict quota.[79]

In late March 1978, Hannon asked the state for a month's delay for Chicago's desegregation plans. He wanted to give the Board of Education an opportunity to vote on the plan at the April 12 meeting. The delay was granted.[80] Prior to Hannon's request for the delay, the federal government announced that it was waiting to see what occurred between Chicago and the state before it would step in and demand more student desegregation. The federal government had just successfully gotten the city to transfer over one thousand teachers.[81]

Also in March, Northwest and Southwest Side parents sued to stop Chicago school desegregation in the Cook County Circuit Court. Similar to the case in Aurora, the suit asked the court to rule that the Illinois State Board of Education and Superintendent Cronin violated the state law with the 15 percent quotas. The litigants also wanted a court injunction to prevent Cronin from enforcing any desegregation rules. The parent group had met with Hannon to ask him to file the suit, but he said he had no authority to do so. The parents filed

the suit themselves, but the case was dismissed.[82] While the Cook County case was dismissed, the East Aurora case effectively limited the state's ability to impose a quota on school districts. Although Cronin had indicated that the 15 percent was an objective rather than a quota, school districts could use the case as an excuse to avoid the type of desegregation Cronin wanted.[83]

ACCESS TO EXCELLENCE

Hannon created "Access to Excellence" based on the CWAC plans "Equalizing Educational Opportunities." However, he removed the mandatory provisions and added other specialty programs. The plan's forward barely mentioned desegregation and instead highlighted the choices Chicago students would have. Hannon focused on quality education. "This challenge has been, and is, to reinvigorate the schools of Chicago, to make certain that every child has access to the best education we can provide, to make the Chicago public school system one of the outstanding examples of what *public* education can be. The challenge is to enhance 'excellence' in our schools and to give each child full and open 'access' to it."[84] Access to quality education had long been a fight for black Chicagoans. However, Hannon's framing of the plan, adopted by the Board of Education at its April 12, 1978, meeting, made it seem as though desegregation was a secondary issue. This had been the trend for plans in former superintendent Redmond's administration, as his desegregation plan listed desegregation third among four objectives. Hannon mentioned the programs were individualized for highly talented students and students who needed more support. "We are reinforcing the importance of each child as an individual, different and special. In doing so we are teaching children to view one another as individuals and to respect and appreciate their differences even while they share common interests." For Hannon, voluntary desegregation, through specialized programs, would provide an important avenue for students to learn to respect each other. This was the crux of desegregation as far as he was concerned. For those who said the plan had gone too far, he said, "To them we say resoundingly, 'not so'" because the plan provided options for the best education. For those who thought the plan did not go far enough, he responded, "to mandate movement of students at this time, as some demand, would negate the right of parents to participate in the educational decisions made for their children." Again the focus was more on presenting choices in a voluntary manner than desegregating the schools although the whole point of creating these programs came from a desegregation mandate from the state.[85]

Hannon defined desegregation as a minimum of 10 percent but no more than 90 percent white or minority students at an individual school. Hannon ignored the state's percentage which had been denounced by the circuit court. According to the 90–10 percent ratio, in the 1977–1978 school year, 35 percent of students (179,628) were desegregated. The plan's goals also came with standards ensuring choice for all students, meeting the needs of students in special education and bilingual education programs, promoting of "multicultural understanding and appreciation," and desegregating the faculty.[86] The five-year plan projected that in the 1978–1979 school year, 210,000 students would be attending desegregated schools or participating in desegregation programs. This would be an increase of 30,000 students over the 1977–1978 school year.[87] The plan added much of the "how to" details to the CWAC's plan so that it could be implemented.

Initial reactions to the plan varied. Cronin, without having read Access to Excellence, said there were some positive features and that he would have his staff go through the plan. The Urban League called it "isolated integration."[88] Citizens School Committee, a watchdog group, questioned whether the plan would actually accomplish desegregation. The Kenwood–Oakwood Community Organization, a neighborhood organization founded by religious and community leaders, called the plan the height of arrogance. Jessie Jackson's Operation Push said the state would have to demand a mandatory backup for the plan. The NAACP threatened to file a suit in federal court because the plan was voluntary. The CWAC also rejected the plan because it lacked the mandatory backup. According to CWAC, Hannon's plan "contravenes the committee's intent," and "compromises the substance of the plan."[89] They voted 14–4 to urge the State Board of Education to reject Hannon's plan as it was and send it back to him to develop a mandatory backup plan. Despite the opposition, the Chicago Board of Education approved the plan in a 6–4 vote. Demonstrators from Operation Push picketed the Chicago Board of Education demanding mandatory provisions.[90]

The State Board of Education sent a warning that the plan may be rejected without mandatory provisions, but Cronin asked the State Board to postpone a decision until May 11, 1978. While yet another extension was granted, on April 13, the State Board of Education voted 12–3 for a resolution that called for Chicago to "move expeditiously in the development and submission" of a plan with mandatory provisions. The State Board put off any further action until its May meeting. One State Board member seriously questioned the commitment to desegregation in Chicago. In response, Hannon was defiant, stating that he would not negotiate with the State Board and would refuse to include mandatory transfers because he did not "see the need for such a thing."[91] Hannon had also been insolent in his interactions with the federal government in their efforts to achieve teacher desegregation. In his interaction with the federal government, he had only acted once the administrative judge ruled that the school district's federal funding could be withheld. But since no similar demand was made by the state, he could comfortably forestall meaningful desegregation without fear of financial sanctions. Cronin was seemingly satisfied with the continued extension of the city's probationary status since the city had finally developed a plan after two years. It was possible that Cronin wanted to wait to see how it would be implemented and what affects it would have.

In the mean time, Hannon wanted the desegregation consultant Welling to resign because he had allegedly faked sickness just as the desegregations plans were being unveiled. Welling had left on sick leave beginning March 23, 1978. He refused to quit and said he would sue if fired. Although Welling's contract expired in August, Hannon suspended Welling until he could get the Chicago Board of Education to officially fire him at its May meeting. Welling attempted to sue for an injunction to keep his job, but the judge refused to hear the case. Finally, the board fired Welling at its May meeting. Welling had made several mistakes in his position, which included the board rejected televised desegregation proposal, the untimely submission of reports, and finally his absence at such a critical time in the desegregation process.[92]

A Technical Assistance Committee formed by Superintendent Cronin and headed by Gary Orfield created a report called "Integration in Chicago: A Report to the Illinois State Board of Education," which questioned the impact Access to Excellence would have on desegregation. The part-time desegregation programs were criticized because both state law and the courts had previously rejected such efforts. The voluntary desegregation procedures were also criticized as ineffective. Mandatory backup plans were seen as necessary in case the voluntary plans were ineffective. The committee also found that the city's 90–10 desegregation standard fell far short of the state standards and insisted that any plan in Chicago should take into account the multiracial aspect of the student population. The report acknowledged the lack of feasibility to acquire complete desegregation of Chicago schools, but argued that a "substantial reduction of racial isolation is possible." It suggested the state create legislation to compel metropolitan desegregation and provide aid to make metropolitan desegregation possible.[93]

Taking the Technical Assistance Committee report into account—and after much debate—the State Board of Education's Equal Educational Opportunity Committee gave Chicago schools until December 1, 1978 to correct the "key deficiencies" in their plan. The deficiencies included the inadequate definition of desegregation, the need for a mandatory back up, and the lack of full-time desegregation programs. The vote was 3–2 with white Equal Educational Opportunity Committee members voting for and black committee members voting against the extension.[94] When the full State Board met, it approved the Equal Educational Opportunity Committee's recommendations and decided 11–3 to give Chicago six and a half months to make changes to its desegregation plans. It did not accept or reject the plan, but said if the changes were not made it would begin the process to cut off $500 million dollars in state funding. Empty threats of this sort had been made by the state before, but garnered little action. A defiant Hannon said he would still go ahead with the Access to Excellence school plan already in place and declared that he was not adding a mandatory backup to the plan.[95]

Prior to school opening in September 1978, 17,000 students had applied for Access to Excellence transfer programs. After school was in session the first week, 9,838 students were participating. This could be attributed to students who did not show up to their new schools and for students sending in applications for multiple programs. Because it did not have accurate records, the board could not distinguish how many students had come from segregated black or Latino schools to attend segregated white schools.[96]

As the program was getting underway, the Chicago Urban League issued a harsh report about the Access to Excellence program, which they also titled "Access to Excellence." The report began: "The adoption of 'Access to Excellence' by the Chicago Board of Education is a clear signal to the minority and poor communities in Chicago, that true quality and equality of educational opportunities remain more a hope than a reality. From our perspective, 'Access to Excellence' can only by misnomer be termed a desegregation plan."[97] The Urban League did not disagree with the entire plan. However, they had problems with the lack of a mandatory provision, elitism in the plan, and the continued isolation of students of color. In terms of mandatory provisions, the report questioned the ability to desegregate when the choice was left up to students and parents. They also found that only four of the Access to Excellence options were deliberately set up to ensure desegregation. Using Hannon's 90–10 percent desegregation standard, the Urban League found that 339 elementary schools were still out of compliance and seven administrative districts did not have any schools in compliance. Of those seven districts, five were only scheduled for programs within the segregated administrative district. Those five districts were 99.2 percent black and Latino.[98] Thus, voluntary measures were not even designed to acquire even minimal desegregation.

The report called Hannon's Access to Excellence elitist because "the improvements it offers are primarily intended for a select minority of preferred relatively elite students." The plan was "business as usual" for poor students and students of color. The basic instructional programs were designed to serve less than 10 percent of the students. Over 90 percent of the programs were designed for more academically talented students. "Educational improvements aimed especially at the pupils who are already better educated—whether they are black or white——cannot be tolerated." Many of the programs offered were located outside of the poorest districts. About "40% of all black students will continue to attend schools in districts where no programming has been provided to attract new students." After evaluating the data on the total slots available in a group of districts with high and low percentages of black students and the available programming slots, they concluded, "that there was/is not significant intention to upgrade the overall educational quality in the predominantly black districts, but instead, as mentioned earlier, to provide some limited opportunities for 'escape' for the chosen few."[99] The Urban League also asserted that there would be continued isolation of students because a number of the programs in Access to Excellence were only existing programs "that have failed the majority of our students in the past and have brought public education in Chicago to the crisis we now face."[100]

The report then evaluated each program. One of the most interesting findings was of the advanced placement (AP) courses. Fifteen predominantly black and Latino high schools, with fewer than 15.4 percent white students, had no AP courses. Yet all predominantly white schools had at least one AP course.[101] The report ended: "Under this proposal, integration will indeed be most voluntary while the pervasive and devastating segregation of 87% of the black and minority students in this system will remain mandatory. If these are the seeds the Board chooses to sow, then they must be prepared to reap the tragic social harvest that will inevitably result from policies that systematically isolate and separate a group of people from the mainstream of the society in which they live."[102]

The Urban League's detailed analysis highlighted the shortcomings of Access to Excellence and exposed the severe educational limitations black and Latino students faced in isolated schools. Only those who were savvy enough could escape to schools offering college preparation curricula. It was also clear, as it had been when the plan was introduced, that desegregation was not the main focus. Again, Chicago would have had difficulty with any plan attempted because of the housing segregation that existed in the city. Entire areas of the city were all or predominantly white, black, or Latino. Still, Hannon's plan did not go far enough.

Recognizing this, Hannon said, "It is obvious the current state guidelines cannot be achieved realistically within the geographic boundaries of the City of Chicago." As the December 1, 1978 deadline approached, Hannon indicated that he would push for city–suburban busing. He suggested that Governor James (Jim) R. Thompson arrange a meeting with superintendents in the Chicago metropolitan area. He sent the State Board a detailed progress report of Access to Excellence, instead of new plans.[103] Hannon's report showed that 30 percent of the first year goals for voluntary desegregation had been met. When the State Board of Education met December 14, they voted 11–2 to give Chicago yet another three months to fix its desegregation plan. The resolution called for state and city officials to work together to "identify deficiencies in the plan and outline necessary steps to remedy them."[104]

Gary Orfield, at the time a political scientist at the University of Illinois at Urbana-Champaign and consultant for the State Board of Education, submitted a report to Cronin about Chicago's schools. The report titled "Voluntary Desegregation in Chicago," discussed Chicago's segregation, analyzed Access to Excellence, and suggested possible changes to the state desegregation rules. According to the report, the Midwest was the most segregated area in the nation and was twice as segregated as the Southeast, which included states that were once the bastion of segregation. Chicago was the most segregated urban area in the nation at the time and was therefore a test case for the state's ability to create realistic rules to deal with desegregation.[105] Orfield plainly stated that in spite of the publicity associated with the program,

Access to Excellence has failed. Its impact on Chicago segregation has been negligible. After implementation of the plan the city's segregation remains higher than many communities before they began desegregation. The city's minority children remain the most segregated in the

U.S. There are serious charges that the plan has made the city's separate education more unequal by locating the challenging educational programs outside the areas where black and Latino children remain in segregated schools. Nor has the plan stabilized white enrollment. That decline is large and it increased this school year.[106]

Orfield said that the press had been inaccurate and "intentionally misleading" in its reporting of the progress with Access and he indicated that according to the Chicago Board of Education's own data, "97 percent of the city's black students and 87 percent of the Latino students remain in predominantly minority schools."[107] Black students were segregated from both whites and Latinos, particularly at the elementary level. Whites and Latinos were more likely to be in school together than the other groups primarily because they lived in less intensely segregated areas. Cronin's own analysis of Access to Excellence in early 1980 agreed "that some 'Access' schools, even after recruitment, remained one race schools."[108] Access failed to reach the projected number of students and many students were desegregated only in part-time programs.

The report examined magnet schools and permissive transfers. According to Orfield, magnet schools had done a poorer job of desegregating in Chicago than cities like Milwaukee and Cincinnati. The magnet school programs actually declined in enrollment, and white flight was a major part of that decline. The permissive transfers were more effective. Access to Excellence had projected 4,500 transfers of minority students, but only 2,570 had transferred—and it was unclear how many of those students were from the targeted group. The transfers had a limited impact on white schools. The Technical Assistance Committee had estimated that Access to Excellence would have desegregated 2 percent of students in full-time programs—ultimately, Access to Excellence had not accomplished even that goal. Much of the desegregation could in fact be attributed more to neighborhood racial change than to the programs created.[109]

Part of the reason Access to Excellence shied away from mandatory desegregation was the fear of white flight. White students in Chicago's schools declined by 7.3 percent during 1970–1976, despite having a segregation index of 90. Comparatively, Detroit lost 13.3 percent of whites in that same time and had a segregation index of 63. Washington, DC had the second highest index of 84 and lost only 5.5 percent of its whites. Chicago has had a rapid racial change that dates back to the 1930s. A combination of factors including suburbanization, the housing market, high property taxes, and lackluster city services led to the decline in whites in Chicago and other cities. Access to Excellence was supposed to help maintain the white population in the schools. But in his report, Orfield determined that, "Mandatory busing does not appear to be the central factor in white population decline." Chicago's programs did not help to maintain the white student population—instead, the most effective maintenance of whites came from a quota type system at Gage Park and Morgan Park High Schools. Those schools maintained stable desegregation for quite some time by limiting the number of minority students. Chicago was unusual for having few desegregation efforts and rapid white flight.[110]

Orfield's critique was not taken lightly. Superintendent Hannon claimed Orfield's "credibility as a scholar is replaced by that of a 'drummer' for his book on mandatory desegregation." According to Hannon, Orfield was one of the creators of the Los Angeles mandatory desegregation program and many critics called that plan a failure.[111] For his part, Orfield noted that it was conflicting court decisions that had left Los Angeles' plan in disarray.[112] Cronin's response was that Chicago had seen progress in desegregation, though not enough. He still wanted the Chicago Board of Education to create a new plan that would further desegregate an additional 20,000 students in the next school year.[113]

Not long after Orfield's report, another report from the Joint Staff Committee on Access to Excellence (made up of officials from the Illinois Office of Education and the Chicago Public Schools) was released by Superintendent Hannon and State Superintendent Cronin. According to the report, 34 schools with 16,649 students were desegregated. Racial balance had improved in 179 schools encompassing 139,688 students. In accordance with Chicago's minimum desegregation guidelines, 38.2 percent (224 schools) achieved the standard. Hannon said, "More than 25,000 students are voluntarily participating [in desegregation programs] and 16,000 of this number are in full time programs."[114] It is interesting to note that even though the state did not agree with Chicago's 90–10 guidelines, the Joint Staff Committee reported on the success of Access based on those guidelines. This added to the difficulty the state would have to force the city to meet the state's guidelines.

Late in 1978, Cronin became aware of the real possibility of federal intervention in Chicago student desegregation. In a November 17, 1978 letter to David S. Tatel, director of the Office of Civil Rights (OCR), Cronin wrote, "This office has recently received reports relating to possible action by OCR in the near future on the issue of student assignment in the Chicago schools." He went on to state that the reports also indicated there was "the possibility of intervention on behalf of the Department of Justice as well." Cronin was attempting to buy time so that Chicago school officials could submit their plan to "remedy the deficiencies the State Board found in the city's Access to Excellence Plan," and so that the Illinois State Board of Education could meet to decide on the merits of the plan. Cronin wanted Tatel to communicate with his office in case OCR moved on Chicago prior to the State Board's December 14, 1978 meeting.[115] Tatel responded in an undated letter that the OCR investigation was ongoing, and that the preliminary investigation could possibly be completed in January 1979. Once the preliminary conclusions were reached, he would review the evidence with Cronin and Hannon.[116]

The State Board of Education met in April 1979 and decided to have Chicago submit additional desegregation plans by the fall. The state wanted further desegregation of vocational schools, boundary and feeder school pattern changes, desegregation assignments for new schools, improvement in recruitment, and backup plans to reach goals. HEW had just begun to demand student desegregation from Chicago, expressing its disappointment with the city in March 1979, and in April threatened court action if more desegregation did not occur. The State Board said it would cooperate with HEW, and Cronin declared that it would be best to settle the dispute within the state. Chicago would continue on its probationary status with the state for the rest of the year.[117]

* * *

Cronin published these hopeful words in 1978: "Where once the states actually legalized or tolerated school desegregation, in the North as well as the South, increasingly state agencies can be expected to participate in the efforts to achieve quality, integrated education in the schools."[118] Although Cronin recognized the difficult challenges states would have with "resegregation and metropolitan inequalities," he believed that having the correct people in place in state agencies could foster desegregation. Despite Cronin's hopefulness, the reality was that Chicago had not made enough strides to desegregate its schools. The political and demographic landscape in Chicago and the unwillingness of the Chicago Board of Education and the school superintendent complicated the efforts to desegregate schools in Chicago. Cronin found out how difficult it was for the state to implement the rules and procedures it had set up when there was no real consequence for not complying. Since September 1972, Chicago was put on notice that it was out of compliance with the state rules. The city was on an extended probation from 1976 to 1979 without any sanctions. While the state had the policies in place to require desegregation from the city, the lack of its own enforcement was perhaps a major reason why Chicago continued to evade its responsibilities. Cronin's "dream" highlighted his philosophy about how to acquire desegregation. A court case could lead to desegregation, not the withholding of state and federal funds. Perhaps withholding funds was too politically risky, or perhaps Cronin was pragmatic about the devastating impact such a withholding would have for a school district already facing financial difficulties. Whatever the case, the lack of financial sanctions meant Hannon could brazenly defy the wishes of the State Board and state superintendent. According to board member Edgar Epps, Cronin did not have "sufficient political clout...I don't know if he had personal commitment to [desegregation] or if he was using it as a personal political ploy; but I don't think he had sufficient political clout to get it done even if he wanted to."[119] Because the state failed in its efforts, the federal government became involved in requiring student desegregation in Chicago. After years of pressure, the state lost its ability to force Chicago to meet its guidelines.

CHAPTER 4

Federal Involvement with Student Desegregation

In 1969, activist Thomas N. Todd, one of the lawyers handling the Justice Department's faculty desegregation efforts against Chicago, resigned. Although Todd had the opportunity to bring the first criminal case (*United States v. Gorman*) against a Chicago policeman for denying an individual's civil rights while in the US Attorney's Office in Chicago, Todd indicated that he was interested in working on larger issues than what the Justice Department was currently pursuing.[1] He believed that the Justice Department should also focus on student desegregation, inequitable school funding, poor facilities at black schools, and the bias certification process for teachers and principals. Similarly, Leon Panetta, Nixon's first Office of Civil Rights (OCR) director, was forced to resign in 1970. Panetta began his political career as an assistant to California senator Thomas H. Kuchel in 1966 and assistant to HEW secretary Robert Finch in 1969 before being tapped to briefly head OCR in 1970.[2] The *Washington Daily News* featured a front-page headline "Nixon Seeks to Fire HEWS Rights Chief for Liberal Views."[3] Though Republican, Panetta was viewed as a liberal for his "tough stand on school desegregation."[4] Panetta's response was, "I had just been fired from a $30,000-a-year Government job for taking that job too seriously."[5] The resignations of both Todd and Panetta highlighted Nixon's calculated response to civil rights. Nixon favored a restrained approach to desegregation and those moving too quickly or wanting more civil rights and desegregation efforts were at odds with his administration.

Gary Orfield argued that Nixon's slowed emphasis on civil rights policies undermined OCR's efforts. Prior to Nixon's administration, the Department of Health, Education, and Welfare (HEW) had set a rigid September 1969 deadline for school desegregation throughout the South. If desegregation did not occur by the deadline, federal funds could be withheld. President Lyndon B. Johnson was uneasy with such a deadline, but he would not be in office when the deadline occurred. After Nixon came into office, his administration urged the Justice Department and HEW to file school desegregation suits instead of withholding funds—an approach that weakened the enforcement and effectiveness of OCR.[6]

Nixon's relationship with civil rights and desegregation efforts was perplexing. Nixon disagreed with forced integration through busing, but actively pursued affirmative action policies to assist with employment opportunities. Historian Dean J. Kotlowsky asserts that Nixon did more for civil rights than critics have given him credit for: "Nixon opposed discrimination which prevented blacks from attending the nearest school or owning a home in a neighborhood of their choice. But he would not 'force' races together. 'I am convinced that while legal segregation is totally wrong, forced integration of housing or education is just as wrong,' the president wrote in 1970."[7] Nixon advised his administration to move quietly. Prior to 1969, only 186,000 of three million black students attended desegregated schools. After 1969, Justice Department suits led to 600,000 blacks attending desegregated schools. In 1970, after the *Alexander v. Holmes* (1969) Supreme Court ruling, two million blacks were in desegregated schools. Kotlowsky surmised that, "A confluence of presidential leadership, federal persuasion, Supreme Court rulings, Justice Department lawsuits, and the threat of HEW denying holdout districts federal aid broke white southern resistance...In this sense, Nixon was the greatest school desegregator in American history."[8] Indeed, during Nixon's administration, the South became more desegregated than during Johnson's administration. Contrary to Kotlowsky's revisionist history, one could just as easily argue that desegregation successes resulted from initiatives that commenced during the Johnson administration and through court rulings. In fact, desegregation occurred in spite of Nixon's policies, not because of them.

Still, through both the Johnson and Nixon administrations, Chicago schools remained segregated. Federal officials had been unwilling to move decisively to demand student desegregation for Chicago schools in the late 1960s and early 1970s—and segregation continued to plague the city throughout Gerald Ford's administration as well. The Ford administration maintained Nixon's focus on Chicago teacher desegregation. When President Jimmy Carter took office, however, it seemed the federal government took a renewed interest in correcting the segregated Chicago school system. Although Title VI enforcement under Carter was not vastly different than previous Republican administrations,[9] it was nonetheless effective for Chicago.

President Carter assembled a team of committed civil rights advocates to head up HEW and the Justice Department's Civil Rights Division. He selected Joseph A. Califano Jr. as secretary of HEW in 1976. Since 1961, Califano had worked in government agencies beginning with John F. Kennedy's administration in the Department of Defense. He then worked as a special assistant to Lyndon B. Johnson and the *New York Times* jokingly dubbed him "the Deputy President of Domestic Affairs."[10] In his book, *Governing America,* Califano writes, "It was imperative to breathe life into HEW's Office of Civil Rights, and the first step was to make my own commitment clear. In my own confirmation hearing, I called for 'full speed ahead' on desegregation." He argued that "the most disgraceful thing that has happened in this country is that we have shattered a generation of black children, largely in urban schools but also in rural schools. These schools have been segregated and ill-cared for."[11] To match his commitment, Califano appointed others who were just as dedicated to civil rights. David S. Tatel became OCR's director, and a friend of Califano's commented, "You picked one helluva tough guy in Tatel. He's going to burn up the road on civil rights."[12] Tatel had been the director of the Chicago Lawyers' Committee for Civil Rights under Law from 1969 to 1970, the director of the National Lawyers' Committee for Civil Rights under Law in Washington, DC from 1972 to 1974, and had also worked in private practice.[13] Along with selecting Califano, Carter also chose Drew S. Days. Days was appointed to the assistant attorney general position in 1977, after serving as a lawyer in the NAACP's Legal Defense Fund where he tried school desegregation and other discrimination cases.[14] With a team dedicated to civil rights, the battle against Chicago school desegregation was revitalized during Carter's administration.

In the past it was difficult to compel Chicago schools to desegregate because of a lack of commitment by previous administrations and the powerful influence of Mayor Richard J. Daley. But when Mayor Daley died in December 1976, his Democratic Machine unraveled and no longer had the strength to obstruct federal plans. OCR had begun an investigation of student segregation in 1977 without the knowledge of the Board of Education fearing they would "drown [investigators] with information" as they had in the past. The board and administrators would also use political leverage from Mayor

Daley's office to stop portions of investigations.[15] As OCR completed its investigation, and as it became increasingly apparent that the State of Illinois was not effective at enforcing desegregation efforts, OCR officials stepped in to enforce student desegregation in Chicago.

Meanwhile, the historically defiant Board of Education members and superintendent were experiencing unexpected school administrative changes beginning in late 1979. A school financial crisis led to the resignation of Superintendent Joseph Hannon and a reconstitution of the Board of Education. It is interesting to note that the federal government accused the Chicago Board of Education of purposeful segregation, but expected the same administrative body to create new policies to end segregation. Although these expectations were similar in other districts, the school leadership changes resulting from the financial crisis, likely made possible a quickly negotiated consent decree between the Board of Education and the Justice Department.

HEW/OCR Report Condemns Chicago Student Desegregation Efforts

Holding true to his commitment to charge 'full speed ahead' with desegregation efforts, HEW secretary Califano wrote a letter accusing Chicago Public Schools of purposeful segregation. An unsigned "confidential draft" of the letter was leaked and published by the *Education Daily* on February 28, causing some scandal—but Califano held his ground and sent an official, signed letter to the city in April 1979. It stated, "OCR has concluded that racially segregated conditions existing in the public school system result from various past policies and practices of the Chicago school system. Specifically, the location of new, permanent and temporary facilities; the establishment and alteration of school boundaries; the transportation of pupils; and the assignment of faculty and staff have contributed to the assignment of minority children to segregated and overcrowded schools."[16] These conditions were in existence from the time there were substantial numbers of black students in the school system. An appendix of just over 100 pages accompanied Califano's letter. The documents also served as notice that the city was again ineligible for the Emergency School Aid Act (ESAA) funds.

OCR had concluded that Chicago school officials intentionally created and maintained a racially discriminatory and dual school system.[17] The investigation was conducted through the use of board minutes since 1939 and racial composition statistics of schools since the early 1960s.[18] A regional office of OCR conducted the investigation of Chicago and had a tremendous amount of evidence of the city's purposeful segregation. In the appendix attached to Califano's formal letter, Chicago's schools were found to be racially identifiable; school officials either acted or failed to act in ways that led to the creation or maintenance of segregation; school official's actions were "through time and across virtually the whole geographic face of the system."

The overwhelming and detailed study convincingly pointed to the purposeful segregation of black children across two decades of policies and through three different superintendents' administrations. Superintendent Benjamin Willis was firmly supportive of constituents who advocated neighborhood schools, and as a result, stood as the symbol of segregation during the Civil Rights Movement in Chicago.[19] Superintendent James R. Redmond, on the other hand, believed that anchoring whites in the city was of the utmost importance, but was willing to experiment with small desegregation plans. Superintendent Hannon also believed in keeping whites in the city, and only attempted voluntary desegregation with parental choice as the focus. Of these three superintendents, Willis had been in the best position to acquire desegregation because during much of his administration whites were still in the majority. However, he chose to do nothing—in spite of the sizable protest demonstrations led by the Coordinating Council of Community Organizations that occurred from 1963 to 1965. As the black and Latino population in the schools outpaced whites, Willis's successors had less to work with.

There were a variety of ways by which the federal government assessed Chicago's purposeful segregation of students and racial discrimination in the allocation of resources. Some of the most persuasive evidence OCR provided was the use of mobile units. Mobile classrooms were used to reduce overcrowding and were supposed to be temporary. However, mobiles were predominantly placed at black schools, largely because the growth in the number of black students in some areas led to overcrowding. The mobiles were dubbed "Willis Wagons" by civil rights advocates and often served as permanent fixtures. According to the OCR report,

> At the same time mobiles were placed at black schools, there were white schools in the same area with classroom space or with space for mobile units themselves. The growing black student populations could have been assigned to these schools in ways that reduced the overcrowding of black schools more satisfactorily and that eliminated the racial identifiability of nearby white schools.
>
> Instead of adopting such less segregative alternatives, the District has used most mobiles to contain black students in large identifiably black

schools. Moreover by placing most mobiles at such schools, the Board has provided these black students with an inferior educational environment...In addition adding temporary facilities to a campus has diminished space for playgrounds. Finally, by diminishing the desirability of these schools, the Board actually promoted segregation by encouraging white students to abandon or avoid predominantly black and racially changing schools.[20]

Mobile units wasted tax payers' resources, sustained racial segregation, promoted institutionalized discrimination, and resisted desegregation. In the examples given, the board used mobiles at black schools rather than send the students to nearby white schools with space. In the Austin community, as discussed in chapter 1, May and Spencer schools were extremely overcrowded. Twelve mobile units were installed at Spencer and five at May, while there were several underutilized white elementary schools within a two-mile radius. Whites in North Austin were attempting to keep their neighborhoods from changing, and school policies assisted with that process. For all intents and purposes, South Austin had already been lost to racial transition, so school officials did little to alleviate the problems outside of the 1968 busing plan.[21] In spite of the busing plan, the schools remained overcrowded. In another example, Altgeld Elementary, which was 95.6 percent black in 1965, had 16 mobiles. There were three nearby schools that were all or predominantly white across Ashland Avenue. One of the white schools, Barton, had six empty classrooms. OCR concluded that "by placing mobiles only at Altgeld, rather than assigning students to or placing mobiles at nearby white schools, the Board contained the growing black enrollment in the oversized, virtually all-black school, protected white students in the area from integration, and imposed the entire burden of overcrowding on black students."[22]

In the case of building new schools, OCR gave examples of how most of the 10 new high schools and two high school branches built between 1968 and 1977 were created for a particular race. Two of the schools, Whitney Young and Metro, had "racially controlled" admissions policies. The rest of the new buildings were located in predominantly one-race neighborhoods, instead of in areas where desegregation could have been promoted. Seven of the schools were over 90 percent black. Five of these schools also had a majority black faculty. Other schools were predominantly white or Latino. Curie opened in 1973 as a predominantly white school, as its student population was 82.7 percent white, and 78.5 percent of its faculty was white. Clemente was 76 percent Latino and Juarez was 92.7 percent

Latino when they opened in 1974. Both schools had Latino teachers eight and seven times the district average, respectively.[23] New elementary, middle, and upper grade centers, totaling 75, were opened between 1966 and 1977. Of these schools, 45 opened with 90 percent or more black students. There were also 11 that opened with majority white students. These schools also had faculties that were typically the same race of the students, with six of the schools containing all white faculties.[24]

OCR also pointed out that transportation was used to keep races separate. For example, OCR highlighted the 1974 busing of black students from the overcrowded Raster Elementary School (90.8 percent black) to Dyett Elementary School (100 percent black), while ignoring six predominantly white schools in the area, including Marquette, which had nine available classrooms.[25] OCR provided other examples where school officials had opportunities to make better decisions that would have led to desegregation, but they chose to maintain segregation. For instance, when a housing project serving black families was constructed in a white neighborhood, the Board of Education built a new school to serve those children instead of sending them to nearby white schools. In other cases when housing projects serving white families were built in white neighborhoods and housing projects serving black families were built in black neighborhoods, the children simply attended the nearby schools. No new schools were built to serve those students apart from the rest of the community in these cases.[26]

The board's use of permissive transfer plans was also problematic. Although the permissive transfer plans were created first to relieve overcrowding and later to spur desegregation, the lack of transportation, limitation of the class sizes in sending and receiving schools, as well as lack of mandatory reassignments, limited desegregation. The OCR appendix stated, "Thus by imposing these limitations, the Board rendered the program almost totally ineffective. Without mandatory reassignments and District-paid transportation, the [permissive transfer plan] reduced neither overcrowding nor segregation. Furthermore, the Board's limitations on class size in the receiving and sending schools also limited the number of transferees and perpetuated gross disparities between sending schools (usually predominantly black) and receiving schools (usually predominantly white)."[27] The board issued a 1966 resolution that called the permissive transfer plans a "privilege," which had to be earned with good "effort, achievement, and conduct" to "placate fears that black transfer students would be disruptive in white neighborhood schools." If students misbehaved, they would not be allowed to re-enroll in a school.[28] In other words, black students were privileged to attend white schools and thus had to be on their best behavior in order to be accepted by the white school and the white community. On the other hand, this conduct expectation was not placed on students in the attendance area of the school.

The 1963 high school permissive transfer plan was opened to academically talented students in the top 5 percent of their classes. Those students could move to schools that had honors and advanced placement courses their current schools did not provide. Parents at some receiving schools—Bogan, Austin, and Washington High Schools—protested against the possible transfers, and those schools and others (Hyde Park and South Shore) were taken off the transfer list. The board later restored Hyde Park and South Shore schools to the list when black parents with children at Hirsh High School protested. But Superintendent Willis held up the transfer of Hirsh students to those schools. Black parents sought a court injunction for the transfers and Willis resigned. In order to placate the superintendent, the board rescinded Hyde Park and South Shore from the list, and Willis withdrew his resignation.[29] That the board sided with Willis, who had slowed desegregation efforts, rather than side with the black parents is yet another example of the board's lack of dedication to desegregation.

The board allowed all students to participate in the transfers beginning in 1964, in an effort to relieve overcrowding and spur desegregation. While this was perhaps intended to expand opportunities to all black students, the most egregious OCR finding was that white students used the transfers to escape predominantly black schools. Superintendent Willis's own report to the board in May 1966 similarly noted this occurrence. "From the data...it can be concluded that the transfer plan has integrated some schools but in other instances may have hastened resegregation. This is substantiated by reports received from district superintendents whose observation is that integration at Waller, Farragut, Hyde Park, and Hirsh has been adversely affected by the permissive transfer plan." White students used the permissive transfers "to transfer from these schools which are or were integrated leaving them more predominantly Negro than they were previously."[30] Despite these findings, the board did not act until April 1967 to exclude "integrated" high schools from the program to prevent "resegregation."

The findings of the report were quite compelling, although Superintendent Hannon denied guilt on the part of his and previous administrations. [31] Over 100 pages of allegations, coming from the board's own sources, were hard to refute. While housing segregation was often blamed for schooling patterns, OCR's report exposed the actions of the Board of Education and its superintendents in a detailed and comprehensive manner. The report uncovered the patterns of segregation that went beyond mere housing segregation and were the result of official action. Still not all were ready to hold the board responsible.

A *Chicago Tribune* editorial argued that without a fuller understanding of community demands, OCR's views of deliberate intent may actually be a case in which a particular community insisted a new school be built or demanded alterations to desegregation plans. The article referenced Juarez and Clemente High Schools as examples of new schools built as a result of community demands.[32] One of the examples OCR listed as an opportunity for desegregation squandered was the proposed Southeast Side busing plan in 1968. OCR alleged that Superintendent Redmond did not do what was necessary to integrate those schools. However, both blacks and whites in those communities opposed the version of desegregation proposed by Redmond's administration. In this instance, the Board of Education's actions were prompted by the fact that Redmond's staff had actually ignored alternative proposals from the community. The board, however, endorsed the plan busing black Austin students to the Northwest Side despite vigorous opposition from Northwest Side residents and their politicians. This demonstrates that in some instances, OCR's view of intentional segregation may have resulted from community requests and not necessarily the Board of Education's intentions. Nonetheless, a board largely opposed to desegregation would more easily be willing to acquiesce to minority demands for separate community schools.

The use of mobile units, site selection for new schools, and permissive transfer plans intensified purposeful segregation and overcrowding of black schools while protecting white schools from desegregation. Some school authorities feared the departure of whites from the school system and the city. Others, like Superintendent Willis, wanted to maintain segregation. Evidence collected by OCR highlights the intentional containment of black children at black schools that went beyond neighborhood segregation. Civil Rights advocates had long protested these segregative acts and the dual system of education that result from such discriminatory actions. The federal government, armed with such clear evidence of intentional segregation, unencumbered by a powerful mayor, headed by civil rights advocates, and propelled by the courts to enforce the law, had little choice but to act.

ACTIVITIES AFTER THE ISSUED
LETTER AND APPENDIX

Although Hannon had initially pledged to work with the federal government to solve the problems of the school system, he and the Chicago Board of Education decided to fight the federal governments' allegations instead. The board was given two choices to receive ESAA funding: attend a hearing to address charges that were incorrect or ask for a waiver and correct the deficiencies that had been alleged. Since the second option was viewed as an admission of guilt, the board chose the hearing.[33] Just over a dozen school officials and six aldermen from the City Council's Education Committee attended a May 4, 1979, HEW "show cause" hearing on school desegregation in Washington DC. The hearing was an opportunity for Chicago school officials to refute the charges of purposeful segregation that had led to the denial of ESAA funds. Hannon and school board attorney Michael Murray spoke at the hearing. Murray called HEW's charges inaccurate and incomplete. He insisted that Chicago was not operating a dual system of education. As for Hannon, the defiant attitude he maintained when dealing with the state had not changed for federal officials. Hannon declared, "We are integrationists and we are an integrated school system." He touted Access to Excellence as a working program based on a "demographic reality."[34] Hannon also asked that the federal government identify what compliance looked like. Interestingly, Hannon's admission of a "demographic reality" contradicted his insistence that Chicago was integrated.

Aldermen attending the hearing had conflicting interpretations of Hannon's performance. Alderman Clifford P. Kelly called the performance the "Hannon hustle." Hannon had gotten into a verbal dispute with black city aldermen because a few weeks prior to the hearing, some of the aldermen had proposed a resolution to fire Hannon in order to increase desegregation in the city. Hannon accused the aldermen of being racists, saying, "I abhor black racism as much as I abhor white racism." Alderman Clifford P. Kelly, who supported the resolution, responded, "Calling us racists just because there are those of us in the City Council who want black children to get as good an education as white children is ridiculous, as is his administration."[35] Clearly, neither side was going to see eye to eye on the situation. In support of Hannon's performance at the hearing was white alderman Roman Pucinski, a former US congressman, who called it a "superb presentation." Pucinski had been an outspoken neighborhood school proponent since 1968 and was among the political leaders against busing. He had also worked with Mayor Daley to demand the release of federal funds initially held by HEW in 1965. The aldermen's views of desegregation determined how they interpreted Hannon's hearing presentation.

Along with presentations at the hearing, Hannon submitted a written response to HEW's allegations, in the hopes of getting the denied 15 million dollars in ESAA funds released to the city. Responding to the allegations that the location of new schools and mobile classrooms contributed to segregation, Hannon argued that since the 1973–1974 school year, buildings funded by the Illinois Capital Development Board had to be fewer than 90 percent one race. As for the mobile units, Hannon cited Access to Excellence's commitment to remove all mobile units by 1981, and noted that half of them had already been removed. Since OCR officials had alleged that Chicago used transfer programs and transportation to maintain segregation, Hannon pointed to the permissive transfer enrollments by which 4,000 students had transferred, fostering an end to all white schools. In addition, he highlighted cases where schools used racial quotas to maintain racial balance insisting that magnet schools in particular were being created and used as a means to desegregate schools. Hannon also noted that the allegation of faculty being assigned to racially identifiable schools was no longer the case as teachers and principals had been reassigned to promote desegregation.[36] He put a positive spin on the accomplishments in Chicago.

Although Hannon bragged about the transformative powers of Access to Excellence, both state and federal officials had found the largely part-time desegregation measures incomplete, and the measures Hannon referenced as not going far enough to correct the extreme and historic school segregation in the city. Controlled enrollment at magnet and other schools, along with permissive transfers, were woefully limited in achieving school desegregation. While these programs were largely ineffective, the board continued them. In spite of numerous critiques of Access to Excellence, the Chicago Board of Education voted in a May 1979 meeting to expand it.[37]

The expansion of Access to Excellence did little to impress HEW officials, who denied Chicago's appeal for the ESAA funds because federal officials were not convinced by the arguments Chicago officials made at the hearing. They believed the arguments provided little evidence to refute the allegations made by HEW.[38] Although he expressed disappointment with the decision, Hannon said he would talk to federal officials to increase student desegregation.[39]

Hannon received a letter from OCR director David S. Tatel on June 5, 1979, in response to Hannon's request to see what compliance

looked like. Tatel's staff created guidelines with Chicago's demographics in mind, which were purposely vague so that it could further be
negotiated before a comprehensive plan was created. The guidelines
provided numerical definitions of desegregation and suggested techniques to desegregate. The letter ended with the following statement:
"The department recognizes that no desegregation plan provides for
every contingency and that exceptions from these criteria will be necessary. The burden is on the District, however, to justify any devia-
tion on the basis of educational and practical considerations."[40]

Hannon responded to Tatel's letter saying that he was delighted
that the guidelines were flexible, but still he continued to insist on
voluntary desegregation programs. The *Chicago Tribune* quoted
Hannon saying, "I would not consider anything mandatory. I think
we've been very consistent about that." He again reiterated that he
believed Access to Excellence was a great plan and said he would still
be willing to negotiate with the federal government.[41] Hannon and
OCR director Tatel met to negotiate a plan in order to avoid a court
suit. Tatel stipulated that mandatory desegregation needed to be a
part of the negotiations.[42]

As they negotiated, President Jimmy Carter forced HEW secretary
Joseph Califano to resign in July 1979. Carter was slipping in the
polls and was looking for ways to boost his ability to be reelected—
though Califano's dismissal came as a shock to many. Califano was
known as an outspoken and independent thinker.[43] According to the
New York Times, he was renowned for taking on controversial issues
such as school desegregation (he also took on the tobacco industry at
a time when it was not popular to do so).[44] Califano assumed that fric-
tion between him and White House staffers was one of the causes for
his dismissal. In his book, Califano writes that Ralph Nader equated
Carter's actions with "firing Mickey Mantle because he couldn't
get along with the bat boy." Texas representative Charles Wilson said
at the time, "They're cutting down the biggest trees and keeping
the monkeys."[45] Califano's supporters did not see Carter's logic in
removing an effective leader while retaining staff members who they
presumed were not of the same caliber as Califano.

Califano was replaced by Patricia Roberts Harris,[46] who became
the first black woman in a presidential cabinet. President Jimmy
Carter appointed her as secretary of the Department of Housing and
Urban Development (1977–1979) prior to her position as secretary
of HEW (1979–1981). She had also served in other federal government positions since 1960, including ambassador to Luxembourg,
and in various positions at Howard University, including dean of the

Law School. She was the first black female ambassador and dean of Howard's Law School.[47]

However, appointment of a black woman did not necessarily mean she was a strong ally for desegregation, and some initially questioned her priorities. Harris had an early political stumble as her comments to HEW officials that "political sensitivity should be considered in pursuing civil rights," caused controversy. Thomas Adkins of the NAACP declared, "We view with alarm, approaching outrage, any efforts by anyone, including Pat Harris to sidetrack, undermine, slow down, or in any way impede the efforts underway in school desegregation systems."[48] In the midst of President Carter's re-election, Harris's comments seemed to indicate that Carter's election was more important than civil rights enforcement. Yet, in a later interview with the *Chicago Tribune*, Harris appeared as dedicated as her predecessor to desegregation. She called the use of white flight as an argument against desegregation "unacceptable," since it was equivalent to asking the government to disregard civil rights laws.[49]

As the shake up in HEW occurred, Hannon released an Access to Excellence status report in July 1979. According to the report, desegregation by the board's 90–10 standards rose 10 percent as 231 of 582 schools met the standards. The number of segregated white schools was reduced from 53 to 18. Though Hannon intended to highlight the program's accomplishments, even with the program there were still 21.5 percent of schools with 90 percent or more white students and more than 50 percent of schools with less than 10 percent white students. Dismissing Hannon's report, the federal government questioned the success of Access to Excellence and continued to push Hannon and his staff to develop better plans.[50]

Amidst these disagreements, Chicago's new mayor made a controversial recommendation. In her desire to shake things up, Mayor Jane Byrne asked the entire Chicago Board of Education to turn in their resignations by August 1979. Byrne blamed the board for many of the school system's failures, and she wanted them all to resign so that she could reassess their performance. Byrne's request came at a time when HEW negotiation deadlines were approaching and Superintendent Hannon's contract was up for renegotiation. Board members simply ignored Byrne's request.[51]

Jane Byrne had risen quickly through the ranks of the Chicago Democratic Machine as Mayor Richard J. Daley continually promoted her. She began working with Head Start in 1965, and moved to the personnel department of the Chicago Commission on Urban Opportunity. In that position she witnessed the inner working of the

Democratic Machine's reward and punishment system as committee-men and precinct captains were rewarded with jobs or fired based on their abilities to deliver party votes. Daley met with Byrne periodically and soon promoted her to commissioner of the Department of Sales, Weights and Measures. She became the first woman Daley named to his "All Chicago" reelection committee in 1967. In 1972, Daley suggested Jane Byrne for the Resolutions Committee of the National Democratic Party. Three years later, he appointed her co-chair of the Democratic Central Committee of Cook County. While it was clear to everyone Daley was not sharing power, machine regulars resented her quick ascent and the fact that she had not paid enough dues.[52] Despite benefitting herself from Daley's machine, in the 1979 election, Byrne ran as an anti-machine reformer and won largely because of the vote of the black middle class. After her election, she quickly renewed ties with party regulars—but according to Daley's biographer Roger Biles, she desired independence and fired some department heads, clashed with city agencies, and quarreled with the press. Members of the press called her "Calamity Jane" and "Attila the Hen."[53]

Byrne's desire for independence and her request for the resignation of the Chicago Board of Education had little impact on school desegregation negotiations. HEW had given Hannon and the board until September 15, 1979, to create a school desegregation plan. As the deadline approached, HEW drafted its own plan for Chicago, which would reduce the percentage of whites to 60 percent or less at each school. The plan included clustering and pairing schools, and HEW considered it a feasibility study rather than a plan the city had to implement. HEW's proposed study called for the busing of 114,000 students around the city and would desegregate 60 percent of the city's schools.[54] However, while the intention was to provide examples of ways in which desegregation was possible in the city, the study still left many segregated black schools untouched. Though the feasibility study did not impact enough schools, Mayor Byrne thought it went too far. She called the federal government's plan impractical and expensive, and thought that neighborhood schools should be preserved.[55]

Latino leaders came out against the feasibility study as well because it did not include their input. They alleged that OCR had met and worked with representatives from the Urban League and Operation Push to create the feasibility study, but often missed meetings with representatives from the Latino community. An HEW official stated that the agency had met with Latinos concerning bilingual education.

Mary Gonzales, director of race relations for Ada S. McKinley Community Services stated, "I see large movements in Latino schools and very little movement in predominantly black schools…Both groups, black and white, are capable of using us for their own needs. We will not allow Latino children to be used as a buffer zone between white and black students."[56] She objected to the disproportionate use of Latinos to desegregate white schools. Mario Aranda, executive director of the Latino Institute, indicated that a plan not inclusive of the Latino community would not receive the support of his community. The implications of Gonzales and Aranda's statement are significant, as much of the desegregation in Chicago had been seen as a black/white issue—Latinos were largely invisible and remained left out of the process. However, with the growing population of Latinos in Chicago, their voices could no longer be ignored. By 1981, they would outnumber whites in the school system.

Latinos had been historically segregated in the Southwest, and like their black counterparts, had fought against school segregation for decades. Since 1925, desegregation court cases were filed in Texas, California, Arizona, and Colorado on behalf of Latinos. *Mendez v. Westminster* (1946) was a K-12 case which used the denial of Fourteenth Amendment rights as an argument. The NAACP had already used the Fourteenth Amendment in higher education cases, but *Mendez* predated *Brown v. Board of Education*, which was won using that same argument. The NAACP submitted a brief in support of the *Mendez* case.[57] Unfortunately, in other cases, Latinos had been used as pawns. In Houston, as elsewhere in the country, Mexican Americans were often legally considered white—and so Latinos were used to desegregate with blacks, leaving traditional white schools mostly untouched. Unlike the Houston situation, however, Latinos in Chicago were considered minorities and used to desegregate schools because of their close proximity to white schools.[58] Latino organizations such as ASPIRA and the Latino Institute, had long worked in Chicago to find compatibility between bilingual education and school desegregation. These groups wanted to make sure desegregation plans would be beneficial to Latinos.[59] They did not want their children used as pawns in desegregation plans.

Like Latino leaders and Mayor Byrne, Superintendent Hannon also disliked the study. He called the feasibility study unworkable. Hannon stated, "Would I recommend to the Board of Education that X number of children be taken on a ride eight to nine miles simply for the sake of exchanging numbers and making statistics work? The answer is no."[60] He further complained that the movement of children would be costly and that the government did not offer educational improvements. As far as Hannon was concerned, OCR was more concerned with racial balance than improving education. He was not alone in his thinking. Many blacks, whites, and Latinos wondered if the mere movement of students would mean quality education for those involved and questioned what it would mean for those students who would be left out because they would not be desegregated. When comparing the government's plan to Access to Excellence, Hannon touted the fact that Access did not leave students out. Since the government's plan left approximately 35 percent of students untouched, Hannon stated, "That could never be acceptable."[61]

Vernon Jarrett, a black columnist, wrote a September 9, 1979, editorial in the *Chicago Tribune* exposing the racism in Chicagoans' commentaries against busing. Jarrett ironically titled his article "Joseph Hannon: Resistance Fighter." He highlighted Hannon's outright defiance of the federal government. But more importantly, Jarrett demonstrated that busing had been a normal part of transporting students for years, causing speculation as to why there was so much opposition in this case. In 1976 to 1977, the National Center for Educational Statistics documented that 55.2 percent of all school children in America were bused. Of that number, about 3 percent were bused for the purpose of desegregation. Moreover, as many argued the high cost of busing, Jarrett responded, "Americans go to all sorts of extremes to enforce the law, regardless of cost. But this is not so when it comes to integration of schools." Jarrett used the high costs of prisons as a comparison for enforcing the law. Lastly, he stated, "Insistence that desegregation is not needed where there is a minimum of white students tells us something about the frame of mind of those who make such statements. Why must whites always be in the majority when desegregation is involved?"[62] Jarrett's words would not impact Hannon.

In response to the government's feasibility plan, Hannon revised Access to Excellence, incorporating some of the ideas from OCR. While the new plans were sent to OCR by their September 15 deadline, they were not officially approved by the Board of Education until September 19.[63] In Access to Excellence II, Hannon indicated that the Board of Education was not opposed to busing, but was more concerned about what was being offered at the school in which a child would be transported.[64] The new Access called for voluntary busing and increased the number of full-time desegregation programs, since the initial Access was made up of largely part-time programs. These plan additions were far less expansive than the

OCR plan, primarily because Hannon refused to carry out mandatory busing.[65]

Access to Excellence II was also another attempt to receive ESAA funds. HEW secretary Patricia Harris denied the city the funding, but said that they could reapply for the 1980 funding. The waiver was denied because the Chicago Board of Education had not approved the Access II prior to it being submitted, and Harris refused to give the city yet another extension for ESAA funding. Access II was still deficient because it had not dealt with racially segregated and overcrowded schools. Harris told David Tatel of OCR to notify the city that it had 30 days to prove that it was not in violation of Title VI.[66] In spite of the rejection of ESAA funds, Hannon was still confident that negotiations with HEW would go well.[67] Yet when Secretary Harris met with Hannon on September 21, 1979, she did not approve the city's desegregation plan. The Board of Education's approval of Access to Excellence II was still considered unacceptable, and it needed substantial revisions before the new deadline of October 17.[68] This deadline was to demonstrate the city was not in violation of Title VI.

As the board debated about how it would deal with HEW's demands, it renewed Hannon's contract for four years. His salary was raised from $56,000 to $82,500. Hannon set student achievement as one of the goals for his new term, and he set out to establish programs that would meet the educational needs of all students, including improved attendance and safety.[69] His reappointment and substantial raise showed the board's approval of his leadership on school desegregation.

On October 12, 1979, Hannon received a letter from Tatel asking the board to approve three criteria in order for negotiations to continue. These criteria included the development of a desegregation plan, which first met slightly revised numerical criteria. Second, OCR wanted a plan submitted to HEW by November 17 and open for community input. Finally, the revised plan would have to be submitted to HEW by December 17, 1979. These three points had to be agreed upon in order for negotiations to continue. If not, HEW would send the case to the Justice Department sooner than the December 17 deadline.[70]

Hannon took issue with the racial guidelines and the short period for plan revisions and community participation. He had the understanding that negotiations could be made in terms of racial percentages. In addressing the federal government's numerical guidelines, Hannon insisted that "The excessive stringency and impracticality of these standards are evidenced by the fact that 55 percent (152 of 275) of the schools 'desegregated' in OCR's feasibility study fail to meet OCR's own standards for desegregation."[71] Moreover, he stated in his response to Tatel's letter that one month for community participation in reviewing the plan and subsequent revision of the plan was quite inadequate. Hannon expressed dismay that his office and HEW/OCR staff had been meeting throughout the summer, reached agreement on a set of criteria, and now another set of criteria was developed that did not include agreed upon points. As far as he was concerned, Access to Excellence II was developed based on the agreed upon criteria. In a statement to the Board of Education, Hannon insisted that "The imposition of preconditions and arbitrary and unrealistic deadlines does not serve the cause of increased desegregation . . . We do not want to go to court, but if we must, we are prepared to argue our case before the judiciary."[72]

On October 17, 1979, the Board of Education voted against a motion by member Edgar Epps to develop a desegregation plan consistent with Tatel's letter. Instead they voted to send a defiant letter, written by Hannon, to Tatel.[73] Hannon and the board's insolence were seen as practical by one congressman interviewed by Stephen C. Halpern, author of *On the Limits of the Law*. According to the congressman, "Now if the school board officials know that at the end of the road OCR is simply going to ship its case to Justice it makes no sense for them to lay themselves bare and provide information which will then get fed over to Justice and be used against them should Justice litigate."[74] While the congressman may have seen defiance as strategic, board member Epps believed that the composition of the board caused opposition to desegregation: "The black board members and the liberal board members voted one way and the others, conservatives, voted the other way. And for everything having to do with desegregation, they [conservatives] had a majority. In other words, the conservatives blocked the majority of every important vote dealing with desegregation."[75]

While the board was deciding the fate of the desegregation plan, President Carter commented at a town meeting that it would be best that the courts handle the situation in Chicago. According to the *Chicago Sun-Times*, some community leaders viewed President Carter's response as "passing the buck." Leon Finney of The Woodlawn Organization, a Saul Alinksy styled, community empowerment organization, said, "For Carter to suggest letting the federal courts decide is only to delay to a time when there are fewer whites than there are now in the schools." James Compton of the Chicago Urban League said President Carter's statement was "clear evidence of abdication of any real leadership on his part." Others agreed with President Carter that a court fight would be a positive move. Robert L. Lucas of the Kenwood Oakland Community Organization thought a court fight would be best since negotiations had stalled.[76]

On October 18, 1979, HEW secretary Harris indicated at a press conference that Chicago's refusal to accept HEW's guidelines for desegregation would be the basis for her to send the case to the Justice Department for litigation. In reviewing the Chicago case, she listed the deadlines the Board of Education missed. The board had until October 17 to submit evidence to rebut "the presumption that it is in noncompliance with Title VI of the Civil Rights Act of 1964." However, the board had submitted a weak plan in September that "contained inadequate provisions for insuring that desegregation goals would be met and insufficient detail to determine the amount of desegregation that would be accomplished." In addition, Harris disagreed with the voluntary proposals preferred by the board. She countered that, "Compliance cannot be secured by voluntary means, and I cannot in good conscience agree to further delay in the guise of negotiation." She further stated that, the nation "has made great progress in desegregating our schools" since the 1954 Supreme Court decision outlawing "separate but equal." "But, as evidenced in Chicago, separate but equal—indeed separate but unequal—schools still exist."[77] She gave the board a 10-day waiting period as required by the Civil Rights Act.

Harris made her decision based on the defiant letter from Superintendent Hannon, which stated, "The Board of Education of the City of Chicago is not and has never been adjudged a dual system and has not engaged in de jure discrimination...Accordingly, any charge that the Board of Education of the City of Chicago has in any way violated...the Civil Rights Act of 1964...is specifically denied."[78] When Harris ruled that Chicago schools were in violation of desegregation mandates, Hannon responded that, "I think the federal government...feels...that negotiation is 'sit down and do what we tell you to do and get into line.' I think we're saying something different."[79] Hannon would not allow the federal government to dictate how desegregation would occur without his view of how negotiations should take place.

As one of his last acts as director of OCR, Tatel sent a letter to Hannon on October 18, informing him that the case would be turned over to the Justice Department. Tatel's letter cited the requirements of *Brown v. Califano* (1978), which stipulated that when a district is denied ESAA, the district has 30 days to rebut the accusations of noncompliance. The district was given 30 days and only provided Superintendent Hannon's letter to Secretary Harris, which was a mere denial rather than an evidentiary rebuttal. In his letter, Tatel stated, "I have determined that the Chicago Public School District is in violation of Title VI...as a result of its creation and maintenance of racially segregated and overcrowded schools." He had reached this conclusion based on "the district's failure to adopt and implement a legally acceptable desegregation plan."[80] Although HEW could commence an administrative hearing to terminate funding as it had done with faculty desegregation, the 1978 Eagleton–Biden Amendment prevented HEW from requiring transportation of students beyond the schools closest to their homes. The Chicago case would require transportation, and consequently a HEW administrative hearing would be ineffective in establishing desegregation. The Department of Justice was not limited by this amendment.[81] The Eagleton–Biden Amendment to Title VI of the Civil Rights Act was considered by Stephen C. Harpern to be "the death knell for Title VI in elementary and secondary education because it eliminated the enforcement mechanism that made Title VI effective: the termination of funds after administrative hearings."[82] HEW officially turned the case over to the Justice Department on October 29, 1979. Tatel resigned two days later.[83]

Drew S. Days III, assistant attorney general of the Department of Justice and head of the Civil Rights Division also released a statement on October 18 stating that upon receipt of the referral from HEW, "the Civil Rights Division will review the matter promptly and make a recommendation to Attorney General Benjamin R. Civiletti as to appropriate action." Days continued, "The Justice Department and all others associated with the matter have a responsibility to insure the system is operated in conformity with the Constitution and federal law."[84]

FINANCIAL PROBLEMS AND LEADERSHIP CHANGES

Chicago was in the midst of deep financial problems as the case was turned over to the Justice Department. The escalating fiscal problems led to unforeseen changes in school leadership, which would eventually make Justice Department negotiations with the new school leadership much easier. In late November 1979, Superintendent Hannon resigned from his position, to the shock of board members. Board member Epps remembers, "Superintendent Hannon walked into a board meeting one day and surprised us all by turning in his resignation. And only after he turned in his resignation did we discover that we had the budget crisis."[85] Board member Margaret Wild was "floored and flabbergasted" by Hannon's resignation.[86] The board voted 9–1 not to accept his resignation,[87] but Hannon would not return, continually giving vague reasons for his resignation. There was speculation that Mayor Byrne was upset with him as a result of the financial crisis. Soon after Hannon quit, others fled as well. Board of Education president John D. Carey resigned, as well as two financial officers for the school system.[88]

The school system had been financially insecure since Superintendent James Redmond's administration. When the Chicago Teachers Union bargained for a raise in 1967, Mayor Daley stepped in and negotiated a $500 a year raise with funds the school system did not have. Daley promised to convince the Illinois State Legislature to increase school funding, but was unsuccessful, leaving the school system in deficit spending.[89] To add to the financial problems, the Chicago schools had lost nearly 100,000 students as their enrollment dropped steadily from its height at 573,000 in 1971 to 477,000 in 1979. Buildings were being under-utilized, and the superintendent had difficulty trying to close schools as parents, representative aldermen, and school employees protested closures. Also, the number of custodians could not be reduced, as their contract was based on the square footage of the buildings—not student enrollment. Other financial difficulties resulted from unfunded federal and state mandates. Even though HEW had negotiated teacher desegregation and costly bilingual education programs, schools did not receive sufficient funding because HEW added student desegregation as a requirement before Chicago schools could be eligible for ESAA funds. Programs for disabled children were also a federal mandate that lacked commensurate funding. Additionally, Hannon's Access to Excellence program had added to the continued employment of 25,000 teachers—despite drops in student enrollment. Furthermore, Chicago had a central office with 3000 employees, a Board of Education radio station, and a certification office separate from the state.[90] With increased spending on employees, coupled with the loss of students and unfunded mandates, the district struggled to pay for its expenses.

According to journalist Casey Banas, with the use of shady accounting schemes, the school system managed to "rob Peter to pay Paul" for a number of years until it became clear that the funding was unavailable. Chicago lost millions of dollars in revenues since Cook County could not collect property taxes from businesses, and Mayor Daley had been opposed to raising additional property taxes on individuals. Therefore, school accountants would borrow money from different pots and try to repay them once other revenues came in—in the hopes that by the time they were audited, the money would be back in place.[91] Epps recalled, "We found out that the accountant had not been telling us the whole picture. They had been putting stuff in an appendix and those of us who were not accountants didn't read that appendix. We didn't know what they had been hiding. So it came as a big surprise, not only were we broke, but our bond rating was going down the toilet."[92]

The board had a traditional practice of selling municipal bonds twice a year that would tie them over until the next state revenues came. In 1979, however, the borrowing had reached such an unsecure level that school officials were selling bonds just to pay for the bonds they had already sold as well as to pay financial obligations like employee pay. Then the board received the lowest rating from Moody's Investors Service as a result of this unstable practice and no one would buy the bonds. Hannon had met with the Mayor Byrne a couple days after Moody lowered the rating to ask her for loan guaranteed with city assets, but Mayor Byrne refused. State senator Arthur Berman acknowledged that "During all of those years of Daley's tenure, the bond rating agencies, S&P, Moody's, never really dug into the practices of the school system. As long as he was around, things got by. He passed away, [so] the rating houses blew the whistle."[93] Byrne did not possess the same clout as her predecessor. The Democratic machine could no longer shield the school financial officer's shady accounting practices.

On January 3, 1980, Governor James (Jim) R. Thompson called around 40 officials from the state, city, school board, bankers, and unions to the governor's mansion and held them for three days until a bargain could be struck. Governor Thompson, a Republican, had been a US attorney general for the Northern District of Illinois from 1971 to 1975, prior to being elected the thirty-ninth governor of Illinois in 1976. He would become the state's longest serving governor, serving for 14 consecutive years (1976–1990).[94] In the governor-initiated negotiations, the board agreed to cut $60 million in expenditures in 1979–1980 and $160 million in 1980–1981; this included the layoff of 3,000 workers. The Chicago School Financial Authority was created by the state legislature to handle the school district's finances. The city, state, and union agreed to raise $125 million, and the new financial authority would raise an additional $500 million. The legislature also called for the resignation of all Chicago Board of Education members by April 30, 1980. Mayor Byrne had finally gotten her wish. As journalist Casey Banas asserted, downstate Illinois politicians, annoyed with bailing out the city's schools, had taken a rare but strong swipe at a Chicago governing board.[95] The entire board was let go even though most did not have knowledge of the shady financial dealings.[96]

The layoffs resulting from the governor's negotiations led to a Chicago teachers' strike beginning January 28, 1980. Also, Chicago Public School teachers had missed three pay checks in a row because of the financial crisis. They also went on strike because they believed that teachers were unfairly targeted as other staff, including custodians and administrators, would not be dismissed in the same proportions. Teachers were given their missed pay after one week but continued to strike for a total of ten days in protest of the layoff of thousands of workers. Mayor Byrne called the union and the school board officials to her office and negotiated the reinstatement of 504 jobs, but 2,496 were still lost. The board also agreed to pay striking teachers for nine of the ten missed days and cut costs from other areas. The board soon met its obligation of reducing the $60 million deficit.[97]

To further complicate Chicago's financial problems, the Supreme Court had recently ruled that New York City could not recuperate millions of dollars in ESAA funds because the schools—intentional or not—practiced teacher segregation. According to Justice Harry A. Blackman, "To treat as ineligible [for ESAA funds] only an applicant [school district] with a past or conscious present intent to perpetuate racial isolation would defeat the stated objectives of ending de facto, as well as de jure segregation." In other words, school districts that were not desegregating could not be rewarded funds established for desegregation. The court ruling could also apply to Chicago since the city had also lost millions in potential funding. Consequently, Chicago would not be able to regain ESAA funding it had missed out on in the past as a result of teacher and student segregation and inadequate bilingual education programs.[98]

Angeline Caruso became the interim superintendent replacing Hannon. Caruso had been a part of the school system for 35 years and had served as the district's curriculum expert. Still, her appointment caused some controversy among black leaders, as she was picked instead of Deputy Superintendent Manford Byrd, her superior.[99] This was the second time Byrd had been passed over.

JUSTICE DEPARTMENT READY FOR ACTION

The Justice Department had been kept abreast of HEW's dealings with Chicago since May 1978. Title IV of the 1964 Civil Rights

Act gave the Justice Department the authority to file suit to desegregate public schools. Assistant Attorney General Drew Days sent a memorandum to his superior, Attorney General Benjamin Civiletti, a few days prior to HEW secretary Harris's announcement that the case would be turned over to the Justice Department. The memorandum briefed Civiletti about the situation in Chicago, and the strong grounds the Justice Department had for a case. According the memo, Days acknowledged that, "the Eagleton–Biden Amendment's threat to HEW's enforcement power provided the impetus for close interagency cooperation." He had also begun to lay out his strategy for a "meaningful" remedy within the district. However, Days indicated that he did not want to sue for a metropolitan remedy right away, writing, "We believe there is substantial evidence of state involvement in racially discriminatory housing practices which have contributed greatly to city-suburban residential segregation."[100] Days wanted to confront desegregation in the Chicago Public Schools first, before gathering evidence for metropolitan violations.

The memo continued that the attorney general could coordinate a federal task force to "develop concrete proposals to give minority residents of Chicago better access to suburban jobs, homes and schools and to attract white students to the central city" based on Executive Order 11764.[101] Days believed "that the Chicago school situation provides a timely and appropriate opportunity for the Federal Government to attempt, for the first time, a coordinated approach to the variety of problems posed by the racial segregation in large urban districts." He recognized the difficulty of accomplishing Chicago desegregation and wanted to involve "various government agencies to attack the racial isolation which makes the traditional methods less workable in large urban areas."[102]

Finally, Days concluded, "I believe that it is critically important for the Justice Department to act promptly…to reinforce not only HEW's, but this entire Administration's commitment to evenhanded enforcement of prohibitions against segregation in public education."[103] Days's memo indicated his personal level of commitment to ending discrimination not only in schools, but also in housing, transportation, and employment. He called for a coordinated agency effort and urged that the Justice Department should act quickly. However, it was unlikely that government departments would work together to end discrimination in all areas of life for inner city blacks, as other departments may not have the same commitment nor political will it would take for such an ambitious effort. Furthermore, many citizens did not support continued federal meddling with local affairs.

Moreover, the political tide of the country had begun to shift away from policies that would further assist blacks. According to historian William C. Berman, "Intense social, cultural, and racial conflicts moved American presidential politics to the populist right after the late sixties." The civil rights agenda of the Democratic Party caused so many white southerners to move to the Republican Party that Georgian Jimmy Carter "could not win back [the southern] white majority in 1976."[104]

The Justice Department sent a report critical of the Chicago Board of Education to school officials announcing that they would pursue a lawsuit in 30 days if the Chicago school system did not offer an acceptable school desegregation plan by December 1979. A *Chicago Sun Times* writer believed the Justice Department report was more critical than the HEW Appendix Chicago received in April. The Justice Department wanted a plan that would reduce the percentage of whites to 50 in each school and would provide mandatory back up provisions.[105]

On April 21, 1980, Days wrote Interim Superintendent Caruso to let her know that their investigation indicated that the board had unlawfully segregated students on the basis of race.[106] Days stated that the Justice Department would like to negotiate with the city and hammer out a plan by early summer. According to Days, desegregation would have to be citywide and be approved by a federal judge in the form of a consent decree. The timing of the letter was important as the school board would soon be replaced and some of the financial volatility had simmered. That same month, Days also wrote the School Finance Authority chairman Jerome Van Gorkom to inform him that the school's financial woes would not be an excuse to prolong segregation. Days wrote, "We are obliged to...insure that nothing is done in the name of economy that will be in violation of the civil rights law."[107]

A few months after Days's letter, a new Chicago Board of Education was appointed. Politics surrounded the entire process of selecting board members, as the Chicago Board of Education was not an elected body, but instead appointed by the mayor. Progressive era changes to boards of education, which replaced appointed boards with elected ones in order to keep politicians from appointing their cronies, had apparently bypassed Chicago.[108] Still, the selection process that had been in place during Mayor Daley's administration had been altered. Before, representatives from various civic groups provided the mayor with a slate of names from which to choose. But the newly elected Mayor Byrne did not agree with that process. Instead she asked an interracial business group called Chicago United to choose the board candidates.[109] Martha Jantho (who would become one of the board members) had been part of the League of Women's Voters—one of the civic organizations that previously participated in the board member selection process, and which still kept watch over Byrne's new process. She revealed that her name had been tossed around but she was at first unwilling to serve. It was not until she attended a meeting with the "Bogan Broads" (they gained their name from leading Bogan High School protests and their tendency to disrupt Board meetings with heckling) that she changed her mind. According to Jantho, one of the Bogan Broads announced at a meeting that she was wanted to be on the Board of Education.

> And I looked at my friend from South Shore...and I said, "Okay, I can't be any worse than she is. You can go start putting my name in." And so my name went in. I had no clue how political this thing was. I thought you were trying to help kids. People [and] organizations took it upon themselves to write letters of recommendation. And when the list was published before it was officially announced, I was an alternate...Harriet O'Donnell...was one of the people who was going to become a board member. At this point in time, the firemen were on strike. Harriet's husband was a fireman. Harriet gave a very frank open interview to a reporter of the *Chicago Sun-Times*. Not a word, not a word. But when the list was officially promulgated from the mayor's office, Harriet was gone. I was in. That's what happened.[110]

O'Donnell's vocal and public opposition to Mayor Byrne caused her to lose the spot on the Board of Education. O'Donnell had been a part of the City-Wide Advisory Committee in the 1970s that created the desegregation plan Hannon changed to Access to Excellence.

Joyce Hughes also recalled her appointment to the board as a political event. She believed that board member Rev. Kenneth Smith had suggested her name. She was acquainted with him as a member of the National Board of the Urban League. Hughes received a call from Mayor Byrne while attending a bank board meeting in Minneapolis, and was asked to be a board member. Hughes remembered,

> I said to her at the time, "Well I have to think about it. I'll have to call my dean [at Northwestern University], and I'll have to get back to you." But she said, "I have to have a response today 'cause it's for the 6:00 news." That's the point in which I realized how much the news dictates when politicians want to do things. This was probably around 3:00 in the afternoon. And she said, "Well I have to know

right now." And I said, "Well, first of all, I have to call my dean and find out whether or not I can do it. I just can't have you go on the news." But I thought about it and decided I would do it. Now if you asked me why I decided to do it, I think I probably had the idea that it was important to impact education. But obviously I was new, relatively new to Chicago at the time...So I obviously didn't know a lot about the lay of the land.[111]

While Jantho and Hughes were approached very differently, they were both introduced immediately to the politics of the process.

The new Board of Education comprised five blacks, including Rev. Smith, the only person from the last board. Mayor Byrne had recently appointed him prior to the reconstitution of the board. There were originally four whites; but one, Thomas Ayres, had to resign because he did not live in the city. Ayers's short stint on the board led to controversy as the mayor and Chicago United staff members, instrumental in nominating the board, wanted Ayers to serve as board president. However, the board majority voted for Rev. Kenneth Smith. Ayers's residency was challenged in court by black community activist Lu Palmer. Pressure from the court challenge and demonstrations against him led Ayers resign after 60 days.[112] He was replaced with a Latino nominee, resulting in a racial makeup of five blacks, three whites, and three Latinos on the board.[113] With a new Board of Education and a new superintendent, much of the opposition to school desegregation had been replaced. The leadership restructuring caused by the financial crisis made it easier to negotiate with the Justice Department in order to create a consent decree. The new board was more receptive to mandatory back up provisions if voluntary desegregation did not work.

On June 11, 1980, the Board of Education authorized its Committee on Student Desegregation to negotiate with the Justice Department. Negotiations occurred between the committee, the Justice Department, and the newly created US Department of Education.[114] The Justice Department and the Department of Education rejected Chicago's denial of charges of intentional student segregation. Because of continued student segregation and declining faculty desegregation, the Department of Education withheld $33 million in ESAA funding Chicago had requested on June 13.[115] Part of the decline in faculty desegregation was due to the school system's $60 million reduction in funds, which eliminated teaching positions. The government, however, contended that there were 106 schools out of compliance even prior to the teacher layoffs.[116] In spite of its findings, Justice Department officials decided to negotiate with Chicago school officials.

CONSENT DECREE

After months of closed-door negotiations, on September 24, 1980, the Justice Department officially filed a lawsuit against the Chicago Board of Education. On that same day, a 20-page consent decree was also approved.[117] The case, *United States v. Chicago Board of Education*, was handled by Judge Milton Shadur. The Justice Department's Drew Days was quoted in the *Chicago Tribune* recognizing Chicago's accomplishment. "Chicago has become the first major school district to see that the way to resolve this matter is not by protracted litigation."[118] The suit was filed so that the negotiations for the consent decree could remain under court order. The consent decree began, "The United States has filed a complaint alleging that the Board of Education of the City of Chicago has engaged in acts of discrimination in the assignment of students and otherwise, in violation of the federal law." While the city was alleged to have engaged in discrimination, the board did not have to admit or deny guilt, but instead, "recognize[d]...that the Chicago public school system is characterized by substantial racial isolation of students," and that the isolation is "educationally disadvantageous to all students."[119]

The consent decree called for a system-wide remedy with the basic objectives of desegregating the schools to "the greatest practicable number of stably desegregated schools," compensatory funding for programs in schools that could not be desegregated, and the participation of all grade levels except kindergarten. The board had the discretion in developing the plan and there were no racial numerical guidelines presented.[120] The agreement insisted on provisions to make sure bilingual education was considered in the plan so that those students in the program would not be left segregated or left without the programs they needed. In order to facilitate the process, the consent decree considered community involvement essential as well as staff training. The timeline called for a completed plan by March 11, 1981, and implementation of the program for the 1981–1982 school year.[121]

The consent decree also stated that the Justice Department would look into the financial responsibility of the State of Illinois and would examine "the extent to which inter-district [metropolitan] remedies for segregative conditions in schools in the Chicago school district may be appropriate." The Justice Department wanted to find out the role state government agencies and suburban governments "may have contributed to the segregation of the races in the Chicago [area] by racially discriminatory use of state or federal housing laws or programs of state or local land use control laws."[122] Faculty desegregation was another area of concern. By November 1, 1981, full-time teachers in each school had to be within 15 percent of their racial make up in the system.[123]

The *Chicago Sun-Times* considered the consent decree a "'weak' pact," which the defunct HEW had previously refused, but the newly created Department of Education accepted. The *Chicago Tribune* reported desegregation proponent Gary Orfield's take on the consent decree. Orfield thought that since the agreement did not have racial guidelines, the federal government may have had confidence in the new Board of Education. But he warned that if the Board of Education did not meet its obligation, Judge Shadur could order a plan implementation.[124] The NAACP was disappointed with the deal and wanted to be involved in further negotiations. Thomas I. Atkins, the NAACP's general counsel, stated, "I am at an absolute loss for words to describe how distressed we are…We're the ones who got the Justice Department involved in the first place."[125] Well aware of previous negotiations with the Chicago Board of Education, the NAACP did not believe that the consent decree would yield meaningful desegregation.

Secretary of Education Shirley M. Hufstedler formed an interdepartmental committee to assist the Board of Education with the development and creation of a desegregation plan. Secretary Hufstedler had served as a lawyer, county and state judge in California, and eventually a judge on the US federal appeals court prior to Jimmy Carter naming her the first secretary of the newly formed Department of Education.[126] Hufstedler indicated, "I am extremely pleased that the Chicago Board of Education has pledged its commitment to a viable solution through a voluntary agreement. The committee I have named today will provide as much support and assistance as possible to help the Board develop and carry out the very complex task of desegregating its schools."[127] The committee would also be responsible for identifying Department of Education funds available to assist with the desegregation planning and implementation and would monitor the development of the plan for the secretary.

Chicago was given a $422,800 planning grant[128] from the Department of Education to help implement its planning, hire an expert consultant and five full-time planning staff, as well as conduct community involvement activities and in-service training for staff.

The first item on the timeline of the consent decree was the hiring of a consultant by October 15, 1980. Michigan State University's dean of the College of Urban Development was hired for the job. Robert L. Green, a black man, had served for a year as the education director for the Southern Christian Leadership Conference and as an education consultant to the NAACP's legal staff. Green had assisted in school desegregation in Memphis, Detroit, Dayton, St. Louis, and Seattle. He indicated that he took the job because he sensed the seriousness of the Chicago Board of Education to create a workable desegregation plan. However, he insisted that his "concern is what youngsters will be faced with [academically] when they get off that bus." This was an issue he believed parents had regardless of race, and it extended beyond desegregation to quality education.[129]

BUILDING CONSENSUS, HIRING A SUPERINTENDENT, AND CHICAGO-STYLE POLITICS

Once all of the people and committees were in place, Chicago school officials had the daunting task of gathering community input and creating a desegregation plan. As stipulated by the consent decree, the Board of Education held eight hearings for public input on the school desegregation plan and to build consensus.[130] The first hearing, held at Whitney Young High School on December 10, 1980, allowed board members and staff to explain the consent decree and invited representatives of 95 groups to speak. The other seven hearings were open to anyone to speak and occurred between December 15, 1980, and January 8, 1981, at high schools in different communities across the city. In the first hearing, invited speakers suggested that the hearings alone were not adequate and wanted a citywide advisory committee to help with the development of the plan. The rest of the hearings revealed discontent with busing from all communities. Some whites threatened to leave the system and the city, as well as protest any forced busing that occurred. Several Latinos who spoke at the hearings focused their concerns on education rather than desegregation. They too were opposed to busing. A number of black parents were concerned that their children would have to bear the burden of busing and asked that some of the magnet schools and high quality programs be placed in their neighborhoods. Other parents supported busing.[131] Desegregation consultant Robert Green who attended the hearings remarked that in Chicago, unlike other cities, many blacks were opposed to busing. He was, however, impressed that most of the speakers at the hearings wanted quality education.[132] He thought the opportunity to create such a plan could help to improve the education for students in the entire system.

Board member Joyce Hughes had been warned about attending meetings in certain areas since she was viewed as the "personification of desegregation." The warnings went far beyond the threat of protest as desegregation efforts moved forward. Personal threats were also made against her, but her response was, "no I have to go. Because when I think about what black people went through years before me, you can't run away." If she had stayed away, she believed it would have indicated that "I'm afraid of you guys…I had to go." At one of the meetings held in 1981 on Chicago's Southwest Side[133] in a school auditorium, board members Hughes and Jantho recalled the tension they felt. They noticed that someone was roaming around in the closed off balcony—and so Hughes summoned one of the police officers to inform him of the suspicious person. It turned out to be a plain-clothed police officer securing the balcony. Apparently, the police were also quite aware of the danger posed to Hughes and other board members. At the end of the meeting, a picture of Hughes with an arrow through her head was found in one of the seats. Once she saw the drawing, Hughes admitted that "Well, if they had shown me that drawing before, I might have changed my mind" about attending the meeting.[134]

Along with the hearings, the Chicago Board of Education approved the creation of two advisory panels as another avenue to build consensus. The first panel was comprised of 29 parents and students leaders. The second panel had 40 members representative of community organizations and businesses. The task of the panels would be to offer their insight on the desegregation proposals before the board approved them.[135] Unfortunately, the advisory committees were sounding boards and were not used as effectively as the City-Wide Advisory Committee just a few years prior.[136] A third aspect consisted of two days of public hearings to discuss the school desegregation plan. The Bogan Broads were the most outspoken at these meetings. Most of the speakers at the hearings were against the draft of the plan.[137]

As the hearings got underway, Drew Days resigned from the Justice Department to take a position at Yale Law School. Days regretted not being able to see the Chicago case to fruition. He revealed that he "saw Chicago all along as the best opportunity we'll see in a long time to demonstrate that school desegregation can be made to work…And it can be made to work by involving many more agencies in the process than has ever been true in the past."[138] The Justice Department was seeking cooperation of various agencies, including the Departments of Education, Housing and Urban Development, and Transportation to provide funding to the city "to attack bias in housing, transportation and other areas that entrench school segregation."[139]

As Days departed his position and in the midst of trying to create a desegregation plan, the Chicago Board of Education also had to hire a new superintendent. The process was filled with controversy, protests, and missteps. Some black and Latino community leaders and students pressed for Deputy Superintendent Manford Byrd to become the superintendent, as Byrd had been passed over for the position twice before. The board, which now had five black members, insisted on a black superintendent—but white and Latino board members did not want Byrd. They preferred an outsider. According to board member Hughes, "I'm not sure how we arrived at this, but it was clear that the new superintendent was going to be black. Love was black; so was Manford Byrd. So it wasn't really race. It was whether you were going to bring an outsider in to run the schools or someone who'd been in the system for a long time like Manford Byrd had been."[140]

Although they were not the majority, Latinos on the Board could tip the balance of power in any direction they chose if they voted as a united group. In choosing a new superintendent, they sometimes voted with whites against the wishes of black board members.[141] Mayor Byrne had apparently calculated correctly in her choice of board members, as the majority minority board did not mean majority power for minorities on the board. According to board member Jantho, Latino board members wanted to unite the different Latino nationalities (Mexican, Puerto Rican, and Cuban) so that they would not exacerbate the tensions between the groups. Sociologist Felix M. Padilla asserts that Mexican and Puerto Rican groups in Chicago created a Latino ethnic identity as a strategic response to needs of the group.[142] Latinos on the board were aware of the importance of a Latino identity and the strength it could produce. In the case of desegregation, many Latinos preferred quality education over school desegregation and many resented being used as pawns in school desegregation issues. Latino board members working together could help strengthen bilingual education and make sure desegregation worked in the best interest of Latino students.

Hughes recognized certain issues, including the selection of superintendent, were more complicated than simply Latinos siding with whites. For example, she pointed out that black board member Michael Smith was against busing. "Obviously here was a black man very concerned about the education of black children. So it was not necessarily no concern about black children verses concern. It was really how best to accomplish it. I remember the most heated discussions were with Michael because of his total disdain for any form of busing. Again I looked at it from the stand point of how you are going to ensure that students get the education they need."[143] Smith did not remain on the board long enough to dictate what would become of the school desegregation plan. However, Hughes's point was that it wasn't simply an issue of Latinos against blacks, but rather differences in ideas about who would be the next superintendent and how best to desegregate students. Some of these issues just happened to fall along racial/ethnic lines.

Meanwhile, Jesse Jackson of Operation Push mobilized community members and students. They disrupted board meetings, picketed in front of board members' homes demanding that Byrd be the next superintendent. But the board refused to cave in to public protest and ignored the pickets. The board first attempted to persuade Detroit's superintendent Arthur Jefferson to take the job, but he did not want to leave his position in Detroit. Then board members voted to offer the job to Frederick Holliday, superintendent in York, Pennsylvania, who Jantho believed would make a great superintendent, but he did not take the chance. With pressure from Jesse Jackson, and a lack of support from black board members, Holliday turned down the job. The third candidate offered the job was Ruth Love, the superintendent of Oakland, California.[144] Love accepted the position with a $120,000 salary. She also negotiated to gain back input in the school financial dealings that had been stripped from the superintendent position with the creation of the School Financial Authority. She was given permission to hire a business advisor who would be a liaison with the school chief financial officer. Love also wanted to have a say in the desegregation plan. This became necessary because negotiations with the Justice Department had effectively bypassed the superintendent position. In the past, the superintendent led the desegregation efforts. The board gave her an opportunity to make changes and approve the plan before the board gave its approval. Finally, Love negotiated hiring her own chief deputy superintendent.[145] In spite of the negotiations, the first black superintendent did not have the power of past superintendents. The superintendent position was stripped of handling the budget[146] and did not play a central role in school desegregation. In the entire process, both Byrd and Caruso were overlooked for the chief job, and so Love's appointment still upset some black leaders.[147]

In a surprising move in February 1981, Mayor Byrne decided not to reappoint two black board members. She said she would replace all the board members except Raul Villalobos. The *Chicago Sun-Times* reported that it was because they disagreed with her choice for school board president. Villalobos had not served a full term and was not on the board when the board selected Rev. Smith as board president instead of Ayres who left the board due to residency issues. Byrne nominated two white women to replace Michael Scott and Leon Davis: Betty Bonow, an anti-busing advocate, and Rose Mary Janus, a school aid and president of a local school council. In the past, Bonow had attended a Boston convention of the National Association of Neighborhood Schools. Davis thought he was let go because Byrne was attempting to garner votes of the city's whites for the next election, as anti-busing whites had been upset with the mayor for not selecting anyone on the board who represented their views. Byrne insisted that she was simply observing the commitment to rotate board members as their terms expired in order to get representatives from all areas of the city. (The board terms were staggered with three one-year terms, and pairs of two, three, four, and five-year terms.)[148] The *Chicago Tribune* reported that Byrne wanted to follow a pledge made to the state legislature. However, State Senator Richard Newhouse indicated that the intent was for a fresh start with the old board that had been replaced April 30, 1980. Byrne had political motives for her Board of Education moves. She was calculating the support she needed to win the next election. Since black votes were already waning, she wanted to secure the votes of white ethnics. Villalobos was retained to keep the Latino vote. Newspaper analysts questioned whether her decisions would work.[149] In spite of opposition to Byrne's political moves, her two nominees were appointed by the City Council. Both confirmed that they were against busing.[150]

*   *   *

The disposition of the President Carter, the firings, and resignations of key officials from federal agencies responsible for enforcing desegregation policies complicated and transformed desegregation policy articulation and implementation. Demographic transformations such as significant increases in the Latino population and significant decreases in the white population underscored the impact that broader environmental factors had on policy implementation.

In spite of the changes in federal agency leadership and city demographics, the federal government's involvement with Chicago schools led to progress that the State of Illinois was unable to meet. The timeliness of the schools financial upheaval led to the resignation of Superintendent Hannon and the reconstitution of the Board of Education. While such drastic changes in school leadership may be devastating because of a lack of institutional memory and a lack of continuity, it was clear in the situation in Chicago that this was a necessary change both for the schools' financial health and for the federal government's school desegregation negotiations with the city. The recalcitrant board and superintendent had ignored the demands of OCR. The Justice Department was able to make less stringent demands on the new Board of Education with the consent decree that would have been extremely ineffective with the old board and superintendent.

CHAPTER 5

Chicago Desegregates Predominantly White Schools

The consent decree was negotiated with the Justice Department under Jimmy Carter's administration. However, by the time Chicago's school officials began to develop their desegregation plan, the national political winds had blown to the right. As Ronald Reagan's administration took over, the Justice Department's politics also shifted. The shifting political climate made it easier for the Justice Department to approve the city's desegregation plans because the city would not be held to the same Carter administration standards for desegregation.

The right turn in American politics began in the late 1960s and early 1970s as conservatives claimed the civil rights policies had gone too far. They expressed concern that the meaning of civil rights had gone from the rights of individuals to the rights of groups. Since the rights of individual whites were trumped for the rights of blacks as a group some viewed affirmative action as reverse discrimination. President Ronald Reagan shared this sentiment, and told the American Bar Association, "The promise in the Declaration of Independence, that we are endowed by our creator with certain inalienable rights, was meant for all of us. It was not meant to be limited or perverted by special privilege, or by double standards that favor one group over another."[1]

Historian Raymond Walters argues that Assistant Attorney General William Bradford Reynolds, appointed by Reagan to head the Justice Department's Civil Rights Division, was the purveyor of Reagan's policies. Reynolds was a direct descendent of Puritan Governor William Bradford and came from a well-to-do family. He attended private schools, including the prestigious Phillips Andover Academy, Yale University, and Vanderbilt University School of Law. Reynolds had worked for a prominent New York law firm and for the solicitor general of the United States where he tried cases before the Supreme Court. He was also a partner at a Washington firm. In his appointment as assistant attorney general, he was in a position to change the meaning of civil rights, and his contacts in the position led him to influence judicial nominations.[2] Reynolds's agenda for civil rights policy was as follows: "I think we should bring the behavior of the government on all levels into line with the idea of according equal opportunity for all individuals without regard to race, color, or ethnic background. In my view this means that we should remove whatever kinds of race- or gender-conscious remedies and techniques that exist in the regulatory framework, to ensure that the remedies that are put in place are sensitive to the non-discrimination mandate that is in the laws."[3] In terms of school desegregation, Reynolds asserted, "The Supreme Court has told us, I don't know how many times that there is nothing wrong with a school that is racially imbalanced. That's not unconstitutional at all. It's only unconstitutional when that's a forced situation because the school board has basically put in place, intentionally, certain practices and procedures that preclude children from going to one school because of their race."[4]

Some conservatives viewed race- and gender-based policies as a threat to white male privilege because civil rights policies meant that whites would have to compete with everyone. As provocative as the conservative arguments were, they typically disregarded the systematic discrimination that people of color and women have faced in spite of laws that have appeared just. What a number of policy makers and activists found was that having the right laws in place was an important first step to end discrimination—but it was only a first step. Prior to the Civil Rights Movement, southern blacks who migrated to the North in search of jobs and better opportunities often found the laws alone were not enough to end racial discrimination. As they migrated, many faced housing and job discrimination. Since they were racially contained in certain neighborhoods, they faced increasingly segregated schools. Consequently, the federal government set up policies such as affirmative action and passed and enforced laws such as the Civil Rights Act to further correct past discrimination.[5]

The Justice Department under Carter had operated under the assumption that these types of policies were necessary, regardless of the administration's ability to effectively enforce them. Drew Days had certainly set the tone for equal educational opportunity in Chicago by advancing ambitious strategies in the consent decree, including federal interagency cooperation, and state liability and interdistrict investigations. The Reynolds-led Justice Department had a different vision, though, and this was the Justice Department with which Chicago school officials would negotiate.

As the presidential administrations shifted, Chicagoans were in the midst of Jane Byrne's erratic administration. According to political scientist Paul Kleppner, in the first two years of Byrne's governance, three city strikes disproportionately impacted black working-class communities. During a December 1979 Chicago Transit Authority strike, Mayor Byrne tried to break the power of the black-led transit workers unions by refusing to negotiate. Meanwhile, blacks heavily dependent on public transportation had difficulty getting to work. In January 1980, a teachers strike resulting from the public schools financial crisis (and subsequent layoffs and delayed pay), left many black children with working parents unsupervised. Then in February 1980 a firemen's strike left communities unprotected, which resulted in fire-related deaths—the majority of which were in black communities. While Mayor Byrne may not have been directly responsible for these various strikes, many in the black community accused her of handling them poorly. The result was that black residents were disproportionately affected, even resulting in the loss of life.[6]

On the housing front, Byrne initially unveiled a plan that would scatter public housing throughout the city in an attempt to increase integration. However, she later backed away from her plans and decided to upgrade housing units already in place instead of building new units in white communities. In an effort to save her reputation, Byrne and her husband moved into the notorious Cabrini-Green housing projects for three weeks beginning late March 1981. The housing units had been suffering from intensified gang violence. Once she moved to the area, police presence and arrests sharply increased. While her performance rate increased in the polls, Alderman Danny Davis called the mayor out for this move, saying, "My reaction is that the mayor has the perception that symbols with black folks can take the place of substance." In July 1982, Byrne nominated three whites to the board of the Chicago Housing Authority (CHA) which oversaw public housing with a substantial black majority. She had also dismissed two black Chicago Board of Education members and replaced them with two white members, gaining further ire from blacks. Byrne's collective actions only fired up a grassroots movement that would eventually lead to her political demise and the election of Harold Washington, the city's first black mayor.[7] As Byrne carried on with her political antics and opponents geared up to defeat her, the Board of Education worked to develop a desegregation plan.

CREATING A SATISFACTORY DESEGREGATION PLAN

The first version of the desegregation plan was created and revised in a series of closed-door meetings and was unveiled April 3, 1981. This version called for voluntary desegregation with guidelines of a 65 percent limit on whites in any school. It also called for mandatory provisions to be implemented by February 1982 if voluntary plans did not work. Forty-two thousand students would be sent to new schools.[8] A controversial component of the plan was the focus on the desegregation of whites and Latinos—but not whites and blacks—as entire predominantly black areas of the West Side and South Side of the city were not included.

Desegregation advocates thought the plan was not comprehensive enough and opponents thought it went too far. Mayor Jane Byrne spoke out against the plan's use of busing and predicted that both whites and blacks would be opposed to the plan. Alderman William O. Lipinski, an opponent of busing, also predicted that blacks, whites, and Latinos would oppose the plan and that the time of mandatory busing had passed. Rev. Herbert Martin, executive director of the Chicago branch of the NAACP, called the proposal far too conservative as it affected only 10 percent of the total school population. Likewise, the Urban League's James Compton was concerned about the schools that were left untouched in the plan. Frank Watkins of Operation Push said, "Only in Chicago could they use this kind of math—a school system that was only 18 percent white saying that no school can have more than 65 percent white students." Furthermore, Watkins commented that, "This reflected that the School Board's concern was more for the 18 percent [white students] than the black students, who have been victims of historic discrimination."[9] Alderman and former Congressman Roman C. Pucinski expressed concerns about how much the Northwest Side was affected by the plan. He also noted how few blacks were involved in the plan and said that, "We'd rather take this back into the court and take our chances. We don't feel we can do any worse and with a (Ronald) Reagan Justice Department, we might do better."[10]

Newspaper editors and Board of Education members also criticized the plan, developed primarily by outside consultants, as ineffective. Casey Banas, education editor of the *Chicago Tribune* wrote, "For years the cry among civil rights leaders has been to integrate black children of the inner city with whites in outlying neighborhoods. The plan unveiled Friday would not do that."[11] The *Chicago Sun-Times* found that black students who represented more than 60 percent of the student population would only represent less than a fifth of those attending the 90 integrated schools.[12] The *Chicago Tribune* further criticized the plan's proposal of voluntary busing for February 1982, as it fell in the middle of the school year. Furthermore, the clustering and pairing of schools on a mandatory basis would disrupt students and teachers as some schools would have to be restructured from kindergarten to sixth grade buildings to ones just for kindergarten to third grade.[13] Board of Education member Joyce Hughes, who formerly headed the board's Committee on Student Desegregation, commented that the plan did not pin down specifics as it related to teacher training and curriculum.[14] The head of the Committee on Student Desegregation, board member Michael Smith whose term expired April 30, 1981, responded, "The planners did not spend enough time in Chicago and were unaware of the city's particular nuances. Everybody has the feeling that they used techniques from other cities and dropped them on Chicago."[15] He believed that Chicago education insiders were needed to create the plan. One telling example of this was that a school the plan scheduled to close for desegregation purposes had just been remodeled. In another situation, Dever Elementary already had voluntary busing but was left out of the plan.

As people expressed skepticism about the plan's potential effectiveness, Mayor Byrne and Governor James (Jim) Thompson both announced they would not support funding for desegregation. The public schools were short approximately 45 million dollars, and the mayor refused to ask for a tax increase to cover the deficit. In a letter to the City Council Education Committee, Byrne stated, "Any desegregation plan that would further erode our tax base must be judged irresponsible and ultimately, unacceptable."[16] Governor Thompson also indicated that the state would not give the city funding for busing, saying, "There are no state dollars for busing."[17] Of course, state dollars were already being used for busing; but what Thompson meant was that state dollars would not be used for busing for the purpose of desegregation.

Other groups had meetings to express their concerns about the plan. While people from all the major ethnic groups were in opposition to the plan, their reasons varied. A group of Latinos and Asians met to discuss the plan. One Latino representative thought the plan unfairly burdened Latinos, as it did not consider the effects on bilingual education. Additionally, a representative of the Chinese American Service League, David Wong, wanted to know why Asians were disproportionately being reassigned. The two groups were

Latino + Asian group

impacted largely because they were located on the North Side, and much of the student assignment was proposed for that area.[18] On the Southwest Side, a group of black and white parents met together. One black parent indicated, "There is a misconception going around that the majority of black people want busing. Black people do not want busing." Another said, "I don't believe it is necessary that [my son] study along white students to learn."[19]

While there were a number of black parents who were against busing, Charles E. Carter, an associate general counsel of the NAACP, chastised them—especially "educated blacks...who should know better" than to speak out against busing. In an interview with columnist Vernon Jarrett of the *Chicago Tribune*, Carter stated that educated blacks got caught in the anti-busing trap. According to Carter, busing has always been a fact of life in American schooling. He explained,

> But now busing is an ugly word because it is used to help in carrying out the law of the land. The truth is that less than 3 percent of the annual total cost of busing is spent on busing for desegregation. Busing is not the real issue.
>
> The people who cry the loudest about busing are not concerned with transportation. They really don't want integrated education. They don't want integrated communities or schools. They don't want it by bus, bicycle, walking, or jogging.
>
> And any Black person who mouths a lot of talk against busing at this time is playing into the hands of people who want to turn back the clock. The same goes for all this talk about the glories of the neighborhood school.[20]

Carter reminded Jarrett's readers of the history of segregation in the Jim Crow South beginning with the 1896 *Plessy v. Ferguson* Supreme Court decision. As far as he and other school desegregation advocates were concerned, desegregation was not simply moving students around. Rather, he pointed out, segregated education often meant an inferior education for blacks, especially those from lower incomes. Carter and others believed that integration provided children with an opportunity to learn together. Busing was simply the means to accomplish better education for black students.

The NAACP fundamentally believed that desegregation was important to creating access to full citizenship and an open society. Hence, the organization continually fought for desegregation even in the face of black opposition. As the aforementioned black parent on the Southwest Side noted, there is typically the assumption that all black people supported desegregation, but those who have supported desegregation did so in hopes that their children would receive a better education. There were also a number of black people fundamentally opposed to desegregation who fought to improve black schools. When given assurance of quality education at neighborhood schools, many black parents preferred that their children not be bused.[21] Still, for some, the loss of their schools in desegregation was not worth the cost.[22]

The *Chicago Sun-Times* conducted an opinion poll among residents in late 1979. While Chicagoans' views about school desegregation varied widely, the poll revealed that most residents—black, white, and Latino—did not approve of busing. Fifty percent of blacks, 51 percent of Latinos, and 87 percent of whites were opposed to busing. Though nearly 70 percent of blacks and Latinos favored students of different races going to schools together, only 40 percent of whites favored diversity. One of the interesting observations about the study was that quite a few of those surveyed wrote in that they preferred neighborhood schools, though it was not one of the options given.[23] About 24 percent of blacks and Latinos and 47 percent of whites thought neighborhood schools would be best. When asked if they thought Access to Excellence was successful in desegregating Chicago's schools, most replied 'no.'[24]

The poll also asked if desegregation would provide a better education for students. Interestingly, while a number of people in the three largest racial/ethnic groups were quoted in papers as opposing desegregation, surveys revealed that close to 55 percent of blacks and close to 70 percent of Latinos polled believed that desegregation would provide a better education for all groups involved. About 38 percent of whites polled thought desegregation would provide a better education for blacks and Latinos, but only 26 percent thought it would benefit whites. Most surveyed also believed that desegregation was not tied to equal opportunity.[25] With the majority of the citizens opposed to busing, any plan the board developed would have to take that reality into consideration.

The board held hearings to discuss the new plans and found opposition from various organizations. After the hearings about the first version of the plan, the board met again in closed-door meetings in mid-April 1981 to hammer out changes. As they negotiated, some whites and Latinos board members voted together and raised the percentage of whites at each school from 65 percent to 70 percent. Black board members wanted to have more funding for educational programs for schools left out of desegregation. The board had already

accepted the Recommendations on Educational Components prepared by consultant Robert L. Green at its April 15, 1981, meeting.
These recommendations called for upgrading the curriculum and
instruction in regular elementary and secondary schools. The plan
also focused on faculty desegregation and affirmative action. The recommendations barely mentioned desegregation as Green was more
concerned with the quality of education students received regardless
of where they attended school.[26]

In the second version of the plan, the board added student assignment principles, financial aspects, and general policies concerning the
desegregation plan. It defined desegregation as a school with no more
than 70 percent whites or minorities. The voluntary techniques they
proposed were similar to those proposed in the past. Students could
transfer from overcrowded schools to underutilized schools to promote desegregation. Transportation would be provided if students
had to walk further than a mile and a half. The board proposed to
have the magnet school limit at 15–25 percent white by September
1982, to ensure that whites did not get most of the seats at the best
schools.[27]

In an eventual 6–5 vote, the board approved the second version
of the school desegregation plan and submitted it to Judge Shadur.
Three Latinos and three whites supported the plan while three blacks
and the two anti-busing whites voted in opposition. Once the plan
was submitted at the end of April 1981, Judge Shadur set three deadlines for further responses. The board had to file a legal brief saying
why it believed the plan they submitted met constitutional requirements; the Justice Department and other interested parties were given
time to file their comments with the courts; and then the board could
reply to the responses. After the process was complete, Judge Shadur
would give his ruling on the acceptability of the plan.[28]

The Board of Education hired a firm to help advertise the programs and created the Office of Equal Educational Opportunity to
oversee the implementation of student and faculty desegregation. The
office would also take the lead in the development of progress and
evaluation reports and would recommend modifications to desegregation activities to the superintendent.[29] It was funded by a $300,000
Title IV (1964 Civil Rights Act) grant.[30] The board also approved
the closing of over 30 schools for financial reasons and to further
promote desegregation.

In late May 1981, the Board of Education submitted its brief to
Judge Shadur that justified the constitutional requirement of its plan.
The board attorneys argued that the plan was reasonable and within

the range of desegregation plans ruled constitutional by other judges, citing plans in Atlanta, Detroit, Milwaukee, and St. Louis, which had all allowed schools to remain 70–80 percent white. The September 1983 date the board set for mandatory provisions was also seen as "quite a prompt implementation of a desegregation plan" particularly since a court battle would lead to a much slower implementation.[31]

The Justice Department objected to aspects of the board's plan in a July 21, 1981, brief. It stated that the plan "encourages, without any underlying rationale, the existence of schools that are 70 percent white in a system whose total enrollment is 19 percent white, 61 percent black, and 21 percent Hispanic and other minorities." The Justice Department's statistics noted that only 3.7 percent of the black elementary students would attend schools with 30 percent or more whites.[32] The brief further argued, "The Board has not made effective use of [voluntary] techniques... which have the potential for relieving racial isolation in Chicago." The response indicated a list of ways the Chicago Board of Education's plan could break consent decree promises by: (1) combining blacks and Hispanics in a minority category, permitting the board to mix whites and Hispanics instead of whites and blacks; (2) not providing enough specifics; (3) relying too much on voluntary measures which had failed in the past; (4) not spelling out the mandatory techniques; (5) inadequately defining desegregation and giving no rationale for 70 percent white schools; (6) burdening blacks with desegregation efforts by requiring them to transfer to white schools, but not requiring whites to transfer to black schools; and (7) allowing too many black students to remain segregated.[33]

In a July 22 memo to Assistant Attorney General Reynolds, Robert J. D'Agostino, deputy assistant attorney general, stated, "Our critique was based upon the admitted incompleteness of the plan, the failure of the plan to address the impact of drawing nonracially discriminatory district lines, a failure the Board promises to correct by sometime in August." Additionally, D'Agostino noted, "the Justice Department objected to the arbitrary use of percentages by the Board. We have not required nor will we require the Board to meet any particular goal of racial mixing."[34] His additional criticism of the board's plan focused on the insufficient implementation schedule, and emphasized that quality education for segregated schools did not "reduce the Board's obligation to reduce racial isolation... where practicable."[35]

In dissent, school board president Raul Villalobos called the Justice Department's brief "completely inaccurate." He noted, "The Board believes its plan is plainly constitutional and that it will be effective in obtaining a substantial degree of student desegregation, indeed the greatest practicable degree under the circumstances in Chicago."[36] Villalobos and others wondered why Chicago was expected to do more than other cities.

The Justice Department, meanwhile, was experiencing internal struggles over the rejection of the plan (and other civil rights issues). When Reynolds was appointed in 1981, he inherited the Justice Department's Civil Rights Division staffed with close to 170 lawyers. Some of these lawyers had civil rights litigation backgrounds prior to their employment at the Justice Department and were passionate about their work.[37] Furthermore, many had worked on the consent decree prior to Reynolds's time in command. Legally, the Justice Department had agreed to the consent decree under the Carter administration. Now the Reagan administration was bound to those agreements, yet competing visions complicated negotiations with Chicago.

William Taylor, director of the Center for National Policy Review, told *Chicago Tribune* reporters that "if [the Justice Department] had accepted [Chicago's desegregation plan], it would have been generally recognized as a sham and not even in compliance with the consent decree."[38] Former Board of Education member, Patricia O'Hern, had a different view. She saw the federal government's objections to Chicago's plans as unfair because other cities had similar or higher desegregation percentages. Moreover, the objection to not enough desegregation of black schools was called "ridiculous because [HEW's feasibility plan] created in August 1979 also left over 200 Black schools segregated." O'Hern argued, "Each year the white enrollment declines because the federal government continues to threaten the Chicago school system with forced busing. Soon there will be no white children left, and then all 600 schools will be minority."[39] Though white flight occurred in spite of segregation, O'Hern had a point that forced busing could certainly accelerate white flight.

The Board of Education continued its school desegregation planning without much concern about the Justice Department's response to its early plan. The board had until August 28 to respond to the Justice Department. In its August 10, 1981, meeting, the board approved boundary changes for a number of elementary and high schools to help spur desegregation.[40] In most of the boundary changes, black and Latino students would be sent to white schools. However, the board later shifted one of the few boundary changes that would lead to white students attending a predominantly black school.[41] In a brief submitted August 28, the Board of Education predicted that desegregation would occur faster than anticipated. It expected the number of schools with more than 70 percent whites would be lowered from 81 to 28 after the first year.[42]

Prior to submitting their brief, the board submitted a draft of its progress report to the Justice Department on August 18, 1981. In a memo to Reynolds from Alexander C. Ross (special counsel for litigation), Ross noted the dilemma the board faced when it closed all white schools. In two cases, once the board closed a small white school, the students were reassigned to predominantly white schools. There were predominantly black schools nearby these schools, but adding the white students would still leave the black schools 90 percent black. In another case, there were no boundary changes made for two small white schools that were close to larger black schools because desegregation would not "sufficiently" occur. When the board did make some adjustments to a 95 percent white school, some students were moved to a nearby 60 percent white school to make room for black students at the 95 percent white school. Ross wrote, "We cannot insist on rigid application of a neutral, neighborhood-school assignment principle for the same reason the Board avoids it—knowledge that the small numbers of white students involved will leave the system unless other steps, which go beyond the assignment principles, are taken to instill stability. Conversely we cannot condone the failure to act (or the inconsistent application of a neutral principle) because of racially discriminatory considerations."[43] The memo captures the conundrum the board faced, knowing whites did not want their children attending predominantly black schools. In order to maintain whites in the system, the board chose to keep whites in predominantly white schools. Past Justice Department officials would probably have rejected these changes, but the Reagan Justice Department allowed them to continue.

Despite these concerns, a joint statement was submitted to the court August 28, 1981. The Justice Department and the Board of Education announced that their concerns "have been resolved at this stage."[44] The joint statement specified that "Some of the questions raised by the [Justice Department's July 21] response indicated that there had been insufficient communication between the parties as to the Board's planning and implementation of activities."[45] Furthermore, the Justice Department acknowledged that the board was familiar with and sensitive to Chicago's unique situation, and that it would have the discretion to create a plan. The two groups asked Judge Shadur not to make a decision until the city's final desegregation plan was submitted in December. The Justice Department was satisfied with the city's progress, but stated: "It is a great overstatement to say that's the end of the ballgame."[46] It also saw the 30 percent minority enrollment as a minimum rather than a maximum percentage. This had been a sticking point for some Justice Department officials. While communication between the two groups had some impact, the Justice Department's change in position from the July 22 memo in a month's time meant Reynolds's agenda was gaining strength.

South Side Boycotts

Much of the boundary changes the Board of Education initiated in the summer of 1981 led to minimal problems for many schools, largely because the boundary shifts made room at predominantly white schools for more black and Latino students. However, one of the boundary changes in particular created unrest, as it called for a two-way transfer of students from the predominantly white Graham Elementary School in the New City community to all black Hendricks Elementary School in the Fuller Park Community (see map 5.1).[47]

New City was better known for its neighborhoods Canaryville and Back of the Yards. Back of the Yards housed the Union Stock Yard livestock and meatpacking industry made famous in Upton Sinclair's *The Jungle*. Working-class white immigrants, mostly from

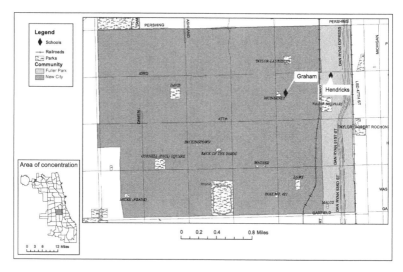

Map 5.1 New City and Fuller Park

Poland, populated the New City community in the 1920s. The area also included Irish, Czechoslovakian, German, and Lithuanian immigrants. Mexicans began arriving in the area during World War I and were 12.5 percent of the New City population by 1970 and 35.7 percent by 1980. The New City community gained a small number of blacks in the 1970s, but increased to 21.9 percent by 1980. [48]

Fuller Park, a community adjacent to New City, was a narrow community surrounded by railroad yards and the Dan Ryan Expressway. The community was 12 percent black in the 1920s. Irish were the major foreign group in the community until the 1930s, when Germans and Austrians replaced them along with some Slavs and Mexicans. The black population grew substantially beginning in the 1940s—though they were forced to live in segregated blocks east of Wentworth Avenue. Then in the 1950s the Dan Ryan Expressway was built directly through Fuller Park, effectively displacing one-third of the community's residents. By 1980, blacks were 98.7 percent of the population.[49]

The schools of New City and Fuller Park were less than a mile apart, but train tracks served as the dividing line between blacks and whites (with some Mexican Americans). Since students would have had to walk through a block-long viaduct, the board called for a bus to transport the students.[50] Vaguely reminiscent of the united black and white opposition to school desegregation in the South Shore community in 1968, both blacks and whites opposed the boundary changes and boycotted the two schools. It was commonly known in both areas that each racial group should stay on their side of the tracks.[51] Filled with mutual fear and racial animosity, both groups were concerned about the safety of their children and met separately to express their discontent. One white parent at Graham said, "It is dangerous to send our kids over there (to Hendricks)...I'd rather keep them at home with me." Another white parent stated, "Those Black kids aren't safe in their own neighborhood. How can my kid expect to be safe over there?" In a different meeting, a black parent stated, "Who's going to protect our children while they're [at Graham] with all those prejudiced people?" Another black parent asserted that, "We've got to worry about someone...turning over a bus, setting it on fire with our babies in it." An additional black parent said, "If you're going to bus our children into a neighborhood where the white people were civilized and had a little more sense, it might make a difference."[52] These remarks indicate the level of fear and disrespect these groups had for each other.

Students boycotted both schools for several days, and both parents and students picketed Graham. On a more interesting note, in

September 1981, both sides joined forces and agreed to allow two lawyers to represent them.[53] A *Chicago Tribune* editorial discussed the irony of the integrated boycott. "Since they have now discovered they can work together to protest and boycott, they may also be able to work together to protect each others' children in their new schools and improve their education. And that could be the beginning of real, lasting integration."[54] When the groups met with board members and other school officials, the board reaffirmed its commitment to the boundary changes and indicated that the federal government would not allow them to change the boundaries because of the consent decree.[55] The board effectively used the federal government's policy as a shield so it would not have to back down to groups protesting their desegregation initiatives—recognizing that if it backed down to this group, it would set a precedent for other groups who opposed boundary changes.

As the boycotts weakened, several black parents sent their children to Graham, but whites did not send their children to Hendricks. Some parents at both schools sent their children to their original assigned schools despite school officials' insistence that they would not be given work, grades, or be marked as present. Eventually, some parents at Graham used different addresses within the Graham attendance area and re-enrolled their children at Graham. Others sent their children to parochial or other private schools. Still others signed their children up for other public schools that were still accepting children. Hendricks parents also sent their children to other schools to avoid having to send them to Graham. In another ironic twist, children from both Graham and Hendricks ended up at Sheridan Math and Science Academy (a magnet school), and actually rode the bus together.[56] In the end, Graham was desegregated, but Hendricks remained predominantly black.

Part of the irony of blacks and whites joining forces to prevent desegregation was not lost on Mrs. Celesting Hughes, the president of the Hendricks School Advisory Council and longtime resident of the Hendricks area. She recalled having to fight whites so that black children could gain access to Fuller Park and its activities in the late 1940s. Mrs. Hughes noted that many who had led the boycott at Hendricks were the very parents who had not been active in the school before. She stated that, "The truth is that black parents have not come together and voted for or against a boycott...What we have is a group of people—people that we can't find to help the schools most of the time—suddenly becoming leaders."[57] For Mrs. Hughes, the parents leading the Hendricks boycott had not considered the history of the community and did not necessarily have full support of black parents at Hendricks. She predicted rightfully that the boycott would not last.

The boycotts at the two schools indicated the level of racial hostility that continued to exist in Chicago. The Graham–Hendricks plan called for an even exchange of black and white students. As the Justice Department noted in its report, whites in schools with declining enrollment were moved to other white schools rather than to become the overwhelming minority at nearby black schools. The white opposition to their children attending predominantly black Hendricks proved that the board knew that whites would not want to attend schools dominated by blacks. The board's plans to desegregate predominantly white schools by using mostly Latinos for that process spoke to the practicality of such a plan, but also the avoidance of dealing with the serious divisions between blacks and whites. While the board hoped to slow the flight of whites from the public schools, its plan left a lot to be desired for the large numbers of black students who would remain isolated—and for whom the plan was meant to help in the first place. The compromised plan that was eventually settled upon was a convergence of white interests and the demands of the federal government, leaving space for only a select number of blacks to be able to participate.[58]

FEDERAL SHIFT IN DESEGREGATION POLICY

The sudden shift in the approval of Chicago's desegregation plans in August 1981, just a month after the July objections to aspects of the plan, was a strong indication that the Reagan administration was changing the federal government's attitude and approach toward desegregation policy. Reynolds gave a speech before educators in Chicago in September 1981 stating, "Forced busing has, in the final analysis, largely failed in two major respects...It has failed to gain needed public acceptance and it has failed to translate into enhanced educational achievement." For Reynolds, it made little sense to 'blindly' continue with a policy that had not worked. The Justice Department's new focus would be to end state enforced segregation and ensure that all students received equal educational opportunities. Reynolds noted, "We are concerned, quite frankly, much less with student relocation than we are with student education."[59] This change had already been underway since the Nixon administration as he and members of Congress found ways to limit busing as a remedy for desegregation. As the person from the Justice Department overseeing the consent decree in Chicago where busing for desegregation would be necessary, Reynolds's comments were troubling. Reynolds made it clear that he would not enforce mandatory busing if it became necessary to meet the even minimal desegregation criteria in Chicago. Instead of busing, techniques such as voluntary transfers, magnet schools, curriculum enhancement, faculty desegregation, school closings, faculty training, changing attendance boundaries, and new school construction would be used to spur student desegregation. Of course, these were many of the initiatives Chicago already had in place with limited success.

In a testimony before a subcommittee of the House Judiciary Committee in November 1981, Reynolds announced another policy shift. The Justice Department would "not rely on the *Keyes* [*v. Denver* Supreme Court ruling] presumption, but will define the violation precisely and seek to limit the remedy only to those schools in which racial imbalance is the product of intentional segregative acts of state officials" before pursuing litigation. In the *Keyes v. Denver* (1973) case, Reynolds observed, "The Supreme Court held that a finding of state imposed racial segregation in one portion of a school system creates a presumption that racial imbalance in other portions of the system is also the product of state action." Reynolds claimed that "the *Keyes* presumption had been unfairly used to desegregate schools where there was no independent evidence showing that racial imbalance resulted from an official policy or intentional segregation." So Reynolds determined that the burden of proof for the Reagan administration would be more stringent than that identified by the Supreme Court. Furthermore, Reynolds stated that people have an opinion about wanting to be integrated or not. "We are not going to compel children who don't choose to have an integrated education to have one…Every kid in America has a right to an integrated education where he wants it, but I don't think that means the government can compel an integrated education." Reynolds insisted that neither the Constitution nor the Supreme Court suggested that the government can compel integration.[60]

Critics of the Reagan administration were appalled by the overall reversal of civil rights. In an article, former assistant attorney general Drew Days expressed his belief that the Reagan administration went out of its way to reverse civil rights gains, which "successive administrations, irrespective of party, attempted to build upon." Days argued that, "Despite differences in ideology, each administration was willing to alter its initial views on civil rights enforcement in the face of reality: techniques that proved ineffective were abandoned in favor of more potent approaches."[61] One example was the recognition that voluntary school desegregation techniques had failed, so mandatory backups including busing was viewed as appropriate to achieve desegregation. Days indicated, "President Carter was personally opposed to busing. But he made it clear that his appointees were to follow the law, not his personal preferences."[62] Additionally, "no administration openly challenged the authority of Supreme Court rulings...or announced publically an intention to ignore the dictates of those decisions in undertaking to 'faithfully' uphold the law."[63] The NAACP's Benjamin Hooks stated that the Justice Department's Civil Rights Division "launched an all out attack on civil rights." Hooks further noted that their actions were an "unprecedented, aggressive, and unnerving campaign to reverse more than two decades of well established policies." The Urban League's Vernon Jordan called the policies a "clear and present danger" for blacks. More than one hundred lawyers within the Reynolds- led Civil Rights Division sent Reynolds a signed letter disagreeing with the administration's reversal of federal policy.[64] Arthur S. Flemming, the chairman of the US Commission on Civil Rights, was fired by Reagan for his outspoken critique of the administration's policies. In a statement, Flemming asserted, "When the passage of the 13th, 14th and 15th amendments to the Constitution created similar opposition in the post-Civil War period, there was a retreat in the civil rights field that lasted 100 years...We hope that leaders in both the executive and legislative branch will think long and hard before they retreat from their civil rights responsibilities under the Constitution by undermining the foundation on which implementation of the mandate under *Brown* must rest."[65]

Since many of the critics were outsiders and not in ultimate positions of power, their strong critiques had little impact on the changing civil rights policies. Stephen C. Halpern pointed out that in spite of the heavy rhetoric on both sides of the arguments, civil rights enforcement had already been severely weakened prior to the Reagan administration. The Eagleton–Biden Amendment had restricted the withholding of federal funds if busing was involved in desegregation plans. The Justice Department was left with the discretion about how to deal with potential complaints and had not done a sufficient job even in the Carter administration.[66] However, the situation in Chicago illustrates a different view. The Carter Justice Department negotiated the consent decree that Reagan's Justice Department had to enforce. While Drew Days drew up ambitious proposals for elimination of discrimination, Reynolds had no intention of fully enforcing those proposals. Furthermore, it was Carter-appointed officials

in OCR who investigated Chicago's student segregation and forced
Chicago to do more to desegregate its students as well as teachers.
While the resulting desegregation was minimal, it was far more than
had been accomplished in the past.

STATE LIABILITY AND INTERDISTRICT INVESTIGATIONS

At a status hearing in mid-November 1981, Judge Shadur ordered the
Justice Department to report on the available space in surrounding
suburban schools as a possibility for metropolitan desegregation.[67]
The Justice Department had been investigating the possibility of state
liability in Chicago's segregation, but state officials would not cooperate by providing the necessary paper work—even though state liability and interdistrict investigations were part of the consent decree.
It suspected the state and municipal agencies of illegally contributing
to segregation in the metropolitan area and the City of Chicago. The
Justice Department began its investigation by sending letters to the
chairman of the Illinois State Board of Education, Donald Muirheid,
and Governor Jim Thompson in October and November 1980 to
solicit support in gathering necessary data.[68] Along with the notifica-
tions, Justice Department officials met with two attorneys representing the State Board of Education in October 1980.[69]

On October 20, 1981, Justice Department attorneys from the
General Litigation Section submitted a memo to their acting chief
Thomas Keeling. In the memo, Burtis M. Dougherty and Linda F.
Thome paid particular attention to the state's segregation and desegregation legislative history, the state's knowledge of segregation and
unequal education in Chicago, and the state's enforcement of the
Armstrong Law. In their investigation, they found that the state had
refused to put Chicago on a nonrecognition status, and instead continually extended its probationary status. Nonrecognition would have
effectively led to the withholding of state and federal funding from
the schools. As explored in chapter 3, former state superintendent
Joseph Cronin did not view withholding funds as a viable option.
When Justice Department officials questioned Cronin about the
lack of action despite recognized deficiencies in Chicago's Access to
Excellence plan, Cronin blamed the State Board of Education leadership. In particular, Donald Muirheid was blamed for his "gradualist
approach." According to Cronin, Muirheid was "willing to maintain
the district's probationary status and take no further action," because
Chicago was negotiating in "good faith."[70]

Dougherty and Thome cited two Ohio cases in which the state was found guilty of knowingly allowing segregation in Columbus and Cleveland and had failed to act to prevent such segregation. As a result, they surmised that, "Proof of active participation in the Chicago Board's segregative actions through approval of funding of school construction projects designed to keep black and white pupils separated will strengthen our case."[71] The memo offered evidence of the state being notified of Chicago's segregation and not investigating the issues, nor enforcing its own policies. The state was only supposed to approve new school building construction if it would not lead to further segregation. In another memo, Thome provided data from the state's Capital Development Board showing that, in spite of reservations, it approved state funding for buildings that would be segregated.[72] The state continually dodged providing the Justice Department with the information to pursue the state liability investigation. Although there was evidence of state liability, the state could not be held accountable.

The metropolitan investigation also resulted in a lack of accountability, but for different reasons. In a comprehensive interdistrict investigation interim report, the Justice Department examined housing and employment issues that led to a predominantly black and Latino city and predominantly white surrounding suburbs. The housing investigation found that a few suburbs were predominantly or all black and that most others were all or predominantly white. When blacks moved to the suburbs, they often moved to suburbs or census tracts which were predominantly black, as housing costs were often a prohibitive factor which kept blacks out of certain neighborhoods. A number of suburbs were only zoned for single family homes or had limited or no subsidized housing. Additionally, discrimination or fear of discrimination was also a prohibitive factor.[73]

Employment opportunities were also limited for blacks who lived in the city. As jobs relocated to the suburbs, the distance to the new jobs and the lack of public or other forms of transportation were preventive factors. There were some municipalities which had residential requirements for public employees. If blacks could not afford to live in those communities, they would be unable to work there. In other communities without residential barriers, there were few black applicants.[74]

Based on the Supreme Court decision in *Milliken v. Bradley* (1974), interdistrict remedies had to be tailored to meet the scope of the violations. The Supreme Court ruled, "Specifically, it must be shown that racially discriminatory acts of the state or local school districts, or of a single school district have been a substantial cause of interdistrict segregation...In such circumstances an interdistrict remedy would be appropriate to eliminate the interdistrict segregation directly caused by the constitutional violation."[75] If there were no constitutional violations on the part of the suburban school districts, then *Milliken* essentially limited the possibility of city and suburban transfers. Yet, the Justice Department indicated that, "a number of interdistrict violations might be found." However, it was difficult to measure "the effects of those violations" and what possible "remedies would be appropriate." The report concluded, "Given the relationship among public employment, residential, and school enrollment patterns, which admittedly is not exact, and the stark racial patterns which emerged in a number of jurisdictions in the Chicago metropolitan area, our investigation into these employment practices pursuant to the 1980 consent decree in this case will continue."[76]

Some Justice Department officials were uncertain about linking housing and schools for the Chicago case. In a memo to Reynolds, Deputy Assistant Attorney General J. Harvie Wilkinson stated that discrimination in one area impacts another. Still, he noted that the courts have rejected the "panoramic view of liability" and have focused more on past school discrimination. Wilkinson indicated that separate housing suits would be more appropriate, as housing desegregation would eventually lead to school desegregation.[77] In response, Reynolds sent a memo to Ross stating that the Justice Department under the consent decree did not have the authorization to launch a housing probe "in the name of school desegregation." He asked Ross to redraft a letter to Illinois Assistant Attorney General Morton Friedman, which would only link state and local housing authorities who acted to maintain or expand segregated schooling.[78]

While the Carter Justice Department supported the linkage between housing and schools—recognizing that if school boundaries were established based on neighborhoods, then segregated schools would persist if segregated housing remained—the Reagan Justice Department did not support those same assumptions. The willingness to separate housing from schools effectively relinquished state and federal government responsibility. Rather than appearing to emanate from racist policy, housing segregation is seen as personal choice. Sociologist Kevin Fox Gotham explained the issue in the following way: "The connection between race, racism, and urban space helps us to understand why racial residential segregation remains a persistent and tenacious feature of US metropolitan areas despite the passage of fair housing and numerous anti-discrimination statutes over the past decades … Racial segregation in housing persists because the majority of participants in the housing industry still adhere to the belief that racially mixed or predominantly black and minority neighborhoods are of lesser value than all-white neighborhoods."[79] Since housing segregation was persistent, Reynolds understood the importance of separating housing segregation from school segregation as the latter could not be effectively tackled without attending to the former. As long as prohibitive housing factors remained in some suburbs, the segregated metropolis would go largely unchanged.

The Justice Department turned in their interdistrict investigation to the court in 1983. First, Justice Department officials found that there had not been interdistrict student exchanges between the city and suburban public schools that would "warrant an action seeking interdistrict relief." Although there were some minor exchanges— including black students transferring to suburban schools without the district's knowledge and suburban students attending Washburne Trade School—the transfers did not "constitute an interdistrict violation."[80] Second, there was also no evidence that the city and other districts planned or refused consolidation. Third, there was no evidence to indicate that public officials selected building sites in a way that would have "significant influence on the racial distribution of students between Chicago and its suburbs." While the Justice Department acknowledged that there were areas outside of housing and employment "in which civil rights violations arguably have had a negative influence on the interdistrict migration of minority families and thus an indirect effect on the interdistrict distribution of public school students by race and ethnicity," it nonetheless concluded, "we have found no basis in fact or law for associating any of these areas with interdistrict school remedies."[81]

Although the Justice Department did not push for interdistrict remedies and separated housing from schools in Chicago, scholars have argued that housing discrimination is directly tied to school segregation. Gary Orfield surmises that restrictive covenants, racial zoning ordinances, home financing discrimination, Federal Housing Administration and Veterans Administration segregation policies, and segregated subsidized housing, etc. have all contributed to increased segregation.[82] The Supreme Court ruled in *Hills v. Gautreaux* (1976) that the CHA and the Department of Housing and Urban Development (HUD) violated the constitution by establishing housing in a segregated manner. The lower courts ordered HUD to establish subsidized housing outside of the city's limits, and the Supreme Court affirmed the ruling because of the constitutional violation and because "a metropolitan area relief order directed to HUD would not consolidate or in any way restructure local governmental units."[83] However, since the ruling did not put blame on any suburb, it was difficult to seek a metropolitan remedy for school desegregation in Chicago.

Critics of metropolitan desegregation have argued that suburban whites were not at fault for the concentration of blacks in central cities, and that busing across districts wastes time and money, and limits local and parental control over schools.[84] While these were certainly legitimate arguments, housing policies have historically limited the opportunity for black Chicagoans to move where they chose, as shown in the *Hills v. Gautreaux* case. The Reynolds led Justice Department, uncommitted to desegregation, was not willing to take on housing discrimination. While it was correct in asserting housing desegregation would lead to school desegregation, without an attack on housing segregation, metropolitan school desegregation was one of the few options for desegregating predominantly black and Latino cities.

Other cities had used metropolitan desegregation with some success. St. Louis, for example, employed interdistrict school desegregation, partly because Missouri law allowed such cooperation. St. Louis County had a "special school district" which provided programs for students with disabilities and two vocational–technical schools (including roughly 6,000 students).[85] Consequently, their school desegregation remedy was a metropolitan plan for the county and was not limited to the city of St. Louis. Another example of metropolitan desegregation occurred in Indianapolis. Indiana consolidated its schools sometimes outside of county lines, but Indianapolis Public Schools (IPS) were unable to consolidate with any surrounding areas. As the parameters of the city expanded for municipal purposes, the state legislature repealed a previous act that called for the expansion of IPS with the expansion of the city's boundaries. Therefore, the school district did not encompass the city limits. The courts ordered metropolitan desegregation in *United States v. Board of School Commissioners* (1980), allowing students to transfer to other districts.[86]

Unfortunately, clear circumstances were not found in Chicago. Furthermore, voluntary metropolitan desegregation, although discussed, was not substantially sought on a local, state, or federal level. This resulted in Chicago being left to find a way to desegregate within its city boundaries.

CHICAGO'S PROGRESS AND FINAL DESEGREGATION PLAN

In early November 1981, Board of Education attorney Robert C. Howard predicted that mandatory busing would probably not be needed in Chicago because the guidelines set could be accomplished without mandatory desegregation.[87] Consistent with Chicago school policy, a report from the Committee on Desegregation acknowledged the importance of white and black children attending school together. Yet, "policies and methods that aggravate the decline of enrollment of white children, in particular schools or in the system as a whole, tend to defeat the goal of student desegregation." Those policies were viewed as "destructive" and counterproductive as they reinforced "the separation of races between city and suburb, to the immense disadvantage of the community as a whole."[88] A school desegregation progress report noted that desegregation had increased from 93 to 114 schools. There were now 76,885 students in desegregated schools out of the 441,000 total students (17.4%). Those numbers rose from the 67,575 who were in desegregated schools in the previous school year. Also, of the nine high schools which were out of compliance with the board's 70 percent ratio in the previous year, four met the standards and another four met the minimum requirements for progress. Of the 72 elementary schools out of compliance, eight had been closed, 33 met the guidelines, and 18 had made minimum progress. Only one predominantly black school, Hendricks, was unable to attract any white students.[89]

While more progress was needed, this was a far better showing than had been accomplished with Access to Excellence in the 1970s. (After the first year of Access to Excellence, only 16,449 students had been desegregated.) In spite of the retreating Justice Department, the new Board of Education members, new superintendent, and the consent decree all converged to make this level of desegregation possible when it had not been possible in the past. The progress Chicago had made occurred at the same time that the number of Latino students surpassed that of whites in the 1981–1982 school year. Blacks were 60.7 percent of the school population with Latinos and whites 19.6 and 17.2 percent, respectively. For Latinos, there was a growing Mexican American student population as there was an influx of Mexican immigrants and Mexican American migrants from the American Southwest.[90]

While the city's progress could be commended, behind the scenes, the Justice Department took a cautionary view of percentages. An internal memo from Ross to Deputy Assistant Attorney General James P. Turner stated that it was difficult to tell the "overall effect of the Board's desegregation measures," for several reasons. First, the board's report focused on percentage change at individual schools rather than "changes in numbers enrolled by race."[91] This made it difficult to tell if the change was simply due to white attrition. Second, minority students were lumped together making it difficult to assess the effect on black students alone. Finally, the racial percentages for magnet schools disregarded the number of students who attended the schools before they became magnet and magnet schools' racial proportion. In examining the statistical data provided by Board of Education attorney Robert Howard, Ross pointed out: "The Board has chosen to measure 'progress' by the decrease in the number of schools which are over 70% whites. Changes in this regard have been accomplished by a 0.5% increase in black transfer students and a decline in white enrollment. Thus there are now fewer white students isolated from 'minority' students but the statistic means little in terms of what has been done to remove additional black students from racially isolated circumstances."[92]

The resulting changes largely came from circumstances beyond the Chicago Board of Education's control. The increase in black enrollment to schools with more than 30 percent whites often occurred primarily as a result of boundary changes at four schools and because the proportion of blacks had increased in certain areas due to changes in residential patterns. This meant that the changes at schools with more than 30 percent whites were occurring because blacks moved into white communities or areas transitioning from white to black. At the same time that approximately 4,000 black students moved to schools with 30 percent or more whites, schools which enrolled about 5,400 blacks "dropped below 5% white, thereby creating a net increase of Black students in the most-segregated category."[93]

Despite these concerns, on December 30, 1981, the board voted 7–4 to approve the third version of the school desegregation plan. The board also scheduled five public hearings to get feedback on the plan.[94] At the public hearings held January 8–12, 1982, many were still skeptical about the plan. The complaints were similar to those of the past. Some black parents thought that improvements at predominantly or all black schools would lead to desegregation in black areas, while some preferred quality education over desegregation. Others did not want their children to leave their neighborhood schools. Like their black counterparts, many Latino parents thought the board should spend the money meant for busing on improvement of their schools.[95]

After the hearings and minor revisions, the final plan was approved and sent to Judge Shadur in January 1982. The plan laid out the legal and demographic context for school desegregation in Chicago. It provided the racial/ethnic demographics through the years to demonstrate that the plan was practical. The Comprehensive Desegregation

Plan also gave background on the instability of desegregation over time because desegregation often occurred in racially transitioning areas noting that, "almost none of the schools that were integrated in 1970 remained so in 1980."[96]

The board's basic objectives were to first "ensure that no segregative acts are initiated or authorized to continue during the term of the plan."[97] Second, the plan "seeks to eliminate, on a system-wide basis, the isolation of white children from other racial and ethnic groups, in a way which avoids resegregation of schools."[98] The focus on white school children drew complaints from black leaders on and off the board. The plan stated, "Because it is practicable to do so, the Board has flatly required that every predominantly white school be desegregated."[99] Although Judge Shadur called for more desegregation of predominantly black schools,[100] the board's plan continued to focus on the desegregation of white schools.

The plan also called for the elimination of mobile units for the instruction of students although they would still be used at schools for special purposes. Mobile units had long been seen as a symbol of racial segregation as civil rights advocates believed that they were used to contain black students at black schools. The board had removed over 1000 units since 1972 when 1,352 were in use at 209 schools. In 1981, only 320 were still in use at 55 schools.[101]

Joyce Hughes, a black member of the Board of Education, criticized the containment of black students, the mandatory measures that limited black student participation in desegregation programs, and the burden placed on black and Latino students. In her critique of permissive transfer plans, Hughes indicated that the transfers called for the movement of black and Latino students to white schools but not the reverse. The controlled enrollment strategy the board used to limit the number of neighborhood children attending neighborhood schools in an effort to keep the schools desegregated was seen as a way to exclude blacks from their neighborhood schools. In terms of majority to minority transfers, Hughes stated that there was a limit of 50 percent on the number of all minority students who could transfer. But for Hughes, the 50 percent limit meant that black and Latino students, who made up 80 percent of students, would have to compete for just half of the slots when whites were just 17 percent of the population. Seeing stability as a code word for black exclusion, she argued, "The rationalization is 'stability' but the reason is to keep Black participation in many of Chicago schools to a bare minimum, while filling up the 'minority' positions with Hispanic, Asians, and other minorities."[102] Hughes's critique of the board's policy was in line with the critiques of Urban League and NAACP representatives who saw the plan's limitation for black students and its preference for white students. Accommodations were made to satisfy the few remaining white students at the expense of black and Latino students.

The board countered that there was "substantial black participation in desegregation programs" already established. Furthermore, it argued that the combined definition of minority was "constitutional." The plan stated, "The Board did not believe that any arbitrary standard could be established that would uniformly quantify what constitutes 'substantial participation' of black students."[103] The participation of black students was determined by the practicality of the situation at each school. According to the board, whites would eventually account for 44.6 percent, blacks 35.3 percent, and Latinos 14.6 percent of the students enrolled at desegregated schools. Magnet schools, meanwhile, were increasingly relied upon to encourage desegregation. Chicago had 29 such schools in operation in 1982, 26 of which were predominantly black schools, and 25 of which were within the desegregation compliance (between 15% and 35% white and 60% and 85% minority).[104] Yet magnet schools failed to significantly add to desegregation.

In February 1982, the Justice Department sent a brief to the court approving Chicago's desegregation plans. The Justice Department believed "that once the plan has been thoroughly implemented the Board will have provided a system wide remedy, established the greatest number of stably desegregated schools, insured that all racial and ethnic groups participated and distributed the benefits and burdens on a fair basis."[105] The Reagan administration's approval was hardly a surprise as Reynolds had previously made clear the administration's views in a Chicago speech.[106] These plans probably would not have been given such praise by the Carter-run Justice Department. However, times had changed, and the board did not have to meet what it believed to be unrealistic goals that had been proposed by former Justice Department leadership. The only hurdle left was the approval of Judge Shadur.

As the desegregation plan was being finalized, a group of white Southwest Side parents called for yet another school boycott. Approximately 2,500 students stayed out of school on January 14, 1982. The students boycotted a number of elementary schools as well as Bogan High School. At Bogan, 79.1 percent of students were absent and at Dawes Elementary 82.6 percents stayed home. The rest of the schools had approximately 55 percent of students absent.[107] The boycott showed the continued resistance of white parents in the Ashburn community. Bogan had remained 95 percent white despite previous desegregation efforts. Even with the limitations of the board's plan, however, white schools previously segregated would now be desegregated. The latest desegregation efforts would force the number of minority students in areas such as Ashburn to at least 30 percent.

Judge Shadur's Decision

US district judge Milton L. Shadur approved Chicago's desegregation plan on January 6, 1983, almost a year after the desegregation plans were submitted to him. His decision approved major issues of contention in the plan. First, Judge Shadur addressed the racial percentages of the board's plan, which considered schools desegregated if they had at least 30 percent minorities or 30 percent whites. He noted, "For the facts are that this aspect of the plan is not only adequate to pass constitutional muster but—vital to public acceptance and support—reasoned and reasonable." The second issue was the minority category, which combined blacks and Latinos together as a single group. According to Shadur, "courts that have dealt with desegregation issues in multi-ethnic school districts have consistently approved plans with an inclusive definition of minorities like that adopted by the Plan. No constitutional requirement has been articulated that blacks must be a substantial part of the enrollment in all schools in a tri-ethnic system." Furthermore, Judge Shadur did not believe that more Latino students were used to desegregate than black students. He rejected the NAACP and Urban League's request for minimum percentages of blacks at each school. A third concern addressed was the undue burden of desegregation on blacks. Judge Shadur stated that "those arguments do not stand up in constitutional terms." He interpreted the NAACP's definition of burden as racial balancing. "Essentially the NAACP's contention is one for racial balance in all schools, which the Constitution does not mandate at all." The final issue was mandatory busing. He noted that, "It may seem bizarre to have gone this far down the road of constitutional evaluation of the plan without talking about busing. Not so. Busing is a concept loaded with emotional content on both sides of the issue, but its significance in the plan is far more symbolic than real." Moreover, the board had made plans to address the issue of busing by June 1983 based on the March 1983 Annual Desegregation Review. That was satisfactory to Judge Shadur.[108] He also found that the other mandatory provisions of the plan, such as boundary changes, properly addressed desegregation.

Appointed by Jimmy Carter, Judge Shadur had previously helped to organize the Lawyers' Committee on Civil Rights and worked on Illinois civil rights legislation with the American Jewish Congress. In spite of his liberal background, historian Raymond Wolters argued that Shadur favored Reynolds's legal arguments and the Chicago Board of Education on all points in contention. Reynolds was in favor of "reasonable" desegregation and against the dispersal of whites throughout the predominantly black and Latino system, which would accelerate white flight from the system, and Judge Shadur agreed.[109]

The Board of Education, superintendent, and Justice Department were satisfied with the judge's decision. Martha Jantho, who headed the desegregation committee, said, "I was very gratified by the judge's decision. It affirms the rights of parents. It's important for parents to have some sense of choice." Superintendent Ruth Love stated in a letter to the board, "The bulk of Judge Shadur's orders reflect an affirmation of both the direction and progress made in the area of student assignment, and reducing racial isolation, particularly in predominately white schools." The Justice Department was also encouraged by Shadur's decision, and released a statement saying, "We remain confident that the proper implementation of this plan . . . can achieve more lasting desegregation than a mandatory decision."[110]

But not everyone saw the plan in such a glowing light. Chicago Urban League member Roger Fox was disappointed with the Judge's decision because the three key provisions the court acknowledged did not go far enough to right the wrongs of past discrimination. NAACP general counsel Thomas Atkins thought Judge Shadur "ignored the rights of a substantial number of children in approving the plan . . . He apparently believes that black folks don't have any rights that white folks are bound to respect."[111] In an interview, Atkins stated that people typically have an easier time desegregating when whites are the majority in the school system. "The trouble is that whites just don't like being a minority. What Shadur approved was a plan which will permit some Chicago schools to be 100 percent black and others 70 percent white." Atkins indicated that "I'm not suggesting that you grab all white students in Chicago and scatter them all over the city. What I object to is the board going out of its way to maintain over-whelmingly white schools." In an effort to act on their dissatisfaction with the plan, the NAACP had filed a school desegregation law suit against the Chicago Board of Education, the City of Chicago, and the State of Illinois. Judge Shadur dismissed the case in April 1983, just days after Chicagoans elected their first black mayor, Harold Washington, after a racially divisive campaign.[112]

A *Chicago Tribune* editorial called Judge Shadur's decision wise and challenged opponents to accept the plan.

> The Chicago settlement marks a major and sensible change in approach to school desegregation by the Justice Department. The agreement worked out under Judge Shadur's jurisdiction concentrates on what improvements in integration can reasonably be achieved in view of an enrollment that now is only 16.3 percent white. It seeks to increase racial balance by the lure of magnet schools and innovative programs rather than by the whip of quota systems and widespread mandatory busing.
>
> Several organizations have been critical of the settlement that Judge Shadur approved. But it would be a tragedy for them to continue to fight it by legal maneuvers. Given current racial, financial, and educational realities, no better plan is possible now. It is time to turn all the caring, good will, effort, energy, and money available to improving the schools, to increasing learning opportunities, to upgrading student achievements and to integrating neighborhoods.[113]

Though NAACP and Urban League representatives probably disagreed with the sentiment of this editorial, the reality was no greater desegregation could be expected in a segregated city with declining white student enrollment.

School Board Sues Federal Government

Once the Chicago Board of Education finally had an approved school desegregation plan in place, it continued to contemplate the difficulties of financing such a plan. In 1981, the board estimated the total cost of the plan to be $17.8 million. That same year and for the first time since the Emergency School Aid Act law was passed in 1972, Chicago was finally granted funding. The city received a $1.8 million federal grant largely because of the consent decree. Chicago had finally demonstrated enough progress in faculty and student desegregation as well as bilingual education to receive the funding.[114] Unfortunately, the ESAA was repealed in 1982 at the request of the Reagan administration, demonstrating the administration's continued opposition to school desegregation. (The administration also wanted to get rid of the Department of Education, but could not convince Congress to do so).[115] To make matters worse, school officials stated that they had received no money from the state, but were expecting the state to reimburse some of the transportation costs. The school budget had already been pieced together for the 1981–1982 school year; half a year before the next budget was due, there were already predictions that there would be a $122 million deficit.[116] Therefore, the board was concerned about how they would pay for their desegregation initiatives, partially because of financial problems, but also because of the lack of or limited financial support from the mayor, governor, and federal government.

Each year the board had to close schools, had difficult negotiations with the Chicago Teachers Union, and struggled to obtain financial solvency. The board decided to sue the federal government to force it to fund the desegregation efforts and filed a petition in the US District Court where Judge Shadur oversaw the matter. The board argued that in the consent decree, the Justice Department had said it would seek federal assistance to fund desegregation and so were "obligated to make every good faith effort to find and provide every available form of financial resources adequate for the implementation of the desegregation plan."[117] The board had only received $1.8 million in ESAA funding. Robert Howard, the board's desegregation attorney stated that the board "has a contract with the United States—the consent decree—that it is asking the U.S. to live up to. The Board is doing its part. It's time the U.S. did its."[118] According to the *Chicago Tribune*, Chicago had received very little financial assistance compared to other cities: Milwaukee had received $14.5 million; Buffalo, $12.4 million; New York City, $17.1 million; and Seattle, $10.4 million.[119]

Judge Shadur ordered the United States to pay at least $14.6 million for the 1983–1984 costs, froze some federal accounts, and ordered the executive branch to assist with ensuring the implementation of the plan. The accounts were frozen to make sure Chicago received its share of the funding. The government appealed the decision. The case ran its course between the district court and the circuit court and was not resolved until July 1987. Congress passed the Yates Bill, promising Chicago $83 million in federal funds over five years. Board attorney Howard indicated that the new law finally ended the funding issues over desegregation. It only awaited US district court judge Charles Kocoras's approval—but President Reagan vetoed the bill.[120] Chicago was left to fund its own desegregation initiatives.

*   *   *

The Chicago Public Schools did what it could to achieve desegregation with the limited number of remaining white students. Although the plan failed to incorporate more black students, it was effective in desegregating white schools. The plan was far more successful than any that had previously been attempted. It desegregated white schools that had been largely untouched with Access to Excellence and permissive transfer plans of the past and led to close to 78,000 students being desegregated in its initial years of implementation. Although the number of white students continued to decline over the years, desegregation did not lead to the massive exodus that many had anticipated. With all of its short comings, the plan was efficient and matched the demographic reality in the city. More black students could have been impacted; however, the movement of white students throughout the city would still have left many black schools segregated.

An interesting aspect of this plan like others created over the years is that blacks were still viewed as undesirable. Time and time again, the various protests and limited aspects of the plans revealed that whites did not want to be the minority at most schools, unless those schools were magnet schools. Most black schools were automatically viewed by many as inferior, and policy makers were not oblivious to this. This suggests white privilege was maintained in the plan and accepted as necessary and reasonable at the expense of many black schools and students and increasingly segregated Latino schools and students. Critics of the plan continually highlighted these issues, but argued that catering to that privilege was not an excuse for leaving so many black children isolated in black schools. An OCR official stated the problem this way:

> It is all there. The wheel-in wagons [used as classrooms], the drawing of school boundaries lines, the schools side by side, a half a mile away—one white, one black. You name it, the case is there—the evidence is nailed down.

> The question in Chicago really is a remedy with a system that is approaching 90 percent minority students in the public school population. It's going to be a case for an affirmative finding and what are you going to do? Are you going to settle for 10 percent whites in each of the schools...and if you're going to do that, are you going to increase white flight? And you will end up with, "Where am I going to get the whites from?"[121]

How does one balance the reality of the situation with creating better opportunities for all students in a desegregated environment? Board member Martha Jantho saw the importance of maintaining whites in the public schools. "For my purposes, I was glad [the Justice Department] approved [the school desegregation plan]. I didn't want to have to impose a mandatory plan on anybody. The plan was approved. I know one of our consultants wanted a more rigid plan and the prognosis was in a year we'll be down to 5 percent white [if a more rigid plan was imposed]. I want to keep as many of these white kids in the schools as I can. And we did."[122] School officials and Judge Shadur did what they thought was going to be the most effective, and the conservative Justice Department also found these limitations acceptable.

Conclusion

The 1964 Civil Rights Act marked a culmination of congressional negotiation and internal pressure from the Civil Rights Movement. The act gave the federal government the power to fulfill civil rights promises to millions of citizens whose race, color, and national origin had prevented full participation in the American society. One of the fundamentally important areas the Civil Rights Act addressed was the desegregation of schools. Schools have been a major target for social policy in the United States—continuing the nation's proclivity to attempt massive social change through its public schools. Reformers have offered schools as a vehicle for equal educational opportunity time and again throughout American history. Though this has not always meant equality or an equal outcome, minimal standards for all has been an essential component for equal educational opportunity.[1]

In regards to desegregation, funding for black schools was grossly inept before and after the *Brown v. Board of Education* decision, limiting the chance for even minimal educational standards to be met. Many southern states continued a state-sponsored Jim Crow system in public and private institutions. But the Civil Rights Act gave the federal government a carrot-and-stick approach to coerce southern states and school districts to provide equality of opportunity that would not have occurred without this statute. Nonetheless, school desegregation implementation was still difficult as southern state and local politicians and citizens rejected school desegregation.

Segregation in the North and West attracted the attention of implementation agencies of the federal government and cast a national rather than regional spotlight on school segregation in a way some signers of the Civil Rights Act never intended. While southern segregation was blatant and unmistakable, northern and western segregation proved more difficult to attack, particularly in large urban areas.

The Chicago school desegregation experience provides a history of implementing a federal civil rights law in the North as enforcers faced shifting federal agenda, local political power, stakeholder opposition, and demographic transitions. As Chicagoans engaged in the Civil Rights Movement exposed the inequalities and segregation in a northern city with a powerful mayor, federal officials had to add additional guidelines to help implement the Civil Rights Act. The political environment caused policy modifications neither intended nor foreseen. The focus on the city brought to the fore the ways in which issues beyond schools impact and dictate the effectiveness schools have in bringing about social change.

Like the South, Chicago's policy makers at the municipal and school district level maintained and enhanced segregation though a myriad of ways. At the city level this was accomplished through urban redevelopment and highway construction. At the school district level, school boundaries were gerrymandered, and attendance areas and mobile units contained blacks at overcrowded schools in black communities while allowing underutilized white schools to exist nearby. Teachers with less experience were concentrated at black schools. As white teachers gained experience they left black schools to seek employment in white areas. Consequently, black students were in overcrowded schools with less experienced teachers and high teacher turnover rates. The city operated a dual system of education that stunted equality of opportunity. While desegregation was seen as an alternative to the dual system, not all constituents were in agreement—especially when it came to strategies (such as busing) for actually achieving desegregation.

Federal agencies, armed with federal law and court rulings, worked to implement school desegregation in Chicago. However, these officials faced numerous obstacles. Presidential administrations changed numerous times, resulting in change in agency leadership and policy goals. Each president had his own beliefs about how the Civil Rights Act should be applied, and some worked to slow or reverse its implementation. Congress continually chipped away at the effectiveness of the Civil Rights Act, even as the courts worked to strengthen the timeliness of federal agency enforcement with *Adams v. Richardson*. In addition to the changes Congress made to the act—including eliminating busing as an option for withholding funding with the Eagleton–Biden Amendment—the Department of Health, Education, and Welfare (HEW), along with the Department of Justice, did not have the personnel to handle the compliance for numerous districts around the country. This resource inadequacy severely limited the capacity of these agencies to articulate and monitor desegregation policy directives. Further, the federal government failed to provide the state and local governments with the resources necessary to ensure successful policy implementation. The Chicago

Board of Education faced with its own limited resources and other constraints had the responsibility of implementing federal policies aimed at undoing institutionalized segregation. Passage of the Civil Rights Act alone was not enough. Without the resources, stability in agency leadership and policy goals, it was a policy destined for limited success if not outright failure.

The federal government had to work with states and local districts to accomplish desegregation. The State of Illinois was less of a hindrance to school desegregation than southern states. The state created policies to achieve student desegregation as the federal government focused on faculty desegregation. Its policy implementation often fell short of federal expectations and even minimal desegregation efforts took years. Superintendents often proposed and implemented only voluntary and token desegregation plans. The Board of Education typically followed the dictates of its superintendent and refused mandatory backup plans when voluntary efforts failed. The Chicago Democratic Machine, which benefitted from segregation, did not allow any ambitious plans while Mayor Daley was in office.

At the local level, both state and federal government officials faced opposition to school desegregation from stakeholders, superintendents, the Chicago Board of Education, the Chicago Teachers Union, and the city's political machine. Private citizens and organizations protested and demonstrated against plans they believed unwise. Although stakeholders were unable to eliminate desegregation plans altogether, most of their protests forced the board to revise aspects of many proposals. The federal and state government officials faced a notable adversary from local government officials and citizens.

Beyond local opponents, the reality of city and school demographics, housing segregation, and the considerable expenses of school desegregation also complicated implementation. By 1980, whites barely comprised half the city's population. In that same year, only 18.4 percent of the students in Chicago Public Schools (CPS) were white. As demonstrated in chapter 3, school desegregation was not the main cause of white flight—whites left the city in spite of its high segregation index. Yet the constant loss of whites meant that the Board of Education had to be astute about any desegregation plans they initiated. Their main focus was to retain whites in the city and the school system, and they feared any ambitious plan to bus remaining white students throughout the city would lead to virtually no whites in the school system. The lack of white students in CPS, just when school desegregation policy was implemented successfully, severely curtailed the promise of social change through Chicago's schools. Whites benefited from attendance at predominantly white schools, and when they attended schools with larger percentages of black and Latino students, these tended to be magnet or transitioning schools. Only two predominantly white schools had more than 70 percent white students by the 1985–1986 school year. Yet that same year, 278 of the district's 596 total schools (46.6 percent) had 95 percent or more black students. Of those schools, 117 (19.6) were 100 percent black.[2] The schools remained predominantly segregated despite years of local, state, and national efforts to create desegregation. Close to half of the schools remained racially isolated. A number of southern districts were able to accomplish far more than this. The Supreme Court inhibited the possibility of metropolitan desegregation in its 1974 *Milliken v. Bradley* decision, leaving Chicago and other predominantly black and Latino cities to fend for themselves.

Housing segregation caused much of the school segregation in the North and especially in Chicago, but efforts to change housing segregation were not effective. Whites simply moved to suburbs or other areas of the city. Housing segregation also made school desegregation efforts expensive. Though busing was a normal part of American schooling, Chicagoans tended to go to local schools and most often used transportation for high schools. The distance between communities along with the creation of special programs and magnet schools made desegregation an expensive endeavor that the federal and state governments were unwilling to finance. As the school system faced repeated financial crises, it could not rely on the federal government to fund desegregation. Funding opportunities only worsened in the 1980s when the Reagan administration eliminated much of the federal funding for school desegregation with the repeal of the Emergency School Aid Act.

The federal government's role as purveyor of public policy in the best interest of the nation has limited power in bringing about social change. Laws passed at the national level have to be negotiated with state and local governments to make implementation possible. Without the cooperation of state and local governments and other crucial implementing agencies such as the school board, change initiatives will fail or have a less substantial impact. Recent actions with the President Barack Obama's healthcare law (Patient Protection and Affordable Care Act), No Child Left Behind, and Race to the Top have once again demonstrated this limitation. States opposed to the laws simply refuse to accept funding or allow implementation in their states. The reach of the federal government is limited and policy implementation is uneven.

Beginning in 2003, district court judge Charles P. Kocoras announced that he thought the Justice Department negotiated consent decree should end. He argued that, "the whole complexion of the city has changed. The school system has changed dramatically."[3] In 2004, he stated, "It can be fairly argued that 23 years is plenty of time to complete whatever can be completed and all the rest is needless trifling. It is not wise for things to go on forever. There's a time for Big Brother to bow out."[4] On September 24, 2009, Judge Kocoras vacated the consent decree. CPS CEO Ron Huberman announced, "The court has held that Chicago Public Schools are in compliance with the Constitution and the laws of the United States in the District's efforts to achieve unitary status. We recognize the importance of promoting diverse learning communities for every student and remain committed to the development of a fair admissions process to achieve that goal even further."[5] Huberman was overly optimistic about the city's accomplishments, as desegregation had never truly occurred in the majority of the city's schools. After the consent decree ended, the Chicago Board of Education changed its race-based assignment policies to socioeconomic-based assignments.[6]

The end of the consent decree occurred within the context of a 2007 Supreme Court decision. The Supreme Court overturned voluntary remedies for desegregation in Louisville, Kentucky, and Seattle, Washington, on the theory that, without a court-determined violation of the law, race neutral policies should determine pupil placement in schools. *Parents Involved v. Seattle School District* came just 53 years after the landmark *Brown v. Board of Education* ruling. In a time of increased resegregation,[7] the Supreme Court's decision makes opportunities for desegregation even more limited.

Fifty years after the passage of the 1964 Civil Rights Act and 60 years after the *Brown* decision, Chicago school officials' focus has moved to accountability and enforcing a neoliberal agenda of weakening teachers unions and closing traditional public schools to open charter schools. The 2012 teachers strike and the protests against the 2013 closure of 50 mostly black schools made national headlines. The promise of the Civil Rights Act brought only momentary relief. For those who could benefit, it helped to create a black middle class, provide better educational opportunities, and opened up the society in ways many could not have imagined. But for so many others, the fight to improve the society through federal public policy bypassed their neighborhoods and communities as continued poverty, deindustrialization, recession, housing crisis, gentrification, drug infestation, and mass incarceration have dimmed the possibility of the American dream.

In 1979, the Chicago Urban League criticized the Access to Excellence school desegregation plan for the continued racial isolation of black students and predicted that, "If these are the seeds the Board chooses to sow, they must be prepared to reap the tragic social harvest that will inevitably result from policies that systematically isolate and separate a group of people from the mainstream of the society in which they live."[8] Skyrocketing murder rates among the city's youth seems to be the harvest the city has reaped from policies which have maintained segregation in spite of the federal government's policy efforts to reduce discrimination and segregation. Yet to demand schools solve social problems created and reinforced by the larger society is both unfair and shortsighted.

This study adds to the narrative about race segregation, racial inequalities and discrimination, and the use of legislation and public policy to overcome these. The Civil Rights Act has had significant value in promoting symbolically, if not also legally, in the national psyche that racial segregation and discrimination are at variance in advancing these United States toward a more perfect union. This book has shown that within the school system at least, segregation persists even as rhetoric and beliefs that suggests otherwise prevail. While adults disagree, the nation's school children were used by its government as harbingers of social change and were being tasked with the responsibility of overcoming years of segregation and discrimination they had no hand in creating. Why despite considerable efforts and historic civil rights legislation does school segregation remain entrenched in America? Is school desegregation still valued or is it an ideal whose time has come and passed? Is public policy enough to bring about lasting social change in a democratic society? This book has hopefully drawn attention to these issues as arenas for further research.

Appendix: Timeline of Chicago Desegregation Efforts

April 1958	NAACP *Crisis* article published
1961, 1963	*Webb v. Board of Education*
1963	Hauser Report, Armstrong Law passed
October 1963	Freedom Day Boycott 1
February 1964	Freedom Day Boycott 2
June 1965	Additional boycotts
July 1965	Congressional Hearing on Chicago segregation
July 1965	CCCO Title VI Complaint
September 1965	HEW withholds federal funds
October 1965	HEW releases federal funds
March 1968	Redmond's busing plan implemented
July 1969	Justice Department demands faculty desegregation
November 1971	State begins interactions with Chicago
September 1972	State finds Chicago out of compliance
May 1975	State places Chicago on notice
October 1975	HEW takes over faculty desegregation negotiations
February 1976	State places Chicago on noncompliance status
April 1976	State places Chicago on probation
February 1977	Administrative ruling on faculty desegregation
June–Sept. 1977	Faculty desegregation
1977	OCR begins student desegregation investigation
January 1978	CWAC plan created
April 1978	Access to excellence unveiled
April 1979	HEW accuses Chicago of purposeful students segregation
October 1979	Case sent to the Justice Department
November 1979	Financial crisis revealed
Jan.–April 1980	Board of Education forced to resign
September 1980	Consent decree approved
January 1982	Board's final desegregation plan sent to Judge Shadur
January 1983	Judge Shadur approves the board's plan

Notes

Introduction

1. Coordinating Council of Community Organizations, "The Chicago Title VI Complaint to H.E.W." *Integrated Education* 3 (December 1965–January 1966): 10.

2. Gary Orfield, *The Reconstruction of Southern Education: The Schools and the 1964 Civil Rights Act* (New York: Wiley-Interscience, 1969), 151–207. For more details, see Alan B. Anderson and George W. Pickering, *Confronting the Color Line: The Broken Promise of the Civil Rights Movement in Chicago* (Athens: University of Georgia Press, 1986).

3. See Mike Royko, *Boss: Mayor Richard J. Daley of Chicago* (New York: Plume, 1971); Adam Cohen and Elizabeth Taylor, *American Pharaoh: Mayor Richard J. Daley, His Battle for Chicago and the Nation* (Boston: Little, Brown, 2000); Roger Biles, *Richard J. Daley: Politics, Race, and the Governing of Chicago* (Dekalb: Northern Illinois Press, 1995); William J. Grimshaw, *Bitter Fruit: Black Politics and the Chicago Machine, 1931–1991* (Chicago: University of Chicago Press, 1992); Dempsey J. Travis, *An Autobiography of Black Chicago* (Chicago: Urban Research Press, 1981).

4. Cohen and Taylor, *American Pharaoh*, 10–11; Lilia Fernandez, *Brown in the Windy City: Mexicans and Puerto Ricans in Postwar Chicago* (Chicago: University of Chicago Press, 2012); Jacobi Williams, *From the Bullet to the Ballot: The Illinois Chapter of the Black Panther Party and Racial Coalition Politics in Chicago*, 31;Royko, *Boss*.

5. Orfield, *The Reconstruction of Southern Education*, 173–174.

6. See Gary Orfield, *Must We Bus: Segregated Schools and National Policy* (Washington, DC: The Brookings Institution); Center for National Policy Review, *Justice Delayed and Denied, HEW and Northern School Desegregation* (Washington, DC: Catholic University of America School of Law, 1974).

7. Interview with Edgar Epps, March 2, 2011.

8. See Dean J. Kotlowski, *Nixon's Civil Rights: Politics, Principle, and Policy* (Cambridge, MA: Harvard University Press, 2001); Lawrence J. McAndrews, "Missing the Bus: Gerald Ford and School Desegregation," *Presidential Studies Quarterly* 27 (Fall 1997). Retrieved February 11, 2013, from http://www.questia.com/library

/1G1-20223418/missing-the-bus-gerald-ford-and-school-deseg regation; Drew S. Days, "Turning Back the Clock: The Reagan Administration and Civil Rights," *Harvard Civil Rights-Civil Liberties Law Review* 19 (1984) 346.

9. Brian J. Kelly, "Half of Blacks and Latinos Reject Busing," *Chicago Sun-Times*, December 30, 1979, 8; Brian J. Kelly, "Access to Excellence Plan Get a Failing Grade," *Chicago Sun-Times*, January 2, 1980, 1.

10. School data for Hispanics were not collected until 1968. At that time, all Hispanics were labeled Puerto Rican. They were labeled Hispanic by 1970. Asians and American Indians have accounted for between 3 and 5 percent of the total student population.

11. The information for Hispanics was not available until 1980.

12. Ronald P. Formisano, *Boston against Busing: Race, Class, and Ethnicity in the 1960s and 1970s* (Chapel Hill: University of North Carolina Press, 2004); Joyce A. Baugh, *The Detroit School Busing Case:* Milliken v. Bradley *and the Controversy over Desegregation* (Lawrence: University of Kansas Press, 2011); Joseph Radelet, "Stillness at Detroit's Racial Divide: A Perspective of Detroit's School Desegregation Court Order, 1970–1989," *Urban Review* 23 (September 1991): 173–190; Jerald E. Podair, *The Strike That Changed New York* (New Haven: Yale University Press, 2002); Gregory S. Jacobs, *Getting Around Brown: Desegregation, Development, and the Columbus Public Schools* (Columbus: Ohio State University, 1998); Jack Dougherty, *More than One Struggle: The Evolution of Black School Reform in Milwaukee* (Chapel Hill: University of North Carolina Press, 2004); Steven J. L Taylor, *Desegregation in Boston and Buffalo: The Influence of Local Leaders* (Albany: State University of New York Press, 1998).

13. Civil Rights Act of 1964.

14. Tracy L. Steffes, *School, Society, & State: A New Education to Govern Modern America, 1980–1940* (Chicago: University of Chicago Press, 2012), 6–7. For research on equal educational opportunity and the federal government's role, see Adam R. Nelson, *The Elusive Ideal: Equal Educational Opportunity and the Federal Role in Boston's Public Schools, 1950–1985* (Chicago: University of Chicago Press, 2004).

15. Carl F. Kaestle, *Pillars of the Republic: Common Schools and American Society, 1780–1960* (New York: Hill and Wang, 1983); Derrick Bell, *Silent Covenants:* Brown v. Board of Education *and the Unfulfilled Hopes for Racial Reform* (Oxford: Oxford University Press, 2004); James T. Patterson, Brown v. Board of Education: *A Civil Rights Milestone and Its Troubled Legacy* (Oxford: Oxford University Press, 2001).

16. Alan B. Anderson and George W. Pickering, *Confronting the Color Line: The Broken Promise of the Civil Rights Movement in Chicago* (Athens: University of Georgia Press, 1986); James R. Ralph Jr., *Northern Protest: Martin Luther King, Jr., Chicago, and the Civil*

Rights Movement (Cambridge: Harvard University Press, 1993); John L. Rury, "Race, Space, and the Politics of Chicago's Public Schools: Benjamin Willis and the Tragedy of Urban Education," *History of Education Quarterly* 39 (Spring 1999); Dionne Danns, *Something Better for Our Children: Black Organizing in Chicago Public Schools, 1963–1971* (New York: Routledge, 2003).

17. Arnold R. Hirsch, *Making the Second Ghetto: Race & Housing in Chicago 1940–1960* (Chicago: University of Chicago Press, 1983); Amanda I. Seligman, *Block by Block: Neighborhoods and Public Policy on Chicago's West Side* (Chicago: University of Chicago Press, 2005).

18. See Michael W. Homel, *Down from Equality: Black Chicagoans and the Public Schools, 1920–1941* (Urbana: University of Illinois Press, 1984), 133–178.

19. "*De Facto* Segregation in Chicago Public Schools," *Crisis* 65 (February 1958), 87–93.

20. Double shift assignments occurred as a result of overcrowding and meant that one set of students came to school in the morning and another set in the afternoon. It also meant that students lost about an hour of school each day so that all the students could be accommodated.

21. "*De Facto* Segregation in Chicago Public Schools," 87–93.

22. Anderson and Pickering, *Confronting the Color Line*, 80–85; "Editorial," *Chicago Defender*, March 13, 1961; *Webb v. Board of Education of City of Chicago* 61C1569, "Filings-Proceedings."

23. *Webb v. Board of Education* 61C1569, "Brief in Support of Defendants' Motion to Dismiss or, in the Alternative, for Partial Summary Judgment, and Suggesting the Necessity for a Three-Judge Court," 3.

24. Anderson and Pickering, *Confronting the Color Line*; *Webb v. Board of Education* 61C1569.

25. *Webb v. Board of Education* 61C1569, "Affidavit in Support of Motion for Preliminary Injunction," 3.

26. Integration was defined as 10 percent or more of the student body at a school being black or white. Philip M. Hauser et al., "Report to the Board of Education of the City of Chicago by the Advisory Panel on Integration of the Public Schools," March 31, 1964, 14.

27. Hauser et al., "Report to the Board of Education," 17–19.

28. Ibid, 27.

29. Cyrus H. Adams, Warren H. Bacon, Thomas J. Murray, Margaret Wild, and Bernard S. Friedman, "Report to the Sub-Committee of the Board of Education. Re: Section 2, Recommendation 2 and Section 1-D, Recommendation 1, of the Report to the Advisory Panel on Integration of the Public Schools (Hauser Committee)," 4.

30. These organizations included the Cook County Physicians Association, Cook County Bar Association, Dearborn Real Estate Board, Teachers for Integrated Schools, Catholic Interracial Council, Presbyterian Interracial Council, Episcopal Society for Cultural and

Racial Unity, Ecumenical Institute, Chicago Area Friends of SNCC, and the Negro American Labor Council.

31. Anderson and Pickering, *Confronting the Color Line*, 99, 114, 129.

32. "Request for Reform of Our School System," Cyrus Hall Adams Papers, box 1–4, Chicago History Museum; James Sullivan, "School Demands Listed: Boycotters Want Willis Backer Out," *Chicago Tribune*, October 21, 1963, 1–2.

33. Paul West, "City School Board Hears Bias Protest: CORE Group Holds Sit-in," *Chicago Tribune*, July 11, 1963, 1–2; Paul West, "Police Remove 10 from Office of School. Board: Daley Supports Action Asked by Roddewig," *Chicago Tribune*, July 19, 1963, 1–2; Betty Flynn, "The Battle of Ben Willis: A Chicago Dilemma," *Renewal* (March 1965): 4; Ralph, *Northern Protest*, 19.

34. Benjamin C. Willis, "Statement to the Education and Labor Committee House of Representatives," July 27, 1965; Philip M. Hauser, "Testimony on De Facto Segregation in the Chicago Public Schools, before the Committee on Education and Labor, House of Representatives," July 27, 1965; James Yuenger, "U.S. Queries Willis on School Bias Study," *Chicago Tribune*, September 3, 1965, 1, 4.

35. CCCO, "The Chicago Title VI Complaint."

1 REDMOND'S SCHOOL DESEGREGATION PLAN AND REACTIONS

1. See Alan B. Anderson and George W. Pickering, *Confronting the Color Line: The Broken Promise of the Civil Rights Movement in Chicago* (Athens: University of Georgia Press, 1986); John L. Rury, "Race, Space, and the Politics of Chicago's Public Schools: Benjamin Willis and the Tragedy of Urban Education," *History of Education Quarterly* 39 (Spring 1999): 117–142.

2. Chicago Board of Education, "Increasing Desegregation of Faculties, Students and Vocational Education Programs," August 1967, 1.

3. See Michael W. Homel, *Down from Equality: Black Chicagoans and the Public Schools, 1920–1941* (Urbana: University of Illinois Press, 1984).

4. Allen H. Spear, *Black Chicago: The Making of a Negro Ghetto, 1890–1920* (Chicago: University of Chicago Press, 1967), 212–216; Gabriela F. Arredondo, *Mexican Chicago: Race, Identity, and Nation, 1916–1939* (Urbana: University of Illinois Press, 2008), 38.

5. Arnold R. Hirsch, *Making the Second Ghetto: Race & Housing in Chicago 1940–1960* (Chicago: University of Chicago Press, 1983), 68–98.

6. Ibid.

7. Beryl Satter, *Family Properties: Race, Real Estate, and the Exploitation of Black Urban America* (New York: Metropolitan Books, 2009), 5.

8. Amanda I. Seligman, *Block by Block: Neighborhoods and Public Policy on Chicago's West Side* (Chicago: University of Chicago Press, 2005).

9. Ibid.
10. The Chicago Fact Book Consortium, *Local Community Fact Book Chicago Metropolitan Areas Based on the 1970 and 1980 Census* (Chicago: Chicago Review Press, 1984), 69.
11. Each community is made up of a group of census tracks. The Local Community Fact Books, cited in this study, used the information from the census tracks to create the neighborhood census. The Chicago Fact Book Consortium, *Local Community Fact Book*, 68–69; Evelyn M. Kitagawa and Karl E. Taeuber, *Local Community Fact Book, Chicago Metropolitan Area 1960* (Chicago: Chicago Community Inventory, University of Chicago, 1963), 65.
12. William Anton Vrame, *A History of School Desegregation in Chicago since 1954* (PhD Diss., University of Wisconsin, 1970), 120–124; Rury, "Race, Space, and the Politics of Chicago's Public Schools," 122–123.
13. Vrame, "A History of School Desegregation," 143–153; The Chicago Fact Book Consortium, *Local Community Fact Book*, 68–69.
14. Vrame, "A History of School Desegregation," 149–153; Seligman, *Block by Block*, 138–140.
15. Vrame, "A History of School Desegregation," 164–167.
16. Saul Alinsky is a legendary community organizer who believed that ordinary people could use confrontational strategies to change their conditions. He organized The Woodlawn Organization and the Back of the Yards Neighborhood Council. Seligman, *Block by Block*, 6, 198.
17. Seligman, *Block by Block*, 198; Vrame, "A History of School Desegregation," 169–179.
18. Chicago Board of Education, "Increasing Desegregation," August 1967, B-17.
19. Ibid., B-19-B-31.
20. Coordinating Council of Community Organization, "The Redmond Board Report and Its Implications," September 8, 1967, 11.
21. Ibid., 10.
22. See Arnold R. Hirsch, "Massive Resistance in the Urban North: Trumbull Park, Chicago, 1953–1966," *The Journal of American History* 82 (September 1995): 522–550; Thomas J. Sugrue, "Crabgrass-Roots Politics: Race, Rights, and the Reaction against Liberalism in the Urban North, 1940-1964," *The Journal of American History* 82 (September 1995): 551–578.
23. Arnold R. Hirsch, *Making the Second Ghetto*; Allen H. Spear, *Black Chicago*.
24. Chicago Board of Education, "Increasing Desegregation," B-16.
25. CCCO, "The Redmond Board Report and Its Implications," 14.
26. Ronald P. Formisano, *Boston against Busing: Race, Class, and Ethnicity in the 1960s and 1970s* (Chapel Hill: University of North Carolina Press, 2004), 20; "Redmond's Career Shows Meteoric Rise," *Chicago Tribune*, May 11, 1966, 5.

27. Henry De Zutter, "Redmond Victory: Busing OKd; Could Start Jan. 29," *Chicago Daily News*, December 28, 1967; Christopher Chandler, "School Busing for Austin and S. Shore OKd," *Chicago Sun-Times*, December 28, 1967, 20.

28. Loraine Green and Warren Bacon are black board members. Paul E. Peterson, *School Politics Chicago Style* (Chicago: University of Chicago Press, 1976), 156–157.

29. Gary Orfield, *The Reconstruction of Southern Education: The Schools and the 1964 Civil Rights Act* (New York: Wiley-Interscience, 1969); Peterson, *School Politics Chicago Style*, 154.

30. Vern K. Richey, "Northwest Side: Pupil Busing Backed by 3 PTA Heads," *Chicago Daily News*, January 4, 1968, 3; "Board Under Fire: Bridge Parents Plan Negro Busing Protests," *Chicago Daily News*, January 5, 1968, 3; Christopher Chandler, "4 More Schools Added to Bus Plan," *Chicago Sun-Times*, January 5, 1968, 3; Christopher Chandler; "Rival Busing Proposal For South Shore Bared," *Chicago Sun-Times*, January 6, 1968, 4; "'We Don't Want Integration': 1500 Protest Busing Plan," *Chicago Sun-Times*, January 7, 1968, 3, 19.

31. Christopher Chandler, "Redmond Discloses the Details of Plans for Busing 1,035 Pupils," *Chicago Sun-Times*, January 9, 1968, 4; Vrame, "A History of School Desegregation," 183, 187.

32. Vrame, "A History of School Desegregation," 204.

33. The Chicago Fact Book Consortium, *Local Community Fact Book*, 38–40, 43–50.

34. Ibid., 116–119; Peterson, *School Politics Chicago Style*, 165; Harvey Luskin Molotch, *Managed Integration: Dilemmas of Doing Good in the City* (Berkeley: University of California Press, 1972), 44; Vrame, "A History of School Desegregation," 197–198.

35. The Chicago Fact Book Consortium, *Local Community Fact Book*, 119–121.

36. There are no clear indication of Mexican views of desegregation in South Chicago from the hearings. Ibid., 123–125; Kitagawa and Taeuber, *Local Community Fact Book*, 106; Peterson, *School Politics Chicago Style*, 166; David Benson, "South Chicago," in *Chicago Neighborhoods and Suburbs: A Historical Guide*, ed. Ann Durkin Keating (Chicago: University of Chicago Press), 270–272.

37. Molotch, *Managed Integration*, 63–65; Peterson, *School Politics Chicago Style*, 167.

38. Chandler, "School Busing for Austin and S. Shore OKd," 20.

39. Chandler, "Rival Busing for South Shore Bared," 4.

40. "2,000 at N.W. Side Rally Map Busing Demonstration," *Chicago Sun-Times*, January 9, 1968, 16; John Linstead, "Northwest Side: 1,000 Delegates Set Protest of Busing," *Chicago Daily News*, January 9, 1968, 1.

41. Edmond J. Rooney, "Hundreds Protest in Corridors," *Chicago Daily News*, January 10, 1968, 1; Christopher Chandler, "Board Delays

Decision on Plan to Bus Pupils," *Chicago Sun-Times*, January 11, 1968, 1.

42. Henry De Zutter, "Daley: 'Let Those in Affected Areas Decide,'" *Chicago Daily News*, January 11, 1968.

43. Rury, "Race, Space, and the Politics of Chicago's Public Schools," 134–135; Roger Biles, *Richard J. Daley: Politics, Race, and the Governing of Chicago* (Dekalb: Northern Illinois Press, 1995), 96–101.

44. Joel Havemann, "Protest school Busing Plan, *Chicago Sun-Times*, January 11, 1968, 1, 32; Chandler, "Board Delays Decision on Plans to Bus Pupils," 1, 32; De Zutter, "Daley," 8.

45. Joel Havemann, "Civic Groups Rally Behind Busing," *Chicago Sun-Times*, January 13, 1968, 3; "U.S. Watching Fate of Busing Here," *Chicago Tribune*, January 13, 1968, 2; Henry De Zutter; "Busing Fight Perils U.S. Aid," *Chicago Daily News*, January 12, 1968, 1.

46. "School Bus Politics," *Chicago Daily News*, January 12, 1968, 6; "Busing Delays School Budget," *Chicago Daily News,* January 17, 1968, 3; Christopher Chandler, "School Tax Levy OK Deferred by Council," *Chicago Sun-Times*, January 18, 1968, 5; "School Tax Levy OKd a Busing Foes March," *Chicago Daily News*, January 30, 1968, 1.

47. Hope Justus, "Angry Reaction Delays, May Kill School Bus Plan," *Chicago American*, January 11, 1968, 4.

48. De Zutter; "Busing Fight Perils U.S. Aid," 1.

49. Chicago Board of Education, *Proceedings*, vol. II., January 24, 1968–January 26, 1968, 1533.

50. Peterson, *School Politics Chicago Style*, 165–166.

51. Chicago Board of Education, "Transcript of Hearings at South Shore High School," February 5, 1968, 3, 4, Cyrus Hall Adams Papers, box 35–4, Chicago History Museum (CHM).

52. Vrame, "A History of School Desegregation," 258.

53. Chicago Board of Education, "Transcript of Hearings at South Shore High School," 23–28.

54. James T. Patterson, Brown v. Board of Education: *A Civil Rights Milestone and Its Troubled Legacy* (Oxford: Oxford University Press, 2001), 42–43.

55. See Vanessa Siddle Walker, *Their Highest Potential: African American School Community in the Segregated South* (Chapel Hill: University of North Carolina Press, 1996); David S. Cecelski, *Along Freedom Road: Hyde County, North Carolina, and the Fate of Black Schools in the South* (Chapel Hill: University of North Carolina Press, 1994); Scott R. Baker, *Paradoxes of Desegregation: African American Struggle for Educational Equity in Charleston, South Carolina, 1926–1972* (Columbia: University of South Carolina Press, 2006).

56. Edwardo Bonilla Silva, *White Supremacy and Racism in a Post Civil Rights Era* (Boulder: Lynne Rienner, 2001).

57. The Chicago Fact Book Consortium, *Local Community Fact Book*, 116–119.

58. Chicago Board of Education, "Transcript of Hearings at Bowen High School," February 12, 1968, 60–61, Cyrus Hall Adams Papers, box 35–4, CHM.

59. Ibid., 62–64.

60. "No Busing," *West Side Torch*, January 19–February 2, 1968, 3; "Westside Speaks on Busing," *West Side Torch*, February 16–March 2, 1968, 4.

61. Carter G. Woodson, *The Mis-education of the Negro* (Trenton, New Jersey: African World Press, 1993), xiii.

62. Black Power included black nationalists, black radicals with Marxist or socialist orientation, as well as those who wanted community control.

63. See Dionne Danns, *Something Better for Our Children: Black Organizing in Chicago Public Schools* (New York: Routledge, 2003); Jakobi Williams, *From the Bullet to the Ballot: The Illinois Chapter of the Black Panther Party and Racial Coalition Politics in Chicago* (Chapel Hill: University of North Carolina Press, 2013); Elizabeth Shana Todd-Breland, *To Reshape and Redefine Our World: African American Political Organizing for Education in Chicago 1968–1988* (PhD Diss., University of Chicago, 2010); Gael Graham, *Young Activists: American High School Students in the Age of Protest* (DeKalb: Northern Illinois Press, 2006); Carlos Muñoz Jr., *Youth, Identity, Power: The Chicano Movement* (London: Verso, 1989).

64. Chicago Board of Education, "Transcript of Hearings at Austin High School," February 22, 1968, 17, Cyrus Hall Adams Papers, box 35–5, CHM.

65. "Veiled Threat of Violence at Rally," *Austinite*, January 24, 1968.

66. See Stephen Kendrick and Paul Kendrick, *Sarah's Long Walk: Free Blacks of Boston and How Their Struggle for Equality Changed America* (Boston: Beacon Press, 2004); Hilary J. Moss, *Schooling Citizens: The Struggle for African American Education in Antebellum America* (Chicago: University of Chicago Press, 2009),164–189; Carl F. Kaestle, *Pillars of the Republic: Common Schools and American Society, 1780–1860* (New York: Hill and Wang, 1983) 176; W. E. B. Du Bois, "Does the Negro Need Separate Schools?" *Journal of Negro Education* 4 (July 1935): 328–335; Davison M. Douglas, *Jim Crow Moves North: The Battle over Northern School Segregation, 1865–1954* (Cambridge: Cambridge University Press, 2005).

67. Dionne Danns, "Racial Ideology and the Sanctity of the Neighborhood School Policy in Chicago," *Urban Review* 40 (2008): 64–75.

68. Chicago Board of Education, "Transcript of Hearings at South Shore High School," February 5, 1968, 34, Cyrus Hall Adams Papers, box 35–4, CHM.

69. Ibid., 43.

70. Ibid., 44.

71. Rod Sellers, *Chicago's Southeast Side Revisited* (Chicago: Arcadia, 2001), 120, 122; Dean Geroulis, "East Side Shows Its Still Made of Steel," *Chicago Tribune*, November 2009, http://articles.chicagot ribune.com/2003-11-09/business/0311090359_1_youth-center -affordable-housing-mills.
72. Chicago Board of Education, "Transcript of Hearings at Bowen High School," 36.
73. Ibid., 11. .
74. Ibid., 13–14.
75. Ibid., 18–19.
76. Richard P. Schnettler, "Status Report: Robert A. Black School South Shore Busing Proposal," 1974, 1–2, Municipal Reference Collection, HWLC.
77. Ibid., 27–28.
78. Letter to Cyrus Hall Adams, February 26, 1968, Cyrus Hall Adams Papers, box 35–2, CHM.
79. Letter to Cyrus Hall Adams, February 16, 1968.
80. For racial violence associated with housing, see Hirsch, *Making the Second Ghetto*; Hirsch, "Massive Resistance in the Urban North," Chicago Commission on Race Relations, *The Negro in Chicago: A Study of Race Relations and a Race Riot* (Chicago: University of Chicago Press, 1922); Spear, *Black Chicago*.
81. Gregory S. Jacobs, *Getting Around Brown: Desegregation, Development and the Columbus Public Schools* (Columbus: Ohio State University Press, 1998) 30.
82. Maryland Elizabeth Perry, "Belmont Cragin," in *Chicago Neighborhoods and Suburbs*, ed. Ann Durkin Keating, 105–106.
83. Vrame, "A History of School Desegregation," 238–239.
84. Chicago Board of Education, "Transcript of Hearings at Steinmetz High School," February 15, 1968, 9, Cyrus Hall Adams Papers, box 35–5, CHM.
85. John P. Spencer, *In the Crossfire: Marcus Foster and the Trouble History of American School Reform* (Philadelphia: University of Pennsylvania Press 2012).
86. Daniel P. Moynihan, *The Negro Family: The Case for National Action* (Washington, DC: Office of Policy Planning and Research, US Department of Labor, 1965); William Julius Wilson, *More than Just Race: Being Black and Poor in the Inner City* (New York: W. W. Norton, 2009), 109–111.
87. James Farmer, as quoted in Patterson, Brown v. Board of Education, 133.
88. Frank Riessman, *The Culturally Deprived Child* (New York: Harper & Row, 1962), 2–3; Hilda Taba and Deborah Elkins, *Teaching Strategies for the Culturally Disadvantaged* (Chicago: Rand McNally, 1966), 1.
89. Riessman, *The Culturally Deprived Child*, 3.
90. Chicago Board of Education, "Transcript of Hearings at Steinmetz High School," February 15, 1968, 39.

91. Chicago Board of Education, "Transcript of Hearings at Steinmetz High School," February 19, 1968, 63, Cyrus Hall Adams Papers, box 35–5, CHM.

92. Ibid., 56–59.

93. Ibid., 14–16.

94. Ibid., 32–34.

95. The Chicago Fact Book Consortium, *Local Community Fact Book*, 50, 68–69.

96. Kevin Fox Gotham, "Urban Space, Restrictive Covenants and the Origins of Racial Residential Segregation in One U.S. City," *International Journal of Urban and Regional Research* 24 (September 2000): 617–618.

97. Jim Carl, *Freedom of Choice: Vouchers in American Education* (Santa Barbara, CA: Praeger, 2011), 9.

98. Kevin Kruse, *White Flight: The Making of Modern Conservatism* (Princeton: Princeton University Press, 2005), 9.

99. Chicago Board of Education, "Transcript of Hearings at Steinmetz High School," February 19, 1968, 40–41.

100. Chicago Board of Education "Transcript of Hearings at Steinmetz High School," February 15, 1968, 43–46.

101. Chicago Board of Education, "Transcript of Hearings at Steinmetz High School," February 19, 1968, 14–16.

102. Ibid., 18–19.

103. Ibid., 19–20.

104. Karen Anderson, *Little Rock: Race and Resistance at Central High School* (Princeton: Princeton University Press, 2010), 56; Formisano, *Boston against Busing*, 8, 89. Jill Ogline Titus, *Brown's Battleground: Students, Segregationists, and the Struggle for Justice in Prince Edward County, Virginia* (Chapel Hill: University of North Carolina Press, 2011) 100–102.

105. The Chicago Fact Book Consortium, *Local Community Fact Book*, 38, 44, 46, 49, 67, 117, 122, 124, 127, 135.

106. Casey Banas, "School Board Rejects Austin Bus Plan, Wants 2d Revised," *Chicago Tribune*, February 29, 1968, 1; Christopher Chandler, "Reject School Busing Plans: Board Orders Redraft of S. Shore Proposal," *Chicago Sun-Times*, February 29, 1968, 3.

107. Chicago Board of Education, *Proceedings*, January 24–June 26, 1968, 1533.

108. "Both Friends, Foes of Busing Unhappy at School Board Vote," *Chicago Tribune*, February 29, 1968, 4.

109. Board of Education, *Proceedings*, March 4, 1968, 1538.

110. Vrame, "A History of School Desegregation," 268–271.

111. George Connelly, "The Austin Area Project: A Pupil Busing Program in District Four, an Evaluation," 1968, 1–2, Municipal Reference Collection, Harold Washington Library Center (HWLC).

112. Vrame, "A History of School Desegregation," 273–276; Connelly, "Austin Area Project."
113. Vrame, "A History of School Desegregation, 280, 282–283.
114. Connelly, "Austin Area Project," 20–24.
115. Ibid., 18.
116. Joseph J. Connery and Jerome H. Glickman, "Austin Area Project: The Pupil Busing Program in District Four: A Seventh Report, 1974, 9, Municipal Reference Collection, HWLC.
117. Connery and Glickman, "Austin Area Project," 1974, 9.
118. Ibid., 8. Similar comments were made in the 1973 report as well.
119. Ray C. Rist, *Invisible Children: School Integration in American Society* (Cambridge: Harvard University Press, 1978), 151, 248.
120. Connery and Glickman, "Austin Area Project," 1974, 6–9.

2 FACULTY DESEGREGATION, 1969–1981

1. Teacher and faculty will be used interchangeably throughout this chapter.
2. *Swann v. Charlotte-Mecklenburg* 402 US 1; Vernon K. Nakahara, "Court Decisions in Key Areas of School Desegregation," 1971, ERIC ED 061 345, 4–6.
3. US Commission on Civil Rights, "Federal Rights under School Desegregation Law," June 1966, ERIC ED 091 374, 13–14; James H. Bash and Thomas J. Morris, *Practices and Patterns of Faculty Desegregation* (Bloomington, IN: Phi Delta Kappa, 1967), 7.
4. Michael Rebell and Arthur Block, "Faculty Desegregation: The Law and Its Implementation," 1983, ERIC ED441662, 2.
5. Rebell and Block, "Faculty Desegregation," 14; Center for National Policy Review, *Justice Delayed and Denied: HEW and Northern School Desegregation* (Washington, DC: Catholic University of America School of Law, 1974), 10–15, 34; Gareth Davies, *See Government Grow: Education Politics from Johnson to Reagan* (Lawrence: University of Kansas Press, 2007), 108–120.
6. Emergency School Aid Act, Title II, Public Law 92–318.
7. Center for National Policy Review, *Justice Delayed and Denied*, 10–15, 34; Davies, *See Government Grow*, 108–120.
8. See Dean J. Kotlowski, *Nixon's Civil Rights: Politics, Principle, and Policy* (Cambridge, MA: Harvard University Press, 2001), 37.
9. Jakobi Williams, *From the Bullet to the Ballot: The Illinois Chapter of the Black Panther Party and Racial Coalition Politics in Chicago* (Chapel Hill: University of North Carolina Press, 2013), 180–188.
10. Paul Kleppner, *Chicago Divided: The Making of a Black Mayor* (DeKalb: Northern Illinois University Press, 1991), 76; Williams, *From the Bullet to the Ballot*, 168. For more details on Fred Hampton's assassination, see also Jeffrey Haas, *The Assassination of*

Fred Hampton: How the FBI and the Chicago Police Murdered a Black Panther (Chicago: Lawrence Hill Books, 2010).

11. William J. Grimshaw, *Bitter Fruit: Black Politics and the Chicago Machine 1931–1991* (Chicago: The University of Chicago Press, 1992), 124–126; Roger Biles, *Richard J. Daley: Politics, Race, and the Governing of Chicago* (DeKalb: Northern Illinois University Press, 1995), 180–181.

12. Robert G. Newby and David B. Tyack, "Victims Without 'Crimes': Some Historical Perspectives on Black Education," *Journal of Negro Education* 40 (Summer 1971): 199; For a synopsis of black teachers' employment rates in the North, see Jack Dougherty, *More than One Struggle: The Evolution of Black School Reform in Milwaukee* (Chapel Hill: University of North Carolina Press, 2004), 14–19.

13. Mary J. Herrick, *Negro Employees of the Chicago Board of Education* (MA Diss., University of Chicago, 1931), 34–35.

14. "Separate Schools," *Chicago Defender* (Big Weekend Edition), July 1, 1916, 8; see also Michael W. Homel, *Down from Equality: Black Chicagoans and the Public Schools, 1920–1941* (Urbana: University of Illinois Press, 1984).

15. Dionne Danns, "Thriving in the Midst of Adversity: Educator Maudelle Brown Bousfield's Struggles in Chicago, 1922–1950," *Journal of Negro Education* 78 (Winter 2009): 3–17.

16. Helen E. Amerman, "Summary of Data Collected by John Winget on Transfer of Elementary Teachers," Prepared for the Technical Advisory of the Public Schools by the Committee on Education, Training and Research in Race Relations, University of Illinois, 1952, 13–16; Homel, *Down from Equality*, 67–69.

17. According to the Hauser Report, those temporarily certified often met Illinois state teaching requirements, but have not passed Chicago's examination. Phillip M. Hauser, Sterling M. McMurrin, James M. Nabrit, Lester W. Nelson, and William R. Odell, "Report to the Board of Education of the City of Chicago by the Advisory Panel on Integration of the Public Schools," March 31, 1964, Municipal Reference Collection, Harold Washington Library Center (HWLC), 17–18; Dionne Danns, *Something Better for Our Children: Black Organizing in Chicago Public Schools, 1963–1971* (New York: Routledge, 2003), 107.

18. James D. Anderson, Discussion at the American Educational Studies Conference in Pittsburgh, PA, 2002.

19. Danns, *Something Better for Our Children*, 106–112.

20. The results of the exam were not given by race. Henry De Zutter, "1,656 Subs Fail Teacher Exams Here," *Chicago Daily News*, August 9, 1968.

21. For more information on black teachers actions to change the conditions in black schools and the movement toward community control, see Danns, *Something Better for Our Children*; and Elizabeth Shana Todd-Breland, *To Reshape and Redefine Our World: African*

American Political Organizing for Education in Chicago 1968–1988 (PhD Diss., University of Chicago, 2010).

22. For information on teachers in New York, see Jerald E. Podair, *The Strike That Changed New York: Blacks, Whites, and the Ocean Hill Brownsville Crisis* (New Haven: Yale University Press, 2002); Daniel H. Perlstein, *Justice, Justice: School Politics and the Eclipse of Liberalism* (New York: Peter Lang, 2004).

23. Dionne Danns, "Chicago Teacher Reform Efforts and the Politics of Educational Change," in *Black Protest Thought and Education*, ed. William Watkins (New York: Peter Lang, 2005), 179–196.

24. See Stephen Kendrick and Paul Kendrick: *Sarah's Long Walk: Free Blacks of Boston and How Their Struggle for Equality Changed American* (Boston: Beacon Press, 2004); Hilary J. Moss, *Schooling Citizens: The Struggle for African American Education in Antebellum America* (Chicago: University of Chicago Press, 2009); Carl F. Kaestle, *Pillars of the Republic: Common Schools and American Society, 1780–1860* (New York: Hill and Wang, 1983), 176.

25. W. E. B. Du Bois, "Does the Negro Need Separate Schools?" *Journal of Negro Education* 4 (July 1935): 328–335.

26. Vanessa Siddle Walker, "African American Teaching in the South: 1940–1960," *American Educational Research Journal* 38 (Winter 2001): 402.

27. See Emma Lou Thornbrough, *Indiana Blacks in the Twentieth Century* (Bloomington: Indiana University Press, 2000).

28. Hauser et al., "Advisory Panel on Integration of the Public Schools," 74; "The Chicago Title VI Complaint to H.E.W.," *Integrated Education* 3 (December 1965–January 1966): 15, 17; *Webb v. The Board of Education of the City of Chicago* (1963) 223 F. Supp. 466.

29. Chicago Urban League, "Segregation in the Chicago Public Schools, 1965–1966," 10, Chicago Historical Museum.

30. Homel, *Down from Equality.*

31. Chicago Board of Education, "Increasing Desegregation of Faculties, Students and Vocational Education Programs," August 1967, A-4, Municipal Reference Collection, HWLC.

32. Chicago Board of Education, "Increasing Desegregation of Faculties," A-5.

33. Ibid., A-14.

34. Joseph Reilly, "Substitute Teachers Face Tests in Math, English," *Chicago Sun-Times*, June 19, 1969, 22.

35. "Proceedings under Title VI of the Civil Rights Act of 1964: Initial Decision in the Matter of Chicago Public School District #299 and Illinois Office of Education and City of Chicago, Illinois," February 15, 1977, ERIC ED 135 931, 36–37.

36. See Jacqueline Jordan Irvine, *In Search of Wholeness: African American Teachers and Their Culturally Specific Classroom Practices* (New York: Palgrave, 2002); Michelle Foster, *Black Teachers on*

Teaching (New York: New Press, 1997); Gloria Ladson-Billings, *The Dreamkeepers: Successful Teachers of African American Children* (San Francisco: Jossey-Bass, 1994).

37. Chicago Board of Education, "Increasing Desegregation of Faculties," A-20–A-27.

38. Emanuel Hurwitz Jr. and Cynthia Porter-Gehrie, "Managing Faculty Desegregation: The Role and Response of Principals in Implementing a Faculty Desegregation Plan," April 1979, ERIC ED 171 821, 4.

39. Joel Havemann, "An Integration Order," *Chicago Sun-Times*, July 10, 1969, 18; Peter Negronida, "City Schools Ordered to Fix Race Balance: U.S. Gives Board Time to Devise Plan," *Chicago Tribune*, July 10, 1969, 1, 2; Jack Schnedler and Hope Justus, "Faculty Segregated Here—U.S.," *Chicago Daily News*, July 9, 1969, 1, 7.

40. Schnedler and Justus, "Faculty Segregated Here," 7.

41. Hugh Hough, "School Board Failed in Attempts to Integrate Teachers," *Chicago Sun-Times* July 10, 1969, 18.

42. Schnedler and Justus, "Faculty Segregated Here," 7.

43. Joel Havemann, "Teachers to Defy Transfer Change: Union Chief Flays Board," *Chicago Sun-Times*, July 11, 1969, 3.

44. "Desmond Wins Presidency of the CTU," *Chicago Tribune*, May 26, 1966, 16.

45. Dennis Sodomka and Jack Schnedler, "Won't Drop Seniority—Desmond," *Chicago Daily News*, July 10, 1969, 1.

46. Ibid.

47. Jakobi Williams, *From the Bullet to the Ballot,* 41; Danns, *Something Better for Our Children*, 64–65, 99–100.

48. Peter Negronida, "Ogilvie Seeks Time in City School Suit," *Chicago Tribune*, July 15, 1969, 6.

49. Joel Havemann, "School Board, Teachers' Union Confer on Faculty Transfer," *Chicago Sun-Times*, July 23, 1969, 20.

50. Frank M. Whiston to John N. Mitchell, Jerris Leonard and Thomas A. Foran, July 23, 1969, in Chicago Board of Education, *Proceedings*, July 23, 1969, 61–64.

51. Whiston to Mitchell, Leonard and Foran; Peter Negronida, "Teacher Race Plan Told by School Board: It Would Modify Transfers," *Chicago Tribune*, July 24, 1969 1; Joel Havemann, "Board Oks Policy Change to Integrate School Staffs," *Chicago Sun-Times*, July 24, 1969.

52. Joel Havemann, "Teachers calls CTU, Protest Desegregation," *Chicago Sun-Times*, July 25, 1969, 27.

53. Joel Havemann, "Integration Talks 'Shock' Left-Out Teachers' Union," *Chicago Sun-Times*, July 29, 1969.

54. Jerris Leonard and Thomas A. Foran to Frank M. Whiston, October 20, 1969, in Chicago Board of Education, *Proceedings*, October 22, 1969, 875–877.

55. Ibid.

56. Ibid.
57. Peter Negronida, "School Board Reacts to U.S. Court Threat," *Chicago Tribune*, October 22, 1969, 6.
58. Joel Havemann, "City Faculty Integration Step OKd," *Chicago Sun-Times*, November 20, 1969, 3; Casey Banas, "School Board to Seek HEW Racial Plan: Move Urged by Justice Dept.," *Chicago Tribune*, November 20, 1969, 6.
59. Joel Havemann, "Integration of Chicago Teachers Shows an Increase," *Chicago Sun-Times*, November 18, 1969, 14.
60. Douglas P. Woodlock, "Tentative Pact Approved for City Teachers," *Chicago Sun-Times*, January 12, 1970, 3, 20; Joel Havemann and Douglass P. Woodlock, "Teacher Pact Hikes Debt," *Chicago Sun-Times*, January 13, 1970, 4.
61. Joel Havemann, "HEW Urges Huge Shuffle of Teachers in Chicago," *Chicago Sun-Times*, July 2, 1970 3, 34; Peter Negronida, "U.S. Proposes Transfers: Teacher Desegregation Plan Affects up to 6000 Faculty," *Chicago Tribune*, July 2, 1970, 1, 5; "Teacher Plan Highlights," *Chicago Tribune*, July 2, 1970, 5.
62. Joel Havemann, "Desmond Hits HEW Suggestions on Teachers," *Chicago Sun-Times*, July 4, 1970, 12; Peter Negronida, "Desmond Hits U.S. Teacher Plan," *Chicago Tribune*, July 4, 1970, 4.
63. Joel Havemann, "School Board Orders Action of Faculty Desegregation," *Chicago Sun-Times*, July 17, 1970, 3.
64. The Board of Education lowered the percentage of teachers needing reassignment from 25 percent to 12 percent. Peter Negronida, "920 Teachers Assigned Here on Racial Basis," *Chicago Tribune*, August 28, 1970, 3; Patrick Koval, "Teacher Shift Plan Modified," *Chicago Sun-Times*, September 15, 1970, 4.
65. Chicago Teachers Union, "Counterproposal to Chicago Board of Education's Proposed Plan to Desegregate Faculties and to Equalize Per Pupil Expenditures for Instructional Staff Salaries through the Assignment and/or Transfer of Teachers," 14 September 1970, Municipal Reference Collection, HWLC; "School Strike if Integration Forced–Union," *Chicago Sun-Times*, September 26, 1970, 3.
66. Danns, *Something Better for Our Children*, 85, 87, 105; Ernest R. House, *Jesse Jackson and the Politics of Charisma: The Rise and Fall of the PUSH/EXCEL Program* (Boulder, CO: Westview Press, 1988) 7, 21–28; Todd-Breland, "To Reshape and Redefine Our World," 48.
67. Sam Washington, "Breadbasket to Oppose Teacher Integration Plans," *Chicago Sun-Times*, September 20, 1970, 7.
68. Mwalimu J. Shujaa and Hannibal T. Afrik, "School Desegregation, the Politics of Culture, and the Council of Independent Black Institutions," in *Beyond Desegregation: The Politics of Quality in African American Schooling*, ed. Mwalimu J. Shujaa (Thousand Oaks, CA: Corwin Press, 1996).

69. James Redmond, "Progress Report: Plan to Desegregate Faculties and to Equalize Per Pupil Expenditures for Instructional Staff Salaries through the Assignment and/or Transfer of Teachers," September 23, 1970, Municipal Reference Collection, HWLC.

70. Joel Havemann, "480 Substitute Teachers Set for Desegregation Transfers," *Chicago Sun-Times*, September 30, 1970, 14.

71. "Teacher Union Alters Demand," *Chicago Sun-Times*, November 11, 1970, 10.

72. HEW called for the faculty at each school to be within 10 percent of the city's average. Therefore, teachers needed to be within 74.2 to 54.2 percent white since white teachers were 64.2 percent of the teachers in 1970. Joel Havemann, "Board Still Fails to Meet Guidelines for the Desegregation of Faculties," *Chicago Sun-Times*, 9, December 1970, 4.

73. "Joint Report of Committee RE United States Department of Justice Communication and the Employee Relations Committee," in Chicago Board of Education, *Proceedings*, June 16, 1971, 3471–3473.

74. Joel Havemann, "A Teacher Integration Plan is Told," *Chicago Sun-Times*, June 10, 1971, 1, 12.

75. Joel Havemann, "Union Unit OKs Faculty Integration," *Chicago Sun-Times*, June 15, 1971, 3.

76. Joel Havemann, "Redmond Tells Integration Blocks, *Chicago Sun-Times*, January 11, 1972, 3.

77. "U.S. Rejects Teacher Integration Plan Here," *Chicago Sun-Times*, April 4, 1972, 3.

78. Grayson Mitchell, "Board: No Faculty Integration Plan," *Chicago Sun-Times*, June 22, 1972, 4.

79. Carolyn Toll, "Learn Teacher Segregation Here Blocked U.S. Funds," *Chicago Sun-Times*, June 14, 1973, 8.

80. Glen Elsasser, "U.S. Expected to Drop Suit on Faculty Bias in Chicago Schools," *Chicago Tribune*, June 17, 1973, 1; "To Drop Bias Charges?" *Chicago Defender*, June 18, 1973, 2.

81. James F. Redmond, "Racial Survey: Administrators and Teaching Personnel," September 30, 1974, Chicago Board of Education Archives. Connie Lauerman, "More Blacks, Latins Teach in Chicago, Survey Shows," *Chicago Tribune*, February 26, 1974, 2.

82. *Adams v. Richardson*, 356 F. Supp. 92 (1973); Andy Shaw, "School Board Ponders Next Faculty Integration Moves," *Chicago Sun-Times*, February 2, 1976, 22; "Another School Crisis to Avert," *Chicago Tribune*, February 1, 1976, A4.

83. Christina Hawkins Stringfellow, *Desegregation Policies and Practices in Chicago during the Superintendencies of James Redmond and Joseph Hannon* (PhD Diss., Loyola University of Chicago, 1991), 49; Lloyd Green, "'Hot-Seat Job' in Schools Nothing New to Hannon," *Chicago Sun-Times*, November 29, 1979, 20; "Jesse Jackson Angry over Choice of School Head," *Jet* XLVIII (August 7, 1975), 7.

84. Andy Shaw, "Hannon Ties Politics, School Desegregation Push," *Chicago Sun-Times*, January 24, 1976, 6.

85. Chicago Board of Education, *Proceedings*, January 21, 1976, 1240–1241.

86. Andy Shaw, "HEW Claims Bias Continues in City Faculty Assignment," *Chicago Sun-Times*, October 8, 1975, 7; Connie Lauerman, "Chicago Schools Face $147 Million Federal Funds Loss, HEW Warns," *Chicago Tribune*, October 8, 1975, 1.

87. Chicago Board of Education, *Proceedings*, January 21, 1976, 1241; Andy Shaw, "Teacher-Bias Suit Near: Schools Face $150-million Setback," *Chicago Sun-Times*, January 18, 1976, 1, 14.

88. Chicago Board of Education, *Proceedings,* January 21, 1976, 1242.

89. Joseph P. Hannon, "Response to the Request from the Office for Civil Rights Department of Health, Education, and Welfare for a Plan to Integrate Faculties, Equalize Professional Staff Services, Provide Special Services to National Origin Minority Children," February 8, 1978, vi, 53, Municipal Reference Collection, HWLC.

90. Andy Shaw, "Hannon's Staff-Integration Plan," *Chicago Sun-Times*, February 11, 1976, 3, 38; Andy Shaw, "Board Adopts Faculty Plan 6 to 3," *Chicago Sun-Times*, February 12,1976, 3, 114.

91. Andy Shaw, "HEW Rejects Teacher Integration Plan, Compromise Seen," *Chicago Sun-Times*, April 1, 1976, 64.

92. "Proceedings under Title VI," 30–31.

93. "Proceedings under Title VI," 44, 54–55; Rebell and Block, "Faculty Desegregation," 28; Cascy Banas, "Teacher Bias Case to be Tried in City July 7," *Chicago Tribune*, June 11, 1976, A1; Casey Banas, "Judge Slashes School Funds," *Chicago Tribune*, February 18, 1977, 1.

94. Board of Education, "Report of the Committee on Faculty Integration," in *Proceedings*, May 25, 1977, 1651–1653; Joseph P. Hannon, "Statement to the Board of Education," in *Proceedings*, May 25, 1977, 1653–1655; Joseph P. Hannon, "Plan for the Implementation of the Provisions of Title VI of the Civil Rights Act of 1964 Related to: Integration of Faculties," May 31, 1977, Municipal Reference Collection, HWLC.

95. Geof Dubson, "Transfer of 2,212 Teachers OKd," *Chicago Sun-Times*, May 26, 1977, 2, 34; Casey Banas, "Transfer of Teachers OKd," *Chicago Tribune*, May 26, 1977, 1, 10.

96. Roberto Suro, "Union Seeks to Block Transfers of Teachers," *Chicago Sun-Times*, August 6, 1977, 3, 42.

97. Lillian Williams and F. K. Plous Jr., "Union Sues on 270 Teachers Transfers," *Chicago Sun-Times*, August 30, 1977, 18; Charles Mount, "Court Hears Teachers Blast Transfer Program," *Chicago Tribune*, September 2, 1977, B1.

98. Lillian Williams, "270 Teachers Transfers Halted," *Chicago Sun-Times*, September 15, 1977, 3.

99. The first program would provide supplemental services for students who were transitioning to English classrooms. Second, special education programs also had to be expanded for bilingual students. Third bilingual education programs would be offered to schools with fewer than 20 bilingual students for the first time. The board would also have to recruit more bilingual teachers.

100. Roberto Suro, "City, U.S. Settle Schools Dispute," *Chicago Sun-Times*, October 13, 1977, 4; Casey Banas and James Coates, "U.S. Approves Teacher Integration Plan," *Chicago Tribune*, October 13, 1977, 1; Roberto Suro, "HEW Ends Teacher-Shift Demand," *Chicago Sun-Times*, October 9, 1977, 3.

101. Augustus J. Jones Jr., *Law, Bureaucracy and Politics: The Implementation of Title VI of the Civil Rights Act of 1964* (Washington, DC: University Press of America, 1982), 159.

102. Mike Anderson, "Faculty Desegregation Progress Last Fall Told," *Chicago Sun-Times*, January 19, 1978, 36.

103. Jay Branegan, "'Age Discrimination' Hit: Faculty Desegregation Nullified," *Chicago Tribune*, November 9, 1978, 3; Betty Washington and Linda Wertsch, "Teacher Shifting Hits a Legal Snag," *Chicago Sun-Times*, November 9, 1978, 3.

104. Linda Wertsch, "Teacher Integration Here Rises," *Chicago Sun-Times*, February 21, 1979, 8; Rebell and Block, "Faculty Desegregation," 36.

105. Joseph P. Hannon to the Principals, June 14, 1977, in Joseph P. Hannon, "Plan for the Implementation of the Provisions of Title VI of the Civil Rights Act," October 12, 1977, 18, Municipal Reference Collection, HWLC.

106. Joseph P. Hannon to Teachers, June 15, 1977 in Hannon, "Plan for Implementation," 21.

107. Robert, Suro, "Teachers Dismayed Over Transfers," *Chicago Sun-Times*, June 16, 1977, 4; Sharon Kornegay, "Teachers with School 'Roots' Uprooted, Says Principal," *Chicago Sun-Times*, June 17, 1977, 38.

108. Dennis D. Fisher, "36 Teachers Sue Board on Transfers," *Chicago Sun-Times*, July 16, 1977, 10.

109. Dennis D. Fisher, "Reject Teacher Bid to Block Fall Transfers," *Chicago Sun-Times*, August 17, 1977, 44.

110. Hannon, "Plan for Implementation," 35–37; Hurwitz and Porter-Gehrie, "Managing Faculty Desegregation," 17–18.

111. See Hurwitz and Porter-Gehrie, "Managing Faculty Desegregation."

112. Hurwitz and Porter-Gehrie, "Managing Faculty Desegregation," 28–30.

113. Connie Putney, interview with author, June 29, 2008.

114. Kimberly Muhammad, interview with author, September 7, 2010.

115. See R. Scott Muirhead, John Q. Easton, Wayne C. Fredrick, and Sarah Vanderwicken, "Teacher and Principal Reactions to an Involuntary Transfer Program to Integrate Faculties in the Chicago Public Schools," 1979, 8–14, Municipal Reference Collection, HWLC.

116. Anna Victoria Wilson and William E. Segall, *Oh, Do I Remember!: Experiences of Teachers During the Desegregation of Austin's Schools, 1964–1971* (Albany: State University of New York Press, 2001); Renarta Tompkins, "Crossing Over: Narratives of Successful Border Crossings of African American Teachers during Desegregation," paper presented at the American Educational Research Association Annual Conference, 2010; Douglas R. Davis, "The Desegregation Experience of Public School Personnel in East Baton Rouge Parish, Louisiana," ERIC ED 436 519.

117. Rebell and Block, "Faculty Desegregation," 45–48.

3 STATE INVOLVEMENT WITH STUDENT DESEGREGATION, 1971–1979

1. Joseph M. Cronin, "How the Chicago Area Desegregated its Schools," *Phi Delta Kappan* 58 (May 1977): 698–699.

2. Joseph M. Cronin, "The State and School Desegregation," *Theory into Practice* XVII (February 1978): 5–6.

3. Some of these cases include *United States v. Missouri, Penick v. Columbus, United States v. Yonkers.* David S. Tatel, Maree F. Sneed, Kevin J. Lanigan, and Steven J. Routh, *The Responsibility of State Officials to Desegregate Urban Public Schools* (Washington DC: Hogan & Hartson, 1987), 8–9.

4. Technical Assistance Committee on the Chicago Desegregation Plan, "Integration in Chicago: A Report to the Illinois State Board of Education," May 11, 1978, i–3. Box Desegregation 1976–1980, Chicago Board of Education Archives.

5. "Remarks of Joseph M. Cronin, State Superintendent of Education, to the State Board of Education, February 26, 1976, Chicago, Illinois," Joseph M. Cronin Papers, box 23, folder 1, Hoover Institution.

6. Gary Adkins, "Joseph M. Cronin," *Illinois Issues* 11 (May 1976): 7.

7. See Carl F. Kaestle, *Pillars of the Republic: Common Schools and American Society, 1780–1860* (New York: Hill and Wang, 1983).

8. See James T. Patterson, Brown v. Board of Education: *A Civil Rights Milestone and its Troubled Legacy* (Oxford: Oxford University Press, 2001); Scott R. Baker, *Paradoxes of Desegregation: African American Struggles for Educational Equity in Charleston, South Carolina, 1926–1972* (Columbia: University of South Carolina Press, 2006); Jill Ogline Titus, *Brown's Battleground: Students, Segregationists, & the Struggle for Justice in Prince Edward County, Virginia* (Chapel Hill: University of North Carolina Press, 2011).

9. Tatel et al., *The Responsibility of State Officials*, 9–14.

10. Some of the northern cases include, *Berry v. School Dist. of Benton Harbor, Oliver v. Kalamazoo, Bell v. Board of Education Akron, United States v. Board of School Commissioners of Indianapolis.* Tatel et al., *The Responsibility of State Officials*, 7.

11. *Illinois Blue Book 1977–1978*, retrieved October 19, 2010, from http://www.idaillinois.org/cdm4/document.php?CISOROOT =/bb&CISOPTR=38030&REC=4.

12. The Armstrong law (H.B. 113) was created to deal with de facto segregation through redistricting. The law was initially ruled unconstitutional in a 1967 Illinois Supreme Court ruling but upheld in a 1968 rehearing.   http://www.uic.edu/depts/lib/specialcoll/services/rjd /findingaids/CArmstrongf.html; "Bakalis to Start Desegregation Plan with Fund Cutoff Penalty," *Chicago Tribune*, November 19, 1971, 1–2.

13. Peter Negronida, "Bakalis Tells Rules to Halt Schools Bias," *Chicago Tribune*, November 20, 1971, N1, N6.

14. Michael J. Bakalis, *A Strategy for Excellence* (Hamden, CT: Shoe String Press, 1974), 56–57.

15. Michael J. Bakalis, "The Bakalis School Integration Plan," *Chicago Tribune*, November 22, 1971, 30.

16. Bakalis, "The Bakalis School Integration Plan," 30.

17. Negronida, "Bakalis Tells Rules to Halt Schools Bias," N1, N6.

18. Joel Havemann, "Redmond Tells Integration Blocks," *Chicago Sun-Times*, January 11, 1972, 3.

19. Joel Havemann, "Bakalis Raps Continuing City School Segregation," *Chicago Sun-Times*, September 13, 1972, 2; Robert McClory, "Schools Still Segregated: Bakalis," *Chicago Defender*, September 13, 1972, 1, 24.

20. Havemann, "Bakalis Raps Continuing City School Segregation," 2.

21. Laurie Joseph Wasserman "New State Education Board's Fight to Assert Independent Role," *Illinois Issues* 11 (May 1976): 9.

22. *Chicago Daily News*, December 11, 1974, 7; Joseph M. Cronin Papers, box 2, Hoover Institution.

23. Adkins, "Joseph M. Cronin," 7.

24. The others were Joliet, Maywood, Rockford, Springfield, and Rock Island. Three of the six were all Chicago metropolitan area districts. Three other school districts in Chicago's metropolitan area with worsening segregation were Proviso District 209, Bellwood District 88, and Aurora District 129. Burnell Heinecke, "State Orders Full Enforcement of '71 Desegregation Rules," *Chicago Sun-Times*, May 9, 1975, 20; Jerry De Muth, "City's school on 'More Segregated' List," *Chicago Sun-Times*, May 10, 1975, 3.

25. Andy Shaw, "Chicago School Integration—The Problem Returns," *Chicago Sun-Times*, June 15, 1975, 6.

26. State Board of Education, "Rules Establishing Requirements and Procedures for the Elimination and Prevention of Racial Segregation in Schools," February 1976, 8, Chicago Board of Education Archives, Box Desegregation 1977–1978, Folder 6; Connie Lauerman, "State Board Charges City Schools with Bias," *Chicago Tribune*, February 27, 1976, 1, 19; Andy Shaw, "School Integration Plan Demanded," *Chicago Sun-Times*, February 27, 1976, 3.

27. Andy Shaw, "State Integration Plan Unrealistic, Hannon Claims," *Chicago Sun-Times*, February 28, 1976, 3; Casey Banas, "School Desegregation Rules Unrealistic: Hannon," *Chicago Tribune*, February 28, 1976, 1.

28. "Schools in City, 2 Suburbs Told: Must Integrate," *Chicago Sun-Times*, April 9, 1976, 1, 6.

29. Andy Shaw, "Illinois Reports Segregated School Districts up 62%," *Chicago Sun-Times*, January 9, 1976, 20; "Segregate Public Schools," *Chicago Tribune*, January 12, 1976, 2.

30. Joseph Hannon Letter, November 17, 1976, University of Illinois (UIC) Special Collections, Series II, Box 261–2616.

31. Geof Dubson, "State Prods Chicago on School Desegregation," *Chicago Sun-Times*, December 10, 1976, 5.

32. Geof Dubson, "Need Time on Integration: Hannon," *Chicago Sun-Times*, December 11, 1976, 4; Geof Dubson, "$127,000 Grant Earmarked for School Integration Plan," *Chicago Sun-Times*, February 23, 1977, 12.

33. Geof Dubson, "Members of School Desegregation Planning Units Listed," *Chicago Sun-Times*, April 23, 1977, 18; Edward A. Welling Jr., "Progress Report and Proposed Equal Educational Opportunities Plan," November 16, 1977, 5, Box Desegregation 1977–1978, Chicago Board of Education Archives.

34. Joseph P. Hannon, "Equalizing Educational Opportunities in the New Chicago: Student Desegregation Planning Process and Progress Report," 37, Box Desegregation 1977–1978, Folder 6, Chicago Board of Education Archives.

35. Ibid., 15.

36. Geof Dubson, "Cronin Indicates Integration Report Inadequate," *Chicago Sun-Times*, April 15, 1977, 11.

37. Meg O'Connor, "City's School Race Plan Viewed as Unacceptable," *Chicago Tribune*, April 29, 1977, 1.

38. Elizabeth Shana Todd-Breland, *To Reshape and Redefine Our World: African American Political Organizing for Education in Chicago 1968–1988* (PhD Diss., University of Chicago, 2010), 35–36, 50.

39. The Chicago Urban League School Desegregation Announcement, Steering Committee Meeting on Public School Desegregation, UIC Special Collections, Series II, Box 261–2616.

40. The Chicago Urban League, "The Purposes and Goals of School Desegregation in Chicago: A Position Statement to the City-Wide Advisory Committee," October 1977, 1, ERIC ED 187 781.

41. Geof Dubson, "Shouts End School-Bias Meeting," *Chicago Sun-Times*, May, 6, 1977 3.

42. "Advisory Committee on Desegregation," 17, Box Desegregation 1977–1978, Folder 12, Chicago Board of Education Archives; Geof Dubson, "More Time on Plan to Integrate Schools," *Chicago Sun-Times*, May 13, 1977, 12.

43. Joseph P. Hannon, "Administrator's Guide to the 1977 Permissive Transfer Program," 1977, Box Desegregation 1977–1978, Folder 1, Chicago Board of Education Archives.

44. Ibid., 2.

45. Advisory Committee on Desegregation, 18.

46. Geof Dubson, "Both Sides Rap Decision on Schools," *Chicago Sun-Times*, June 11, 1977, 6.

47. Ibid.

48. Meg O'Connor, "Hannon 'Committed' to Desegregation Plan," *Chicago Tribune*, June 5, 1977, 18; Geof Dubson, "Hannon Rejects Plea to Drop Bus Plan," *Chicago Sun-Times*, June 21, 1977, 16.

49. See Ronald P. Formisano, *Boston against Busing: Race, Class, and Ethnicity in the 1960s and 1970s* (Chapel Hill: University of North Carolina Press, 2004).

50. Dionne Danns, *Something Better for Our Children: Black Organizing in Chicago Public Schools, 1963–1971* (New York: Routledge), 44.

51. Roberto Suro, "Busing Foes Try to Picket Bilandic," *Chicago Sun-Times*, August 24, 1977, 4.

52. Roberto Suro, "Busing Off to Peaceful Start, But Boycott On," *Chicago Sun-Times*, September 8, 1977, 3.

53. Kay Rutherford and Roberto Suro, "Blacks Jeered at S.W. Side School," *Chicago Sun-Times*, September 9, 1977, 5.

54. Michael Zielenziger, "4 Hit After School Busing Protest," *Chicago Sun-Times*, September 12, 1977, 3.

55. Roberto Suro and Kay Rutherford, "Protesters Delay Pupils; 2 Seized," *Chicago Sun-Times*, September 13, 1977, 3.

56. Kay Rutherford and Roberto Suro, "Bogan Protest Walkout; Arrest 27," *Chicago Sun-Times*, September 14, 1977, 3, 32.

57. Kay Rutherford and Jon Ziomek, "6 Are Arrested Outside Bogan," *Chicago Sun-Times*, September 15, 1977, 3.

58. Roberto Suro, "Busing Rolls On—As Do Protests," *Chicago Sun-Times*, September 18, 1977, 5. Paul Kleppner, *Chicago Divided: The Making of a Black Mayor* (Dekalb: Northern Illinois University Press, 1985), 57.

59. Kleppner, *Chicago Divided*, 57.

60. Formisano, *Boston against Busing*.

61. Michael Zielenziger, "Voluntary Desegregation Plan Lacking, City Told," *Chicago Sun-Times*, October 18, 1977, 9; Meg O'Connor and John Gorman, "State School Chief Cool To Desegregation Plan," *Chicago Tribune*, October 28, 1977, C2.

62. Midwestern Regional Office Staff of the US Commission on Civil Rights, "Analysis of Dr. Edward A. Welling, Jr.'s October Paper on School Desegregation: Chicago," October 31, 1977, 2, Harriet O'Donnel Papers, Box 1, Folder 11, Chicago Board of Education Archives.

63. "Advisory Committee on Desegregation," 20.

64. Zielenziger, "Voluntary Desegregation Plan Lacking, City Told," 9.
65. "Dr. Welling and Dr. Cronin," *Chicago Tribune*, October 30, 1977, A4.
66. Gary Wisby, "Desegregation Advisor Admits Pulling a Boner," *Chicago Sun-Times*, November 3, 1977, 28.
67. The Urban League predicted the tipping point to be schools with 40 percent Whites. Others believed the tipping point occurred once formally when all white schools gained as little as 20 percent blacks. The Chicago Urban League, "The Purposes and Goals of School Desegregation in Chicago," 1–6.
68. Ibid., 4–5.
69. Ibid., 16.
70. Roberto Suro, "Forced Desegregation Urged," *Chicago Sun Times*, November 8, 1977, 3.
71. Hank Rubin, "Amended Report," November 14, 1977, 2, Harriot O'Donnel Papers, Box 1, Folder 11, Chicago Board of Education Archives.
72. Ibid., 5.
73. Welling, "Progress Report and Proposed Equal Educational Opportunities Plan," 15–26; Casey Banas, "5-Year Plan to Integrate Chicago Schools Proposed," *Chicago Tribune*, November 17, 1977, 1; Roberto Suro, "Propose 5-Year Integration Plan," *Chicago Sun-Times*, November 17, 1977, 3.
74. Welling, "Progress Report and Proposed Equal Educational Opportunities Plan," 8.
75. "Advisory Committee on Desegregation," 21–23; Roberto Suro, "Urban League Hits School Proposal," *Chicago Sun-Times*, December 7, 1977, 14; Roberto Suro, "Plan Urges Mandatory Desegregation as Backup," *Chicago Sun-Times*, December 8, 1977, 5.
76. City-Wide Advisory Committee, "Equalizing Educational Opportunities: Proposed Plan," January 12, 1978, 1–2, Box Desegregation 1977–1978, Folder 1, Chicago Board of Education Archives.
77. Geof Dubson, "Judge Nullifies School Bias Rule," *Chicago Sun-Times*, January 14, 1978, 3; Meg O'Connor, "Illinois School Bias Quotas Held Invalid," *Chicago Tribune*, January 14, 1978, B1; Elizabeth Brenner, "City School Desegregation Plan Won't Be Affected by Verdict," *Chicago Tribune*, January 15, 1978, 3.
78. "School Desegregation Appeal Rejected by Court," *Chicago Tribune*, March 4, 1978, F9.
79. Casey Banas, "Plan Hearing on Bias Ruling," *Chicago Tribune*, May 12, 1979, B4; "State School Board Asks Rehearing on School Guide," *Chicago Sun-Times*, January 29, 1981, 18.
80. Mike Anderson, "Ok One Last Desegregation Delay," *Chicago Sun-Times*, March 24, 1978, 5.
81. Casey Banas, "U.S. May Enter City School Bias Fight," *Chicago Tribune*, February 12, 1978, 3.

82. Casey Banas and Charles Mount, "Parents Sue to Halt School Desegregation," *Chicago Tribune*, March 10, 1978, 1.
83. Adkins, "Joseph M. Cronin," 7.
84. Joseph P. Hannon, "Access to Excellence: Recommendations for Equalizing Educational Opportunities," April 12, 1978, ix, Box Desegregation 1976–1980, Chicago Board of Education Archives.
85. Hannon, "Access to Excellence," x–xi.
86. Hannon, "Access to Excellence," 4–5.
87. Hannon, "Access to Excellence," xiii–xiv.
88. Meg O'Connor, "Cronin Pleased; Urban League Isn't," *Chicago Tribune*, April 7, 1978, 14.
89. Linda Wertsch, "CWAC Rejects Integration Plan," *Chicago Sun-Times*, April 11, 1978, 4.
90. O'Connor, "Cronin Pleased," 14; Meg O'Connor, "NAACP Plans to Sue Despite Desegregation Proposal," *Chicago Tribune*, April 8, 1978, B3; Casey Banas, "Panel Asks: Reject Hannon School Plan," *Chicago Tribune*, April 11, 1978, 3; Wertsch, "CWAC Rejects Integration Plan," 4; Linda Wertsch, "Voluntary Desegregation OKd," *Chicago Sun-Times*, April 13, 1978, 3; Casey Banas, "OK Voluntary School Plan," *Chicago Tribune*, April 13, 1978, 1.
91. Wertsch, "Voluntary Desegregation OKd," 3; Linda Wertsch, "All-Voluntary School Proposal 'Not Enough,'" *Chicago Sun-Times*, April 14, 1978, 3; Meg O'Connor, "State Cool to Hannon Plan," *Chicago Tribune*, April 14, 1978, 1; Casey Banas, "Hannon Firm on Voluntary Desegregation Plan, *Chicago Tribune*, April 15, 1978, B3; Karen Koshner and Linda Wertsch, "No Forced Transfers, Hannon Vows," *Chicago Sun-Times*, April 15, 1978, 3.
92. Meg O'Connor, "Hannon Orders Welling to Quit," *Chicago Tribune*, April 16, 1978, 1; Marcia Kramer, "Hannon to Ask Firing of Welling," *Chicago Sun-Times*, April 17, 1978, 5; Meg O'Connor and Bill Grady, "Hannon to Ask Board to Fire Welling," *Chicago Tribune*, April 17, 1978, 3; Linda Wertsch, "Fill Welling Post CWAC Unit Asks," *Chicago Sun-Times*, April 18, 1978, 7; Meg O'Connor, "Welling Defies Hannon, Attends CWAC Meeting," *Chicago Tribune*, April 21, 1978, A1; Linda Wertsch, "Welling Fired By School Board," *Chicago Sun-Times*, May 4, 1978, 5; Casey Banas and Charles Mount, "Board Ousts Welling as Integration Planner," *Chicago Tribune*, May 4, 1978, 1.
93. Technical Assistance Committee, "Integration in Chicago," 37–43, 46–47, 76–78.
94. Linda Wertsch, "City's School Plan Kept Alive," *Chicago Sun-Times*, May 11, 1978, 3; Meg O'Connor, "School Panel Urges Forced Integration," *Chicago Tribune*, May 11, 1978, 3.
95. Linda Wertsch, "Desegregation Go-Ahead for City," *Chicago Sun-Times*, May 12, 1978, 12; Meg O'Connor, "Chicago's School Plan gets State OK, with Reservations," *Chicago Tribune*, May 12, 1978, 5;

Casey Banas, "Hannon Defies State Panel," *Chicago Tribune*, May 12, 1978, 1.

96. Bob Olmstead, "10,000 Enroll in Access to Excellence," *Chicago Sun-Times*, September 20, 1978, 3; Meg O'Connor, "'Excellence' Draws 2 pct. of Enrollment," *Chicago Tribune*, September 20, 1978, A1.

97. Chicago Urban League, "Access to Excellence: An Analysis and Commentary on the 1978–79 Program Proposals," 1, 1979, ERIC ED 187 780.

98. Ibid., 2–3.

99. Ibid., 6–9.

100. Ibid., 14

101. Ibid., 26.

102. Ibid., 68.

103. Linda Wertsch, "Hannon to Push City-Suburb Busing," *Chicago Sun-Times*, December 2, 1978, 7; Casey Banas, "Hannon to Push Area-Wide Bias Plan if 'Access' Ends," *Chicago Tribune*, December 2, 1978, S3.

104. John McCarron and Meg O'Connor, "Schools Get 3 Months to Fix Bias Plan," *Chicago Tribune*, December 15, 1978, 3.

105. Gary Orfield, "Voluntary Desegregation in Chicago: A Report to Joseph Cronin, State Superintendent of Education," February 26, 1979, 1–2, ERIC ED 171 832.

106. Ibid., 3.

107. Ibid., 4.

108. Joseph M. Cronin, "A Personal View—Chicago Desegregation," January 2, 1980. Joseph M. Cronin Papers, Box 23, Folder 2, Hoover Institution.

109. Ibid., 6–7, 10.

110. Ibid., 12–13, 18–19, 50.

111. Joan Zyda, "Hannon Hits Critical Report on 'Access,'" *Chicago Tribune*, March 7, 1979, E1.

112. Orfield, "Voluntary Desegregation in Chicago," 21.

113. Casey Banas, "School Desegregation is succeeding: Cronin," *Chicago Tribune*, March 9, 1979, A5.

114. Joint Staff Committee on Access to Excellence, "Report I: Analysis of Chicago's Progress September 1978–February 1979," March 5, 1979, Box Desegregation 1976–1980, Chicago Board of Education Archives; Leo E. Hennessy, Memorandum to Joseph Cronin, March 22, 1979, Box Desegregation 1976–1980, Chicago Board of Education Archives. "In Reply: 'Access Program Works,'" *Chicago Tribune*, March 11, 1979, A6.

115. Joseph M. Cronin to David S. Tatel, November 17, 1978, Record Group 60, General Records of the Department of Justice Office of the Attorney General, Box 98, National Archives.

116. David S. Tatel to Joseph M. Cronin, undated, Record Group 60, Box 98, National Archives.

117. Mark Polzin, "State Asks New Plan for Integration," *Chicago Tribune*, April 13, 1979, B8; Charles N. Wheeler III, "City School Bd. Still on Probation," *Chicago Sun-Times*, April 13, 1979, 5.

118. Cronin, "The State and School Desegregation," 10.

119. Edgar Epps, interview with author, March 2, 2011.

4   FEDERAL INVOLVEMENT WITH STUDENT DESEGREGATION

1. *United States v. Gorman* ended with a hung jury in 1971. Joel Havemann, "U.S. Lawyer Decides to Quit Faculty Desegregation Case," *Chicago Sun-Times*, November 1, 1969, 6; http://www.njcdlp .org/Thomas_N_Todd.html.

2. http://www.browsebiography.com/bio-leon_panetta.html.

3. Leon E. Panetta and Peter Gall, *Bring Us Together: The Nixon Team and the Civil Rights Retreat* (Philadelphia: J. B. Lippincott, 1971), 350.

4. Glen Elsasser, "HEW's School Integration Chief Resigns," *Chicago Tribune*, February 18, 1970, 3.

5. Panetta and Gall, *Bring Us Together*, 353.

6. Gary Orfield, *Must We Bus: Segregated Schools and National Policy* (Washington, DC: The Brookings Institution, 1978), 286, 291–295; Dean J. Kotlowski, *Nixon's Civil Rights: Politics, Principle, and Policy* (Cambridge, MA: Harvard University Press, 2001), 26–29, 34.

7. Kotlowski, *Nixon's Civil Rights*, 8, 26–29.

8. Ibid, 37.

9. Stephen C. Halpern, *On the Limits of the Law: The Ironic Legacy of Title VI of the 1964 Civil Rights Act* (Baltimore: Johns Hopkins University Press, 195), 137.

10. http://www.allamericanspeakers.com/celebritytalentbios/Joseph -A.-Califano,-Jr.

11. Joseph A. Califano Jr., *Governing America: An Insiders Report from the White House and the Cabinet* (New York: Simon and Schuster, 1981) 219.

12. Califano, *Governing America*, 219–220.

13. http://www.cadc.uscourts.gov/internet/home.nsf/content/VL +-+Judges+-+DST.

14. "Assistant Attorney General Drew S. Days, III, Assistant head of the Civil Rights Division's Statement," October 18, 1979, Records Group 60, Box 98, National Archives; http://www.mofo.com/drew-s-days/.

15. Linda Wertsch, "Timing of Order to Desegregate School Baffling," *Chicago Sun-Times*, April 16, 1979, 5, 28.

16. Linda Wertsch, "School Get U.S. Bias Warning," *Chicago Sun-Times*, April 11, 1979, 5; Meg O'Connor, "City Faces School Bias Suit by U.S.," *Chicago Tribune*, April 11, 1979, 1.

17. "Appendix to Letter of Ineligibility to the Chicago Public School District under the Emergency School Aid Act," 7, Record Group 60, Box 98, National Archives.

18. Wertsch, "Timing of Order to Desegregate School Baffling," 5, 28.
19. See Alan B. Anderson and George W. Pickering, *Confronting the Color Line: The Broken Promise of the Civil Rights Movement in Chicago* (Athens: University of Georgia Press, 1986).
20. "Appendix," 26.
21. Ibid., 29–30; See Amanda I. Seligman, *Block by Block: Neighborhoods and Public Policy on Chicago's West Side* (Chicago: University of Chicago Press, 2005); William Anton Vrame, *A History of School Desegregation in Chicago since 1954* (PhD Diss., University of Wisconsin, 1970).
22. "Appendix," 15–16.
23. Ibid., 15; Casey Banas, "U.S. Lists Cases of Bias in Schools," *Chicago Tribune*, April 12, 1979, 1.
24. "Appendix," 15; "U.S. Says Chicago School Bias No Accident," *Chicago Tribune*, April 15, 1979, A1.
25. "Appendix," 94; "Where U.S. Says City Schools Fail," *Chicago Sun-Times*, April 12, 1979, 80.
26. "Appendix," 26–31; "U.S. Says Chicago School Bias No Accident," 2.
27. "Appendix," 74.
28. Ibid., 77.
29. Ibid., 78–80.
30. Ibid., 62.
31. Linda Wertsch, "Hannon Denies Deliberate Bias," *Chicago Sun-Times*, April 12, 1979, 7.
32. "Dual Systems and Chicago," *Chicago Tribune*, May 8, 1979, B2.
33. Casey Banas, "Hannon to Fight U.S. Charges of School Bias," *Chicago Tribune*, April 19, 1979, 1, 5.
34. Barbara Reynolds, "Hannon Denies Federal Charges of Segregation," *Chicago Tribune*, May 5, 1979, B3; Linda Wertsch, "'Access' Defended at Capital Hearing," *Chicago Sun-Times*, May 5, 1979.
35. Linda Wertsch and Bob Olmstead, "School Bd. to Fight HEW on Bias," *Chicago Sun-Times*, April 19, 1979, 56.
36. Joseph P. Hannon, "Response to Department of Health, Education, and Welfare on the Eligibility of the Chicago Public Schools for Funding Under the Emergency School Aid Act," May 4, 1979, 11–13.
37. Linda Wertsch, "Schools Broaden Access Program," *Chicago Sun-Times*, May 10, 1979, 6.
38. Barbara Reynolds and Meg O'Connor, "HEW Holds to School Bias Charge," *Chicago Tribune*, May 26, 1979, B9.
39. Linda Wertsch, "Hannon Firm on Voluntary Path to School Integration," *Chicago Sun-Times*, May 30, 1979, 8; Casey Banas, "Hannon Lashes U.S. for 'Pushing' Board," *Chicago Tribune*, May 30, 1979, C11.
40. David S. Tatel to Joseph P. Hannon, "Criteria for an Acceptable Chicago Desegregation Plan," June 5, 1979, Harriet O'Donnell Papers, Chicago Board of Education Archives.

41. Linda Wertsch and Harry Golden Jr., "Hannon Hits New Integration Plan," *Chicago Sun-Times*, June 8, 1979, 4; Meg O'Connor, "Hannon: I'll Reject Mandatory Plans for Desegregation," *Chicago Tribune*, June 8, 1979, D1.

42. Casey Banas, "U.S. to Develop Options for School Desegregation," *Chicago Tribune*, July 26, 1979, B5.

43. Jerome R. Watson, "Califano, Blumenthal get the Ax," *Chicago Sun-Times*, July 20, 1979, 3.

44. *New York Times*, July 20, 1979, A24; *New York Times*, July 22, 1979 E18.

45. Califano, *Governing America*, 443.

46. "Urban League Head 'Welcomes' Harris," *Chicago Tribune*, July 20, 1979, 3.

47. http://www.biography.com/articles/Patricia-Roberts-Harris-205630; http://www.greatwomen.org/women.php?action=viewone&id=200; http://web.archive.org/web/19990128165845/http://www.toptags.com/aama/bio/women/pharris.htm.

48. Augustus J. Jones Jr., *Law, Bureaucracy and Politics: The Implementation of Title VI of the Civil Rights Act of 1964* (Washington DC: University Press of America), 157–158.

49. Barbara Reynolds, "HEW Warns City on School Integration Plan," *Chicago Tribune*, August 26, 1979, 1.

50. Jonathan Landman, "Integrated Schools up in City," *Chicago Sun-Times*, July 27, 1979, 3; Casey Banas, "Access to Excellence Drew 36,000 in First Year," *Chicago Tribune*, July 27, 1979, A1.

51. At least three board members had served since the mid-1960s. The board is selected by the mayor and approved by the City Council. Linda Wertsch, "Some School Board Members Defying Byrne," *Chicago Sun-Times*, August 24, 1979, 10; Karen Koshner and Linda Wertsch, "Byrne Asks School Board to Quit," *Chicago Sun-Times*, August 23, 1979, 3.

52. Paul Kleppner, *Chicago Divided: The Making of a Black Mayor* (DeKalb: Northern Illinois University Press, 1991), 104–105.

53. Roger Biles, *Richard J. Daley: Politics, Race, and the Governing of Chicago* (DeKalb: Northern Illinois University Press, 1995), 235–236.

54. Casey Banas and Meg O'Connor, "U.S. Proposes Busing 114,000 Pupils in City," *Chicago Tribune*, August 31, 1979, 1.

55. Marcia Kramer and Karen Koshner, "Byrne Opposes Citywide School Busing," *Chicago Sun-Times*, September 1, 1979, 3; Robert Unger and Casey Banas, "Can't Bus 114,000 City Students: Byrne," *Chicago Tribune*, September 1, 1979, S1.

56. George de Lama, "Latinos Say Busing Plan Disregards Their Needs," *Chicago Tribune*, September 2, 1979, 5; Peggy Constantine, "Latinos Say HEW Plan Ignores Their Needs," *Chicago Sun-Times*, September 2, 1979, 7.

57. Richard R. Valencia, *Chicano Students and the Courts* (New York: New York University Press, 2008), 13, 24.

58. Gaudalupe San Miguel Jr., *Brown, Not White: School Integration and the Chicano Movement in Houston* (College Station: Texas A & M Press, 2001), 74–94; Rubén Donato, *The Other Struggle for Equal Schools: Mexican Americans During the Civil Rights Era* (Albany: State University of New York Press, 1997).

59. ASPIRA, "Bilingual Education and Desegregation: Conflict or Harmony," a statement before the Chicago Board of Education, December 15, 1976, Chicago Urban League Papers, Series III, Box 91–1001, University of Illinois Special Collections.

60. Casey Banas, "Hannon Won't Seek Forced Busing," *Chicago Tribune*, September 5, 1979, 1.

61. Karen Koshner and Harry Golden Jr., "Busing Plan Not Feasible: Hannon," *Chicago Sun-Times*, September 5, 1979, 12.

62. Vernon Jarrett, "Joseph Hannon: Resistance Fighter," *Chicago Tribune*, September 9, 1979, A6.

63. Banas, Casey, "Hannon School Plan Rushed to U.S.," *Chicago Tribune*, September 13, 1979, 1.

64. Joseph P. Hannon, "Access to Excellence: Further Recommendations for Equalizing Educational Opportunities," September 19, 1979, iii–iv, 4–5.

65. Hannon, "Access," 6–40.

66. Barbara Reynolds, "HEW Blocks School Funds," *Chicago Tribune*, September 16, 1979, 1, 6.

67. Karen Koshner, "Hannon Confident of Acceptable School Plan," *Chicago Sun-Times*, September 18, 1979, 3; Casey Banas, "Hannon 'Optimistic' on OK for Bias Plan," *Chicago Tribune*, September 18, 1979, 3.

68. Ellen Warren, "HEW Rejects Hannon's Desegregation Plan," *Chicago Sun-Times*, September 22, 1979, 3; Barbara Reynolds, "HEW Rejects City Integration Plan," *Chicago Tribune*, September 22, 1979, S1.

69. Casey Banas, "Student Achievement Leads Eight Goals Set by Hannon," *Chicago Tribune*, September 25, 1977, 11.

70. In schools with blacks and whites, the criteria was 35–50 percent white and 50–65 percent black; in schools with the three largest racial/ethnic groups, the criteria was no less than 25 percent and no more than 50 percent Latinos, whites, and blacks. David S. Tatel to Joseph Hannon, October 12, 1979, in Board of Education, *Proceedings*, October 17, 1979, 507.

71. Joseph Hannon to David S. Tatel, October 17, 1979 in Board of Education, *Proceedings*, October 17, 1979, 512.

72. Joseph Hannon, Statement to the Board of Education, Board of Education, *Proceedings*, October 17, 1979, 505.

73. Ibid., 512–513.

74. Stephen C. Halpern, *On the Limits of the Law*, 158.

75. Edgar Epps, interview with author, March 2, 2011.

76. Michelle Stevens, "Blacks Hit Carter School Stand," *Chicago Sun-Times*, October 17, 1979, 3.

77. Ibid., 7–8; Ellen Warren, "Take School Fight to Court—Hew," *Chicago Sun-Times*, October 19, 1979, 1.

78. "Statement by Patricia Roberts Harris, Secretary of Health, Education, and Welfare," October 18, 1979, 6, Records Group 60, Box 98, National Archives.

79. Barbara Reynolds, "HEW Referring School Case to Justice Dept.," *Chicago Tribune*, October 19, 1979, 1.

80. David S. Tatel to Joseph P. Hannon, October 18, 1979, 2, Record Group 60, Box 98, National Archives, 6.

81. Ibid., 9.

82. Harpern, *On the Limits of the Law*, 155.

83. Meg O'Connor, "Official in City's School Case to Quit HEW Post," *Chicago Tribune*, October 23, 1979, 7; Ellen Warren, "School Feud to Justice Dept.," *Chicago Sun-Times*, October 30, 1979, 4.

84. Statement from Drew S. Days, October 18, 1979, Record Group 60, Box 98, National Archives.

85. Edgar Epps interview.

86. Bob Olmstead and Betty Washington, "Hannon Quits Amid School-Fund Crisis," *Chicago Sun-Times*, November 29, 1979, 3.

87. "Dazed School Board Ask 'Why'd He Quit?,'" *Chicago Tribune*, November 29, 1979, 1.

88. Casey Banas, "The Chicago School Financial Catastrophe," *Phi Delta Kappan* 61 (April 1980), 519.

89. Banas, "The Chicago School Financial Catastrophe," 520.

90. Joseph M. Cronin, "Big City School Bankruptcy," Policy Paper No. 80-C3 Institute for Research on Educational Finance and Governance, Stanford University (1980), 4–5, Joseph M. Cronin Paper, Hoover Institution.

91. Banas, "The Chicago School Financial Catastrophe," 520.

92. Edgar Epps interview.

93. Dorothy Shipps, *School Reform, Corporate Style: Chicago, 1880–2000* (Lawrence: University of Kansas Press, 2006), 93.

94. *Illinois Blue Book 1977–1978*, http://www.idaillinois.org/cdm4/document.php?CISOROOT=/bb&CISOPTR=38030&REC=4.

95. Banas, "The Chicago School Financial Catastrophe," 519, 522; Cronin, "Big City School Bankruptcy," 9, 12.

96. Edgar Epps interview.

97. Banas, "The Chicago School Financial Catastrophe," 522; Cronin, "Big City School Bankruptcy," 11.

98. See Cronin, "Big City School Bankruptcy;" Ellen Warren, "School Decision Will be Felt Here," *Chicago Sun-Times*, November 29, 1979, 25.

99. Casey Banas, "Caruso's Theme—Austerity" *Chicago Tribune*, December 14, 1979, 3; Storer Rowley, "Rev. Jackson Rips Caruso's Selection," *Chicago Tribune*, December 14, 1979, 18.

100. Memorandum for the Attorney General from Drew S. Days III, n.d., 2–6, Record Group 60, Box 98, National Archives.

101. Executive Order 11764 addressed nondiscrimination in federally funded programs and was issued in 1974. Ibid, 8.

102. Ibid, 7.

103. Ibid., 9.

104. William C. Berman, *America's Right Turn: From Nixon to Bush* (Baltimore: Johns Hopkins University Press: 1994), 4, 61.

105. Ellen Warren, "Justice Department Lawyers Push School Bias Suit," *Chicago-Sun Times*, December 14, 1979, 1, 18.

106. Committee on Student Desegregation, "Report," September 24, 1980, 2.

107. Ellen Warren, "U.S. Gives City Ultimatum on School Integration," *Chicago Sun-Times*, April 22, 1980, 3.

108. For progressive era changes, see David B. Tyack, *The One Best System: A History of American Urban Education* (Cambridge: Harvard University Press, 1974.)

109. Shipps, *School Reform, Corporate Style*, 98.

110. Martha Jantho, interview with author, July 9, 2010.

111. Joyce Hughes, interview with author, June 2, 2010.

112. Shipps, *School Reform, Corporate Style*, 98.

113. "Profiles of Byrne's 11 new School Board Nominees," Chicago Tribune, April 16, 1980, 17; Casey Banas, "Council Unit Oks Villalobos," *Chicago Tribune*, July 15, 1980; Casey Banas, "School Bias Talks Breakthrough Seen," *Chicago Tribune*, July 29, 1980, 3; Jonathan Landman, "Schools Likely to Agree to Federal Integration Plan," *Chicago Sun-Times*, July 30, 1980, 22.

114. Committee on Student Desegregation, "Report," September 24, 1980, 3.

115. Jonathan Landman, "$33 Million is Denied to Schools," *Chicago Sun-Times*, June 14, 1980, 4.

116. Meg O'Connor, "U.S. Levels New Bias Charges at City Schools in Faculty Firings," *Chicago Tribune*, June 14, 1980, S1.

117. Allen E. Shoenberger, "Desegregation in Chicago: Settlement without a Trial," in *Justice and School Systems: The Role of the Courts in Education Litigation*, ed. Barbara Flicker (Philadelphia: Temple University Press, 1990), 307.

118. Casey Banas and Jay Branegan, "School Board, U.S. Set Integration Guidelines," *Chicago Tribune*, September 25, 1980, 1.

119. *United States of America v. Board of Education of the City of Chicago*, "Consent Decree," 2–3.

120. Ibid, 4–7.

121. "Consent Decree," 8, 11, 13, Attachment A.

122. Ibid., 14–15.
123. Ibid., 17–18.
124. Casey Banas, "School Board Seeks Expert on Desegregation," *Chicago Tribune*, September 26, 1980, 5.
125. Jonathan Landman, "U.S. OKs 'weak' Pact HEW Refused," *Chicago Sun-Times*, September 25, 1980, 4.
126. Columbia Electronic Encyclopedia, 6th ed. http://www.encyclopedia.com/topic/Shirley_Mount_Hufstedler.aspx.
127. Colleen O'Connor, "United States Department of Education News," September 24, 1980, 1.
128. The grant came from Title IV of the Civil Rights Act of 1964, which provided for funding to employ a specialist to advise with desegregation matters. O'Connor, "United States Department of Education News," 2.
129. Meg O'Connor, "Schools Hire Top Consultant on Desegregation," *Chicago Tribune*, October 9, 1980, 1, 22.
130. G. Alfred Hess Jr., "Renegotiating a Multicultural Society: Participation in Desegregation Planning in Chicago," *Journal of Negro Education* 53 (Spring 1984): 138–139.
131. Casey Banas, "Parents Criticize Mandatory Busing," *Chicago Tribune*, December 16, 1980, D1; Linda Wertsch, "White Parents at Hearing Lash 'Forced Busing,'" *Chicago Sun-Times*, December 16, 1980, 36; Jonathan Landman, "Parents Tell Fears of School Busing," *Chicago Sun-Times*, December 17, 1980; Jack Houston, "Busing Opposed at Pilsen Hearing," *Chicago Tribune*, December 23, 1980, 3; Jonathan Landman, "Bus White Children, Too, Black Parents Tell Board," *Chicago Sun-Times*, December 19, 1981, 64.
132. Casey Banas, "Integration Plan, More than Busing," *Chicago Tribune*, January 11, 1981, 5.
133. "500 S. W. Side Parents Push Attack on Busing," *Chicago Sun-Times*, January 8, 1981, 13.
134. Joyce Hughes interview.
135. Casey Banas, "Parents Urge Citywide Desegregation Committee," *Chicago Tribune*, December 11, 1980; "2 School Panels Planned," *Chicago Tribune*, January 16, 1981, B5; Jonathan Landman "Two Citizen Panels to Aid School Plan, *Chicago Sun-Times*, January 15, 198.
136. Hess, "Renegotiating a Multicultural Society," 138.
137. Ibid., 139.
138. "School Plan Periled, Say U.S. Official," *Chicago Sun-Times*, December 13, 1980, 18.
139. Ibid.
140. Joyce Hughes interview.
141. Meg O'Connor, "Latinos Unite to Obtain Clout in School Politics," *Chicago Tribune*, December 29, 1980, E4.

142. Felix M. Padilla, *Latino Ethnic Consciousness: The Case of Mexican American sand Puerto Ricans in Chicago* (Notre Dame, IN: University of Notre Dame Press, 1985.)

143. Joyce Hughes interview.

144. Casey Banas, "Unrealistic Approach to Selection of School Chief," *Chicago Tribune*, January 7, 1981, E2.

145. Casey Banas and Meg O'Connor, "Love Gets School Post on 8–2 Vote by the Board," *Chicago Tribune*, January 14, 1981, 1; "Dr. Love's New Contract," *Chicago Tribune*, January 16, 1981, B2.

146. Paul Kleppner, *Chicago Divided: The Making of a Black Mayor* (DeKalb: Northern Illinois University Press, 1985), 137.

147. Rich MacArthur and Michael Anderson, "Many Blacks Still Bitter over Choice of Love," *Chicago Sun-Times*, January 14, 1981, 11.

148. Harold Golden Jr. and Linda Wertsch, "2 School Bd. Blacks Dumped for 2 Whites," *Chicago Sun-Times*, February 12, 1981, 1; Casey Banas and Robert Davis, "2 Black Dropped from School Bd.," *Chicago Tribune*, February 12, 1981, 1.

149. Vernon Jarrett, Byrne's Deliberate Insult to Blacks," *Chicago Tribune*, February 15, 1981, A6; Casey Banas, "Examining Motives in Shakeup of Board," *Chicago Tribune*, February 18, 1981, E2; Peggy Constantine and Harry Golden Jr., "Byrne Gain in School Move Doubted," *Chicago Sun-Times*, February 14, 1981, 6.

150. Kleppner, *Chicago Divided*, 140–141; Harry Golden Jr., "Panel OKs Mayor's 2 School Bd. Nominees," *Chicago Sun-Times*, March 25, 1981, 9.

5 CHICAGO DESEGREGATES PREDOMINANTLY WHITE SCHOOLS

1. Quoted in Raymond Wolters, *Right Turn: William Bradford Reynolds, the Reagan Administration, and Black Civil Rights* (New Brunswick, NJ: Transaction, 1996), 2.

2. Ibid., 6–7.

3. Quoted in Robert R. Detlefsen, *Civil Rights under Reagan* (San Francisco: Institute for Contemporary Studies Press, 1991), 3.

4. Ibid., 131.

5. Affirmative action and school desegregation are linked because they represent policies used to correct past discrimination. The actions and discussion against these policies demonstrate the Reagan administration's reversal of civil rights.

6. Paul Kleppner, *Chicago Divided: The Making of a Black Mayor* (DeKalb: Northern Illinois University Press, 1991), 136–139.

7. Ibid; Dempsey J. Travis, *An Autobiography of Black Politics* (Chicago: Urban Research Press, 1987), 533–543; Elizabeth Shana Todd-Breland, *To Reshape and Redefine Our World: African American*

Political Organizing for Education in Chicago 1968–1988 (PhD Diss., University of Chicago, 2010), 185–186.

8. Linda Wertsch and Jonathan Landman, "School Plan Sets Whites Limit at 65%," *Chicago Sun-Times*, April 3, 1981, 3.

9. Michael Zielenziger and Linda Wertsch, "Byrne Rips Busing: Plan Draws Fire from Both Sides," *Chicago Sun-Times*, April 4, 1981, 1, 6.

10. Brian J. Kelley, "Pucinski Finds Ire at School Proposal," *Chicago Sun-Times*, April 6, 1981, 5.

11. Casey Banas, "School to Mix Whites, Hispanics–Few Blacks," *Chicago Tribune*, April 5, 1981, 1, 14.

12. Jonathan Landman and Linda Wertsch, "Black–White Mix Small in School Plan," *Chicago Sun-Times*, April 5, 1981, 4.

13. Casey Banas, "Flaws in the Desegregation Plan," *Chicago Tribune*, April 15, 1981, 25.

14. Banas, "School to Mix Whites," 6.

15. Casey Banas, "School Aide Rips Bias Plan," *Chicago Tribune*, April 9, 1981, 1, 18.

16. Harry Golden Jr. and Linda Wertsch, "Byrne Rules out Aid on School Plan," *Chicago Sun-Times*, April 7, 1981, 3; Harry Golden Jr. and Linda Wertsch, "Won't Back School Tax Hike: Byrne," *Chicago Sun-Times*, April 8, 1981, 3.

17. G. Robert Hillman, "No Funds for City Busing: Thompson," *Chicago Sun-Times*, April 9, 1981, 3.

18. Jerry Crimmins, "As Hispanics Hit Bias Plan," *Chicago Tribune*, April 8, 1981, 2.

19. Michael McCabe, "S.W. Side Parents Hit School Plan," *Chicago Tribune*, April 7, 1981, 13.

20. Vernon Jarrett, "Busing Isn't the Issue," *Chicago Tribune*, April 19, 1981, A4.

21. Christine J. Faltz and Donald O. Leake, "The All-Black School: Inherently Unequal or a Culture-Based Alternative, in *Beyond Desegregation: The Politics of Quality in African American Schooling*, ed. Mwalimu J. Shujaa (Thousands Oaks, CA: Corwin Press, 1996), 233–234.

22. See David S. Cecelski, *Along Freedom Road: Hyde County, North Carolina, and the Fate of Black Schools in the South* (Chapel Hill: University of North Carolina Press, 1994); Derrick Bell, *Silent Covenants: Brown v. Board of Education and the Unfulfilled Hopes for Racial Reform* (New York: Oxford University Press, 2004).

23. Brian J. Kelly, "Half of Blacks and Latinos Reject Busing," *Chicago Sun-Times*, December 30, 1979, 8.

24. Brian J. Kelly, "Access to Excellence Plan Get a failing Grade," *Chicago Sun-Times*, January 2, 1980, 1.

25. Brian J. Kelly and Jacqueline Thomas, "Desegregation, Equal Education not Tied: Poll," *Chicago Sun-Times*, January 6, 1980, 16.

26. Robert L. Green, "Student Desegregation Plan for the Chicago Public Schools: Recommendations on Educational Components. Chicago Board of Education approved April 19, 1981, Chicago Board of Education Archives.

27. Chicago Board of Education, "Student Desegregation Plan for the Chicago Public Schools, Part II: Student Assignment Principles, Financial Aspects, General Policies Concerning the Desegregation Plan," April 19, 1981, 3–6, Chicago Board of Education Archives.

28. Casey Banas, "School Board OKs New Bias Plan," *Chicago Tribune*, April 30, 1981, 1.

29. Chicago Board of Education, *Proceedings*, June 24, 1981, 3275.

30. Title IV provided funding for desegregation initiatives. Chicago Board of Education, *Proceedings*, July 15, 1981, 3295.

31. Casey Banas, "Judge Gets New School Bias Data," *Chicago Tribune*, May 27, 1981, 4.

32. Michael Hirsley, "School Board Bias Plan Hit by U.S.," *Chicago Tribune*, July 22, 1981, 1, 23.

33. Linda Wertsch and Jonathan Landman, "U.S. Hits Board's School Bias Plan," *Chicago Sun-Times*, July 22, 1981, 3, 12.

34. Robert J. D'Agostino to William Bradford Reynolds, July 22, 1981, Record Group 60, Box 205, Folder 904, National Archives.

35. "Special Litigation Counsel Weekly Report," January 21, 1981, Record Group 60, Box 205, Folder 904, National Archives.

36. Banas, "School Board Bias Plan Hit by U.S.," 23.

37. Wolters, *Right Turn*, 7, 9.

38. James Worsham and Glen Elsasser, "Bias Plan Too Weak for Regan," *Chicago Tribune*, July 26, 1981, 14.

39. Patricia O'Hern, "Objections to Chicago Desegregation Plan," *Chicago Tribune*, August 6, 1981, 26.

40. Chicago Board of Education, *Proceedings*, August 10, 1981, 3439–3461.

41. Linda Wertsch, "Teacher Shifts to Meet Bias Plan Approved," *Chicago Sun-Times*, August 26, 1981, 18.

42. Jonathan Landman, "Fast Desegregation of Chicago School Predicted," *Chicago Sun-Times*, August 28, 1981, 6.

43. Alexander C. Ross to Wm. Bradford Reynolds, August 19, 1981, Record Group 60, Box 205, Folder 904, National Archives.

44. Jonathan Landman, "Desegregation Gain Wins U.S. Nod," *Chicago Sun-Times*, August 29, 1981, 3.

45. "Joint Statement of the United States and the Chicago Board of Education," Draft *United States v. Board of Education*. Record Group 60, Box 205, Folder 904, National Archives.

46. Casey Banas, "School Desegregation on Track: U.S.," *Chicago Tribune*, August 29, 1981, S3.

47. Chicago Board of Education, *Proceedings*, August 10, 1981, 3459–3460.

48. The Chicago Fact Book Consortium, *Local Community Fact Book Chicago Metropolitan Areas Based on the 1970 and 1980 Census* (Chicago: Chicago Review Press, 1984), 156–158; Erik Gellman, "New City," in *Chicago Neighborhoods and Suburbs: A Historical Guide*, ed. Ann Durkin Keating (Chicago: University of Chicago Press, 2008), 231–232; James R. Barrett, "Back of the Yards," in *Chicago Neighborhoods and Suburbs*, ed. Ann Durkin Keating, 103–104; Alan Solomon, "Back of the Yards: Chicago's History Lives On in This One-Time Home of the City's Stockyards," http://www.explorechicago.org/city/en/neighborhoods/back_of_the_yards.html, retrieved December 18, 2010.

49. The Chicago Fact Book Consortium, *Local Community Fact Book*, 101–103.

50. Chicago Board of Education, *Proceedings*, August 10, 1981, 3459–3460.

51. Don Wycliff, "Behind School Boycott: 'Unwritten Law' Divides Black, White Neighbors," *Chicago Sun-Times*, September 20, 1981, 48.

52. Monroe Anderson, "South Side Black and White Parents Rebel Against Busing," *Chicago Tribune*, September 11, 1981, A4.

53. Andy Knott and Casey Banas, "Blacks, Whites Join in Busing Boycotts," *Chicago Tribune*, September 15, 1981, 1.

54. "An Integrated Boycott," *Chicago Tribune*, September 16, 1981, 18.

55. Linda Wertsch, "Better Programs Vowed at Boycotted South Side Schools," *Chicago Sun-Times*, September 24, 1981, 8.

56. Don Wycliff, "Parents to Defy School Districting," *Chicago Sun-Times*, September 29, 1981, 12; Don Wycliff, "Parents 'Solve' Desegregation Fight on S. Side," *Chicago Sun-Times*, October 8, 1981, 4; Casey Banas, "Busing Protest: Schools Standing Firm," *Chicago Tribune*, October 11, 1981, 8.

57. Vernon Jarrett, "Tale of Two School Boycotts," *Chicago Tribune*, September 20, 1981, A5.

58. Derrick Bell makes this argument known as the interest convergence theory, where the interests of blacks are met when they converge with white interests. Derrick Bell, *Silent Covenants*.

59. Storer Rowley, "Busing 'Failed': Reagan Aide," *Chicago Tribune*, September 28, 1981, 1, 5.

60. "U.S. Eases School Bias Policy," Chicago Tribune, November 20, 1981, A1, 18.

61. Drew S. Days, "Turning Back the Clock: The Reagan Administration and Civil Rights," *Harvard Civil Rights-Civil Liberties Law Review* 19 (1984) 346.

62. Ibid., 323.

63. Ibid., 346.

64. Stephen C. Halpern, *On the Limits of the Law: The Ironic Legacy of Title VI of the 1964 Civil Rights Act* (Baltimore: Johns Hopkins University Press, 195), 192–193.

65. Vernon Jarrett, "A Step Back for Civil Rights," *Chicago Tribune*, November 20, 1981, A23.
66. Halpern, *On the Limits of the Law*, 234–235, 307.
67. Casey Banas, "Judge Orders School Busing Report," *Chicago Tribune*, November 13, 1981, B1.
68. James R. Turner to Donald Muirheid October 22, 1980; Drew S. Days III to James R. Thompson, November 6, 1980, Record Group 60, Box 98, National Archives.
69. Michael H. Sussman to Files, October 30, 1980, Record Group 60, Box 98, National Archives.
70. Ibid., 21.
71. Ibid., 25.
72. Linda F. Thome to Chicago Files, November 14, 1981, Record Group 60, Box 204, Folder 902, National Archives.
73. *United States of America v. Board of Education City of Chicago*, "Interdistrict Investigation—Interim Report of the United States," Record Group 60, Box 204, Folder 902, National Archives.
74. *United States of America v. Board of Education City of Chicago*, "Interdistrict Investigation."
75. *Milliken v. Bradley*, 418 US 717 (1974).
76. Ibid.
77. J. Harvey Wilkinson to Wm. Bradford Reynolds, September 27, 1982, Record Group 60, Box 206, Folder 905–908, National Archives.
78. Alexander C. Ross to Wm. Bradford Reynolds, November 3, 1982, Record Group 60, Box 206, Folder 905–908, National Archives.
79. Kevin Fox Gotham, "Urban Space, Restrictive Covenants and the Origins of Racial Residential Segregation in One U.S. City," *International Journal of Urban and Regional Research* 24 (September 2000): 630.
80. *United States of America v. Board of Education City of Chicago*, "Factual Findings of the United States Concerning Its Investigation of Interdistrict School Violations," 1–3, Record Group 60, Box 204, Folder 901, National Archives.
81. Ibid., 4–5.
82. Gary Orfield, *Must We Bus: Segregated Schools and National Policy* (Washington, DC: The Brookings Institute, 1978), 408–409.
83. *Hills v. Gautreaux*, 425 U.S. 284 (1976).
84. Robert L. Green, ed., *Metropolitan Desegregation* (New York: Plenum Press, 1985), 16.
85. Missouri Advisory Committee, *School Desegregation in the St. Louis and Kansas City Areas: Metropolitan Interdistrict Options* (US Committee on Civil Rights, 1981), 15.
86. *United States v. Board of School Commissioners, Indianapolis, IN*, 573 F 2d 400 (1978), 637 F 2d 1101 (1980).
87. Casey Banas, "Mandatory Busing in City Called Unlikely," *Chicago Tribune*, November 10, 1981, A11.

88. Chicago Board of Education, "Report of the Committee on Student Desegregation," November 9, 1981, 7–8 Record Group 60, Box 204, Folder 902, National Archives.

89. Linda Wertsch, "School Bias Progress Told," *Chicago Sun-Times*, November 19, 1981, 3; Casey Banas, "Chicago Raises its Grade on School Desegregation," *Chicago Tribune*, November 19, 1981, D1.

90. Chicago Board of Education, "Racial/Ethnic Survey: Students as of October 10, 1981," 2, ED 266,213; Casey Banas, "Latinos Outnumber White Pupils in City," *Chicago Tribune*, December 30, 1981, A1, 14; "Hispanic Pupils Outnumber Whites," *Chicago Sun-Times*, December 30, 1981, 3.

91. Alexander C. Ross to James P. Turner, December 16, 1981, Record Group 60, Box 204, Folder 902, National Archives.

92. Ibid., 3.

93. Ibid., 3–4.

94. Casey Banas and Jerry Crimmins, "New Bias Plan for School Hit," *Chicago Tribune*, January 1, 1982, 1; "School Bias Plan: A 20 Year Controversy," *Chicago Tribune*, January 1, 1982, 4.

95. Betty Washington, "Racial Busing under Black Attack," *Chicago Sun-Times*, January 9, 1982, 17; Alan P. Henry and Larry Weintraub, "Parents Rip School Busing Plan at Hearings," *Chicago Sun-Times*, January 10, 1982, 54.

96. Board of Education, "Comprehensive Student Assignment Plan," vol. 1, January 22, 1982, 38.

97. Ibid., 41.

98. Ibid., 42.

99. Ibid., 132.

100. Linda Wertsch, "Desegregate Black Schools: Judge," *Chicago Sun-Times*, November 13, 1981, 8.

101. See Alan B. Anderson and George W. Pickering, *Confronting the Color Line: The Broken Promise of the Civil Rights Movement in Chicago* (Athens: University of Georgia Press, 1986); Board of Education, "Comprehensive Student Assignment Plan," 300.

102. Joyce A. Hughes, "Statement of Joyce A. Hughes on Final Desegregation Plan," December 31, 1981, 3; Joyce A. Hughes, "Statement of Joyce A. Hughes: Revised Final Desegregation Plan," January 23, 1982, Chicago Board of Education Archives.

103. Board of Education, "Comprehensive Student Assignment Plan," 179–180.

104. Chicago Board of Education, "Comprehensive Student Assignment Plan, 1982." Municipal Reference Collection, Harold Washington Library.

105. Rudolph Unger, "School Bias Plan Wins Test," *Chicago Tribune*, February 13, 1982, B1.

106. Don Wycliff, "U.S. Approval of School Plan Is No Surprise," *Chicago Sun-Times*, February 14, 1982, 58.

107. Linda Wertsch and Don Wycliff, "8 Schools on S.W. Side Affected by White Boycott," *Chicago Sun-Times*, January 14, 1982, 20; Casey Banas, "Boycott by White Pupils Hits Desegregation Plan," *Chicago Tribune*, January 14, 1982, A16.

108. *U.S. v. Board of Education*, 554 F. Supp. 912.

109. Wolters, *Right Turn*, 373–374.

110. Thomas Hardy, "U.S. Hails School Plan; Urban League Critical," *Chicago Tribune*, January 7, 1983, 2; Ruth Love, personal communication to Raul A. Villalobos and members of the Board of Education, January 10, 1983, Chicago Board of Education Archives; Hardy, "U.S. Hails School Plan," 2.

111. Don Wycliff, "NAACP Lawyer Blasts School Ruling," *Chicago Sun-Times*, January 8, 1983, 8.

112. Vernon Jarrett, "School Bias Fight Not over Yet," *Chicago Tribune*, January 12, 1983, 19; Sarah Snyder, "NAACP's Chicago School Suit Dismissed," *Chicago Sun-Times*, May 18, 1983, 19; Kleppner, *Chicago Divided*, 196–220.

113. "Judge Shadur's Wise Decision," *Chicago Tribune*, January 8, 1983, W6.

114. "City Schools Get First Grant for Desegregation," *Chicago Sun-Times*, October 1, 1981, 56.

115. Linda Wertsch, "School Board to Sue for Help on Plan," *Chicago Sun-Times*, April 14, 1983, 19.

116. Don Wycliff, "Deficit of $122 Million Estimated for Schools," *Chicago Sun-Times*, February 17, 1982, 22.

117. *United States of America v. Board of Education*, "Consent Decree," 12.

118. Sarah Snyder, "Schools Sue U.S. for Desegregation Aid," *Chicago Sun-Times*, June 2, 1983, 3.

119. Jean Latz Griffin, "City School Sue to Get U.S. Funds for Desegregation," *Chicago Tribune*, June 2, 1983, B3.

120. Allen Shoenberger, "Desegregation in Chicago: Settlement without a Trial," in *Justice and School Systems: The Role of the Courts in Education Litigation*, ed. Barbara Flicker (Philadelphia: Temple University Press, 1990), 330–336; Linda Lentz, "City Schools Will Get $83 Million from U.S.," *Chicago Sun-Times*, July 14, 1987, 14; Casey Banas, "Schools Get $83 Million from U.S.," *Chicago Tribune*, July 14, 1987, 1.

121. Halpern, *On the Limits of the Law*, 160.

122. Martha Jantho, interview with author, July 9, 2010.

Conclusion

1. Tracy L. Steffes, *School, Society, & State: A New Education to Govern Modern America, 1980–1940* (Chicago: University of Chicago Press, 2012).

2. The numbers were calculated based on information provided in G. Alfred Hess Jr., Christina A. Warden, Lisa Korte, and Linda

Loukidis, "Who Benefits from Desegregation: A Review of the Chicago Desegregation Program 1980 to 1986," (Chicago: Panel on Public School Policy and Finance, December 1987), I–VIII.

3. Dan Weissmann, "Judge Signals End of Desegregation Case," *Catalyst*, February 2003.

4. Rosalind Rossi, "Judge Says It May Be Time to End Desegregation Deal," *Chicago Sun-Times*, March 2, 2004.

5. Chicago Public Schools, "More than 20-Year-Old School Integration Case Now Closed," September 25, 2009, http://www.cps.edu/News/Press_releases/2009/Pages/09_25_2009_PR1.aspx.

6. Chicago Public Schools, "Socio-Economic Data Will Be Used Instead of Race-Based Criteria," November 10, 2009, http://www.cps.edu/News/Press_releases/2009/Pages/11_10_2009_PR1.aspx.

7. Gary Orfield and Susan E. Eaton, *Dismantling Desegregation: The Quiet Reversal of Brown v. Board of Education* (New York: The New Press, 1987).

8. Chicago Urban League, "Access to Excellence: An Analysis and Commentary on the 1978–79 Program Proposals," 1, 1979, ERIC ED 187 780.

Index